OUR 100 YEARS

A FEMINIST HISTORY SOCIETY BOOK

Our 100 Years

The Canadian Federation of University Women

DIANNE DODD

Second Story Press

Library and Archives Canada Cataloguing in Publication

Title: Our 100 years : the Canadian Federation of University Women / Dianne Dodd.
Names: Dodd, Dianne, 1955- author.
Description: Series statement: A Feminist History Society book | Includes bibliographical
    references and index.
Identifiers: Canadiana (print) 20190185295 | Canadiana (ebook) 20190185309 | ISBN
    9781772601275 (softcover) | ISBN 9781772601282 (EPUB)
Subjects: LCSH: Canadian Federation of University Women—History.
Classification: LCC LC1551 .D63 2020 | DDC 378.0082/0971—dc2

www.FeministHistories.ca

Edited by Andrea Knight and Kathryn Cole
Book design by Melissa Kaita
Original series design by Zab Design & Typography

Every effort has been made to secure permission and provide appropriate
credit for photographic material. The publisher deeply regrets any omission
and pledges to correct errors called to its attention in subsequent editions.

Printed and bound in Canada

*Second Story Press gratefully acknowledges the support of the Ontario Arts Council
and the Canada Council for the Arts for our publishing program. We acknowledge
the financial support of the Government of Canada through the Canada Book Fund.*

Published by
Second Story Press
20 Maud Street, Suite 401
Toronto, ON M5V 2M5
www.secondstorypress.ca

For CFUW members, past and present
...for my family and
...for Rhona

CONTENTS

A NOTE ON FOOTNOTES
The footnotes supporting the author's extensive research
can be accessed online at: http://secondstorypress.ca/resources

FOREWORD

How I would have enjoyed being a fly on the wall on several CFUW occasions in the past century, as the organization evolved alongside feminism, society, and Canada itself.

I would like to have been in Niagara Falls in 1921 to watch federation members welcome Dr. Marie Curie when she stepped onto the stage to give a CFUW-sponsored public lecture. I can imagine the excited buzz from the audience as the soft-spoken scientist spoke about her discovery of the radioactive element radium. Here was the perfect CFUW role model back then: a woman who had overcome barriers, doggedly pursued first a university education and then a career, and had won two Nobel Prizes. And she had also fulfilled traditional expectations as a wife and mother.

The federation had fewer than two thousand members in the 1920s, and, for that tight little group of middle-class blue-stockings, CFUW meetings offered a rare chance to mingle with other university graduates. "Be less curious about people and more curious about ideas," was one of Dr. Curie's repeated sayings. For her listeners, she was a gratifying reminder of the importance of scholarship and their own intellectual potential.

I would like to have been at the University of Toronto, a few years later, when the president suggested to the redoubtable Mossie May Kirkwood, dean of women and professor of English, that she should resign from the university since her husband had a job and could therefore support his family. The suggestion had barely been made before the CFUW came forcefully to Dr. Kirkwood's defence. Not only was this blatant discrimination, the federation pointed out, it was also a waste of the taxpayer dollars invested in women's education. The president backed off. Dr. Kirkwood stayed.

Education. Fairness. Mutual support. The women who got the federation up and running in the first half of the twentieth century gained much from the CFUW, but they gave much too. They were progressives who felt a commitment to serve the community and help those less privileged than themselves. They ran for positions in community organizations and all levels of politics; they collected clothes and toys for needy families. And they lobbied federal and provincial governments for improvements in women's working conditions, including equal pay and a federally supported daycare program—but only *after* they had prepared a carefully researched brief. They mirrored the homogenous and rather cautious society that typified Canada until after World War II.

The big change came when a new and more assertive feminism emerged in the 1960s. Once again, the CFUW was in step with the times on the issues: federation president Laura Sabia was in the vanguard of those calling for a royal commission on the status of women to make more radical demands. Another occasion when I would happily assume my fly-on-the-wall stance is the moment when Sabia, a take-no-prisoners campaigner, flippantly suggested that she might organize a two million-woman march on Ottawa. She herself admitted that it was an idle threat, but she was viciously pilloried in the press. Recognizing misogyny for what it was, she called it "an astonishing display of a prejudiced, untruthful, and even vicious attitude toward women."

The royal commission endorsed many of the recommendations made in the CFUW's fact-filled, well-argued briefs. However, Canadian politics were growing steadily more fractious, and so was the women's movement. The federation watched other, more aggressive groups grab the headlines; in Sabia's words, hobnail boots replaced white gloves. CFUW quietly carved out a niche at the moderate end of the feminist spectrum. Its balanced and deeply researched input on issues ranging from the Charter of Rights to drug patent protection, child pornography, landmines, and reproductive technologies carried weight in government debates.

More recently, the CFUW has weathered a shrinking membership and the backlash against feminism. But the aims of this resilient, self-funded organization remain undimmed. How I wish I had been my insect self at the meeting of the Aurora/Newmarket branch a few years ago, when it gave a $1,000 grant to a ward of the Children's Aid Society as she moved out of care and into postsecondary education. I like to imagine the smile on that young woman's face as she realized that this empowering grant (part of a national CFUW initiative) would likely change her life.

As an author, I've often been invited to speak at CFUW meetings, so I know first-hand what to expect: an attentive audience, perceptive questions…and wonderful discussions over refreshments afterwards. Yes, the CFUW has always stood for education, fairness, advocacy, and support. But it has also offered members friendship, laughter, and, as Dr. Curie recommended nearly a century ago, lively conversations about ideas.

Charlotte Gray
August 2019

Charlotte Gray, CM, is the author of eleven bestselling books of history and biography, including a biography of Nellie McClung.

INTRODUCTION

Daniel Wilson, President of the University of Toronto (1880–1892) felt that the system of separate colleges "under lady principals and other efficient oversight… is the one best calculated to promote the refined culture and high intellectual development of women." He was concerned about the moral breakdown that might result from "bringing scores of young men and women into intimate relations in the same institution at the excitable age of 18 to 22."
—Martin Friedland, *University of Toronto: A History*, p. 89.

The Canadian Federation of University Women (CFUW) was born out of the struggle by nineteenth- and early twentieth-century women to gain admittance to Canadian universities. The educational pioneers who became the organization's founders were a small, privileged group of unusually accomplished women—scandalous "blue-stockings" in the eyes of many. But there was another issue that arose almost immediately: once they had graduated, what would they do with their education? Would they forsake motherhood and marriage for the professions, or would they follow more traditional "feminine" roles? This question has driven much of CFUW history.

These early women graduates came together in local clubs, starting with Toronto in 1903 and Vancouver in 1907, in the hopes of preserving their university experience through opportunities to continue learning and maintain friendships with like-minded women. As more clubs formed, in 1919 they decided to create a federation that articulated a founding philosophy of education as a privilege, albeit one that included a social obligation. This notion of *noblesse oblige* reflects their status as white, Euro-Canadian members of an economically, politically, and educationally privileged group in Canadian society. Still, as women, they were restricted from full participation in all aspects of Canadian life and, by fulfilling their obligation to serve their communities, they sought to prove that the resources used to educate them had not been wasted—as their critics too often charged. Through service to their communities, their families, and their nation, they also sought to prove their competence, to wear down entrenched gender prejudices, and eventually improve the status of all women. As such, the federation later known as CFUW, built a longstanding tradition of service, much of it in areas that fit within accepted gender roles and the duty of middle-class women to do "good works"—education, culture, and charitable work. University women's clubs funded local libraries, worked with settlement houses, and raised money for scholarships. By extending their activities further into the arena of political reform, however, a few clubs and club members also began to ally themselves with the first-wave feminist movement in projects that sought to improve women's status. They helped establish political and social policy to support women in the workforce, in the professions, in the family, and in the voluntary sector. On their own and with other organizations, these policy initiatives sometimes led to important legislative reforms. As well, the federation established a unique women-only scholarship program that gave important support to women scholars—truly the centrepiece of the organization's work.

The idea for this book originated with the CFUW board as a way to celebrate the organization's 100th birthday in August 2019. They formed a CFUW History Committee, chaired by President Grace Hollett, with Gail Crawford, Doris Mae Oulton, and Eleanor Palmer. The committee decided to engage a historian and non-member to write the book in order to get a broad perspective on the issues that CFUW has faced over the past one hundred years. While a member would have brought more inside knowledge and personal experience of the organization to the project, they felt that someone with knowledge of the history of the women's movement would be able to view it through a wider lens. As a centennial history, the committee asked that it bring CFUW up to the present day. This was done with some trepidation as writing about the recent past is an exercise fraught with perils. Historians need distance to contextualize and analyze the past, and to take advantage of sources written by contemporaries after the fact. Thus, the reader may find the final chapters read quite differently than earlier ones. Another CFUW initiative to mark the historic occasion is the 100th Anniversary Scholarship Project, which raised more than $215,000 for scholarships and fellowships across the country (a mainstay of the organization), and funded increases to the scope and amounts of the academic awards presented.

The pertinent sources that were used in putting this volume together are the federation publication the *Chronicle*, the CFUW material deposited at Library and Archives Canada (LAC), and secondary historical literature. Happily, conscious of contributing to history, CFUW has kept its records in excellent shape, thus making the work easier. In addition to the archival sources in Ottawa, the author had access to many of the individual club histories and, keenly aware of how unique and special each club is, tried to incorporate as many aspects of these as possible. The author thanks all the clubs who provided material and her only regret is not being able to use all of them. The book unavoidably reflects the author's own areas of expertise and interest in social history and the women's movement and may inadvertently have neglected to explore, for example, the intimate details of the financial or constitutional history of the organization. The aim of this book was to shape a history of this multifaceted organization made up of affiliated clubs across Canada that would focus on its advocacy and community work and highlight its place within the history of the Canadian women's movement. Women's agency in history is too often neglected and we hope the book will instil in its readers—members and non-members alike—a sense of pride in the organization's historic accomplishments and lead to a better understanding of the role CFUW played in the formation of Canadian social, educational, and political institutions.

To document CFUW's changing socio-economic and political realities over its first centennial, the book has been organized in a largely chronological fashion, with chapters following a decade-by-decade progression. Two topics, however, have been treated separately. Chapter 13 deals with the organization's scholarship program for women, trying to highlight, as much as the sources allow, the accomplishments of its winners, all outstanding academic achievers who made significant contributions to research, teaching, and women's entry into academia. Chapter 14 explores CFUW's involvement in international women's and human rights movements, largely through their affiliation with the International Federation of University Women (IFUW), recently renamed Graduate Women International (GWI). These activities include their role in helping Jewish academic women escape from Nazi-controlled Europe prior to World War II and, later, bringing the influence of international human rights—particularly through the United Nations—home to benefit Canadian women.

History always presents challenges with regard to terminology that changes over time. This is especially problematic in the case of married women. The History Committee decided that, wherever possible, the names of members in the book would be expressed using their given names followed by their surnames and only using titles in the case of "Dr." A concerted effort has been made to use women's own names without the "Miss" or "Mrs." notations that were commonly used in the records until at least the 1970s—sometimes longer. While this affects the historical authenticity, the committee felt that it was more respectful to use women's own names in place of their husbands'. Accordingly, we have exchanged an old-fashioned—and to many, offensive—naming tradition for a more modern one. Mrs. R. H. McWilliams, for example, will appear in this book as Margaret McWilliams, and Miss Margaret MacLellan, will appear as simply Margaret MacLellan. However, Dr. Elizabeth Bagshaw will remain Dr. Elizabeth Bagshaw. In those few cases where we cannot find a woman's given name—a casualty of past naming customs—her designation will remain as it is in the source. This is especially apparent in photograph credits. It should also be noted that CFUW sources typically use the title "Dr." to recognize women with honorary doctorates, and the author has, by and large, followed that custom. In addition, an effort has been made to convert historical terms used to refer to Indigenous peoples such as

"Indian"—which was still in use in the 1970s—to the contemporary, inclusive, and generally preferred term, Indigenous. And in an effort to facilitate the ease of reading a book-length text, the writing style is less formal, minimizing the use of capitalization.

As mentioned above, this book places CFUW in the context of the history of the women's movement, specifically that of late-nineteenth-century Canadian women's organizations that were largely made up of middle-class and culturally homogeneous Euro-Canadian women, with whom CFUW shared many goals and initiatives. In an earlier period of women's history, many of these organizations became the subject of academic studies that largely focused on the period of first-wave feminism that led up to World War I. Diana Pedersen has looked at various aspects of the Young Women's Christian Association (YWCA),[1] and Sharon Cook has examined the history of the Woman's Christian Temperance Union (WCTU) in Canada, with its critical support of the woman's suffrage campaign.[2] CFUW shared many common goals with the influential National Council of Women of Canada (NCWC), which has been studied both by Veronica Strong-Boag in the early days of women's history in Canada, and by Naomi Griffiths, who wrote a later centennial history.[3]

By contrast, CFUW has been relatively neglected in the academic literature on women's history with only two theses written—one by Wendy Hubley on the federation from 1919 to 1931, and another by Laurie Smith that takes the organization up to 1960 through the lens of the Ottawa Club.[4] Some aspects of the CFUW story have been incorporated into the larger narrative of women in Canada, such as the role of Laura Sabia in the creation of the Royal Commission on the Status of Women (RCSW) in 1967.[5] However, the trail goes cold there as Sabia left the organization and was critical of it in the years following her departure. Given CFUW's propensity to produce leaders, it is not surprising that some have been the subject of biographies, such as *Margaret McWilliams: An Interwar Feminist* by Mary Kinnear that links her work at CFUW with her active participation in other organizations.[6] Similarly, Helen Gregory MacGill and, more recently, Laura Jamieson, also active in CFUW as well as many other organizations, have been the subject of biographies.[7] These prominent figures in the women's movement who helped give rise to major reforms also brought the CFUW membership into a global community of organized activism.

We hope that this comprehensive history of one women's organization will not only enlighten readers but will also spark interest among future researchers to explore other, more specialized areas of its work. Many possibilities come to mind. As yet, there is no biography of Laura Sabia, nor of the first Canadian woman astrophysicist and first Canadian president of the International Federation of University Women, A. Vibert Douglas. Such a biography may well illuminate Canadian involvement in the heroic support given to female war refugees escaping from Nazism in their home countries. In general, the history of graduate women's organizations at the international level is poorly known, and an academic or popular history of the IFUW/GWI story in the post-1960s era would be most welcome.

Another gaping hole in the literature relates to Margaret MacLellan, a pivotal figure who made early links between post-World War II internationalism, the growing human rights movement, and Canadian feminism at home. As well, the story of CFUW scholarship winners, their subsequent careers, and the organization's efforts to place them in academic positions certainly merits a narrative of its own. A focus for further research might also include studies at the club level—the role of educational reform within the clubs that has been directed at the provincial and school board levels, for example, and the clubs' cultural activities. The satirical plays written and performed by members, often on women's issues, are especially fascinating. These productions, still being written and performed today, are reminiscent of the mock parliaments of suffrage days in which humour was used to make pointed but non-threatening political statements. Amateur artists who occasionally exhibited their work at conferences, or organized their own shows, also remain in the shadows of the organization's history, as does CFUW's role in fostering artistic expression.

What this book can tell us is that CFUW, like some of the more broadly based middle-class women's organizations, brought women together for fellowship and learning, and to influence social attitudes through public education. In its early years, the organization represented the small minority of women with a university education, an elite within an elite, a group of unusually bright and privileged women. Later, as university education became much more common for women, the membership's socio-economic status broadened somewhat, although its dependence on fees makes it inevitably more restrictive than other women's organizations.

With their focus on serving the needs of their communities, CFUW clubs joined other women's organizations in providing low-cost services, relying on volunteer labour and often serving marginalized populations. Some historians who have studied these women's organizations have reduced their efforts to a cynical attempt to instil mainstream, middle-class social values into the "great unwashed" and, in the case of immigrant communities, to Canadianize them. While it is undeniable—and perhaps unavoidable—that they brought their own cultural bias along with the health, educational, and other services they provided, they did fill a need. Their pilot projects sometimes went on to become part of the social welfare and the educational infrastructure that we now value so highly. And the policy that emerged from their resolutions sometimes led to social, political, and legislative reforms that benefitted all women. The activism of CFUW and its affiliates at the local, federal, and later provincial levels was able to help bring about changes precisely because its members could exploit their upper-echelon political and social connections.

In the early studies of suffrage and first-wave feminism, CFUW, like other women's organizations that directed many of their charitable works toward women and children, were labelled maternal feminists. As we shall see, however, the actions of the CFUW from its very earliest days indicate that it also was concerned about equal rights for women and thus comes out looking more modern than many of its contemporaries. The CFUW was not doctrinaire and drew on both maternal feminism and equal-rights feminism as needed in its support for women's suffrage and women's education, as well as for other gains for women. It filled a niche for university-educated women, especially in those early years when the leadership was dominated by a small cohort of academic women. With a significant number of professionals in its ranks, especially teachers, CFUW even occasionally argued for combining careers and motherhood. Starting with the first $1,000 Travelling Scholarship awarded in 1921, the federation established and funded through its own efforts a substantive program of scholarships for women. Not only did it allow promising academic women to pursue advanced degrees abroad, it also tried to place them in academic teaching positions in Canada once they graduated. Later these efforts were extended to other professions and the civil service.

Historians now understand the maternalism/equal rights dichotomy to be a false one and indeed many CFUW members were relatively wealthy mothers and wives who used their education to pursue voluntary roles in the community, often at an elite level. Influenced by maternalism, some pursued family law reforms, sometimes joining forces with other women's organizations to give themselves more clout. Although CFUW primarily focused on teachers and academics, the organization, like the Canadian Federation of Business and Professional Women (CFBPW), worked to defend women—particularly married women—who came under attack for working for wages during the Depression. CFUW also worked with the YWCA, CFBPW, and others to push for the establishment of the federal Women's Bureau in the Department of Labour in the 1950s, one of the first government bodies concerned with research and legislative improvements for women. Under Laura Sabia's leadership, CFUW played a major part in the coalition that led to the appointment of the RCSW in 1967, which in turn ushered in what has come to be known as the second wave of the women's movement.

Most of the academic sources on women's history that relate to CFUW's first century end their analysis at about the time of the RCSW. There are, however, a few exceptions: Jill Vickers, Pauline Rankin, and Christine Appelle have studied the National Action Committee on the Status of Women through the lens of the political scientist, looking at the efforts to implement the RCSW recommendations.[8] As well, there is a growing body of memoirs by individual activists that have begun to appear, including *Ten Thousand Roses: The Making of a Feminist Revolution* by Judy Rebick and *Rebel Daughter: An Autobiography* by Doris Anderson. Histories of organizations rooted in the provinces and territories are scarce, as are histories of organizations devoted to specific issues such as daycare or domestic violence. One of the few exceptions is *White Gloves Off: The Work of the Ontario Committee on the Status of Women*, edited by Beth Atcheson and Lorna Marsden, the study of a post-RCSW women's organization in Ontario. Like this book, it was published through Second Story Press and the Feminist History Society, which is dedicated to documenting second-wave feminism in Canada.

Given this dearth of literature on the women's movement of the modern period, this book, covering one hundred years, offers a rare glimpse into one organization—CFUW—that promoted the status of women from the first wave of the feminist movement to its re-emergence in the 1960s and beyond. It delineates CFUW's role in formulating policy through research and resolutions that drew on input from its clubs and the national level and shows how the organization adapted to changing realities. The Royal Committee on the Status of Women, secured by a coalition led by CFUW president Laura Sabia, set a new tone, and the new women's liberation movement blossomed.

CFUW officially joined the lobby to implement the RCSW recommendations, many of which reflected their own policy resolutions, but the organization also shifted its emphasis toward another of its numerous goals. Stressing women's leadership, CFUW marked International Women's Year in 1975 with a project to promote a roster of qualified women for senior academic, government, and business appointments. In the 1980s, the organization returned to advocacy and defined itself as a "moderate voice in public affairs" in order to distinguish itself from what it viewed as radical women's groups. Focusing on quiet influence and exploiting its elite political and social connections, CFUW established a channel to government through regular consultations. In response to the horrific massacre of fourteen young women engineering students in Montréal, CFUW joined a successful coalition on gun control and later helped bring about an international treaty on landmines, contributing political connections and their usual solid research. Matters again changed course in the millennial years with threats to women's organizations through funding cuts and restrictions on non-profit organizations in the 2010s. CFUW, now an equality-seeking organization, joined the protest coalitions and marches calling for an inquiry into missing and murdered Indigenous women and girls, and an end to women's poverty and violence against women.

Right from its inception, CFUW prided itself on its research capacity—not surprising given its highly educated membership—and contributed several important research reports in the movement toward reform. Responding to its members' changing needs, CFUW conducted a major study on women and continuing education in the 1960s. Despite the domestic mystique, baby boom, and suburban explosion of the 1950s, many members expressed frustration with their inability to use their education or to have their community volunteer work recognized for its true value. This foreshadowed an economic revolution that pulled more married women into the workforce. CFUW demographics were changing.

As more and more women obtained university degrees, its membership began to broaden socio-economically and to include some French-speaking clubs. Its leadership also changed from the academics of the early years to women who identified as mothers and wives, many of whom were affluent enough to forego salaries in order to hold executive roles in voluntary organizations at the community, provincial, and national levels. It is certainly true that the leadership of CFUW is, and has been, largely white, middle-class, Christian, and moderate in its political views. However, the organization is made up of member clubs that control their own membership lists, so it is difficult to know how many ethnically and religiously diverse women are members. Nonetheless, CFUW is aware of the need to do more to attract members to better represent the growing cultural diversity of the Canadian population. There have been efforts to do so in the past but these have largely failed.

Coming full circle from its days of funding and promoting women scholars to fill academic positions, CFUW in 1992, and again twenty-five years later, conducted studies on women's experience at university. The first was a comprehensive look at women's roles as professors and students that recommended ways to improve the environment on campus, and the later study, among other proposals, recommended ways to address the scourge of sexual violence against women on campus.

CFUW has been particularly adept at a certain type of advocacy that draws on political connections, on the importance of good research, and on quiet influence. The organization developed an elaborate resolution and advocacy machinery, had a well-educated membership, and was focused on the political and constitutional process. As such it provided a solid training ground for women who were interested in roles in executive leadership in government, business, and politics. Indeed, many CFUW members have successfully run for office, including such luminaries as Flora MacDonald, Monique Bégin, Thérèse Casgrain, and Elizabeth May. Seen by some women in CFUW as an effective strategy for furthering the status of women and a way to prove women's competence, there are nonetheless members who remain reluctant to embrace politics and the organization is officially non-partisan.

Such contradictions are understandable in an organization such as CFUW that is composed of a network of diverse and autonomous clubs, a federation, and some regional and provincial bodies. A complex organization, it has many, sometimes contradictory, goals. Its core values, rooted in the friendship and lifelong learning that has contributed to the richness of its members' lives, have allowed it to withstand the test of time. At the same time, CFUW has, over the years, pursued its wider goals of advocacy, community service, and improving the status of women to fulfil its founding obligations. CFUW's community projects and advocacy efforts benefit a much wider group than just its own members and its influence has extended locally, provincially, nationally, and internationally. True to the founders who stormed the doors of Canadian universities, CFUW members have tried to make this a better world for all, especially for women and girls, while welcoming women for fellowship and learning.

Chapter 1
A FOOT ON THE LADDER: EARLY CLUBS AND THE FOUNDING OF CFUW

We knew we were being watched closely, so strove to give no cause for criticism.

—Ella Gardiner

These words were recorded in a 1923 survey conducted by the new federation of university women's clubs. Ella Gardiner was one of a small group of determined young women who, after a hard-fought battle, gained admittance to University College, the University of Toronto's non-denominational college, in 1884. Aware of the hostility they engendered, Gardiner and her female colleagues decided to draw up regulations "by which we would be guided in our life at College, so the first Saturday, after we were admitted, the women students met, discussed matters and agreed how we should conduct ourselves and all signed the regulations."[1] These early pioneers, predominantly women of European descent from middle- to upper-class families, were conscious of having done something both special and controversial. As their numbers increased, they founded clubs and eventually, established a federation of university women's clubs, later called the Canadian Federation of University Women (CFUW).

Throughout Canada, Britain, and the United States more and more women gained entry into universities during the 1870s and 1880s. A complex of reasons went into that development, including religious motivations to mould future wives and mothers, changing expectations of women in an industrializing world, and demands from some women for an education equal to that of their brothers. By attending university, Canadian women in turn transformed what had been all-male institutions into co-educational institutions.

In general, Canada did not follow the British or American pattern of founding separate women's colleges to avoid the co-education that many Victorians found offensive. At a time when people believed that women were essentially different from men and should remain in the domestic, private sphere, men and women were not meant to mix, except under strict supervision. In the 1870s, the first Canadian women attended university in the eastern provinces, where such schools as Mount Allison and Acadia had affiliated ladies' academies. These institutions, Wesleyan Methodist and progressive Baptist respectively, were founded on religious convictions that viewed the education of women in a positive light.

Grace Annie Lockhart, who graduated from Mount Allison in 1875 with a BA in science and literature, is thought to be the first female university graduate in Canada. Female students were first admitted to Acadia University in 1879. One woman who studied there in the 1890s was Evlyn Keirstead (Farris), who went on to found a university women's club in Vancouver. Her father, Reverend Miles Keirstead, was a professor at Acadia and believed that men and women were equal in God's eyes and that every woman had a right and responsibility to develop her own talents. Despite being chaperoned to social events, she described her time at Acadia as happy; many of the chaperones were her father's younger colleagues.[2] Women's reception in Canadian universities varied considerably, and Acadia was one of the friendlier ones. They established a women's gymnasium, for instance, which gave Evlyn the opportunity to be captain of a basketball team. Despite his initial opposition to admitting women, Acadia's president Dr. Artemus Wyman Sawyer asked an early female student, J. L. Marsters, to establish the Propylaeum Society for them,[3] named for the ancient Greek word for a gateway to a temple or sacred place.[4] Farris, like many others, obtained admission due to family connections. The family of later fellow Vancouver club member, noted feminist, and judge Helen Gregory MacGill, had also pulled strings so she could gain admittance to Trinity College's new Bachelor of Music program at the University of Toronto.

The universities in central Canada were less friendly and accepted women into their classrooms later than the schools in Nova Scotia. Those with evangelical ties opened their doors first. In Cobourg, the Methodists' Victoria College, which later affiliated with the University of Toronto, graduated its first female student in 1877. One of these students, who later became a member of the University Women's Club of Toronto, was Margaret Addison. Her father, a Methodist preacher with ties to Victoria, and her mother, a former teacher, were both deeply committed to women's education. Like other women who may not have started out with specific career goals but wanted to be sure that they could earn their own livelihood, Addison became a high school teacher in the Ontario towns of Stratford and Lindsay. Teaching positions at the high school level often required a university degree and offered better pay than elementary school teaching, but women were still paid considerably less than male teachers.

Queen's University in Kingston admitted women in 1878. Its principal, George Grant, was an influential advocate of the social gospel, a popular form of Protestant Christianity at the time that stressed social activism over personal salvation. Not a supporter of women's education for its own sake, he believed that "woman should have every possible opportunity to obtain a sound mental training because of her relation to man and the importance of her position as a possible wife and mother."[5] At Queen's, as elsewhere, programs open to women were restricted primarily to the arts and modern languages; professional schools such as law and medicine kept their doors firmly closed. Queen's University did admit women to its medical school, but in 1882, a strike by male students and faculty led to their expulsion, prompting Drs. Jenny Trout and Emily Stowe to establish separate women's medical colleges in Kingston and Toronto. Elizabeth Smith, who was the first president of Queen's Alumnae Association and active in the Ottawa University Women's Club, had also attended this short-lived program and her diary details the obstacles facing women in professional programs.[6]

McGill University in Montréal and the University of Toronto were more resistant, but they ultimately bowed in the face of political and financial pressures. Both Principal John William Dawson of McGill and President Daniel Wilson of the University of Toronto

Margaret Addison, Dean of Women at Annesley Hall.

tried to hold out for separate women's colleges that would allow them to support women's education without actually allowing women to set foot on their campuses. At McGill, women were admitted in 1884 as a result of a generous donation from Donald A. Smith (Lord Strathcona), but Principal Dawson ensured that they were taught in the separate women's Royal Victoria College.

At University College in Toronto, matriculation exams were opened to women in 1877, but they were excluded from the classroom, forced to study on their own or with private tutors. Ella Gardiner recorded that she and several other fourth-year female students were anxious to have "at least one year of College privileges."[7] They sent in their applications along with their fees but were still refused admittance. Influential allies William Houston, a member of the University of Toronto senate, and George Ross, the Ontario Minister of Education, introduced a bill into the Ontario legislature forcing the university to admit women to their arts programs.[8] Still, President Wilson objected that separate facilities were needed as was a chaperone.[9] Gardiner recalled that Wilson himself gave the women their first lecture. Trying to show that he was only opposed to co-education, not women's education, he showed the class the skulls of Roman men and women, pointing out that the women's skulls were just as fully developed as the men's.[10] The hostility toward co-education at the University of Toronto is evident in the creation of women's spaces such as Victoria College's Annesley Hall, which began as a college-like facility meant to protect and separate women on campus. After her teaching career, Margaret Addison served as its dean of women from 1903 on and often opened its doors to the Toronto Club for meetings and social occasions. Similarly, St. Hilda's College, affiliated with Trinity College, was established in 1888, but moved to a co-educational facility in 1894. Both Annesley Hall and St. Hilda's became women's residences.[11]

At the University of New Brunswick (UNB), Annie Tibbets' battle for acceptance was aided by economic factors. She wrote her matriculation exam in 1885 but was refused admittance to the university.[12] Unwilling to accept defeat, she checked the Statutes of New Brunswick and found a section stating that any person who passed the province's matriculation examination and paid the fees would be admitted to the University of New Brunswick.[13] She consulted a

Annesley Hall.

lawyer who assured her that under the New Brunswick statutes she was indeed a "person" and then, with the help of Valentine Ellis, member for Saint John, the legislature decided in her favour. As the UNB Alumnae history notes, "there was nothing like a threat to its provincial funding to get the University Senate moving."[14] An outstanding student like so many of these women, Tibbets became the first female high school principal in the province and head of the Department of English at Hyde Park High School in Boston.

Women's uneven admission to university education in Canada followed the country's patterns of European settlement. In Western Canada, women's academic acceptance was less contentious simply because most universities were not established there until the beginning of the twentieth century, when co-education had significant precedents in eastern and central Canada. Some of the graduates from these latter universities brought the idea of university women's clubs west as they themselves relocated. French Canada followed yet another pattern due to Roman Catholic influence at universities such as Laval—and even the University of Ottawa—initially focussing on training men for the priesthood. Women's religious communities such as the Grey Nuns and Congrégation de Notre-Dame trained women for motherhood and roles in nursing, education, and charitable works, much as their Protestant counterparts did.

Getting into a university was only the first of many obstacles women faced, however. Once they stepped onto the campus grounds and disrupted the previous all-male culture, they were treated with a mix of curiosity and hostility. As Acadia student J. L. Marsters describes it:

> ...the young men had their college customs, societies, sports and pranks, and did not like the idea of having women enter into these or of having to change them on account of women being in the same institution. Their presence implied a certain amount of restraint and the young men wanted to enjoy untrammelled freedoms.[15]

Women were initially subjected to an exaggerated civility—some recalled being sung to, escorted to their chairs, kept separate from the rest of the class, or vigorously applauded when they spoke in class. But as the number of women on campus rose, some male students began to express open hostility. One source of friction was women's academic success: when marks were posted, it often became obvious that many of the female scholars were not only as good as male students, they were often better. Despite the disquiet this caused male students, one can only imagine the boost of confidence it gave female educational pioneers. As female students gained in numbers, they became more assertive.[16] Barred from men's extracurricular societies, they formed their own, many of which were literary societies.[17] Others were devoted to debate, a much-loved pastime at this time. As with sports, debate was considered far too competitive for mixed groups and men and women participated separately.

So who were these female educational pioneers? Studies undertaken by the federation and historians indicate that, like their male counterparts, they were predominantly of northern European descent, spoke English as their first language, and came from families of comfortable, if not privileged circumstances. But unlike the men, they were unique in that they constituted a tiny minority within a tiny minority. In 1901, approximately 5 per cent of the Canadian population attended high school and only 0.5 per cent of these attended university.[18] Of this, an even smaller number were women or girls. In 1900–1901, eleven of seventy-three Mount Allison students were women (16.4 per cent), although by 1910–1911, forty-one of 155 (more than 25 per cent) were women. They were more likely to live locally than were male students, probably because parents were less willing to send daughters far from home.[19] Female students, in disproportionate numbers to male students, also came from wealthier families—families that either had sufficient income to send both daughter(s) and son(s) to university, had only daughters, or valued the education of daughters more highly. Male students included sons of teachers, farmers, clergy as well as professionals and businessmen, in which families had to make greater economic sacrifices to educate them as future breadwinners. As some of the examples above show, many of the pioneer women came from enlightened, privileged families from whom they received financial and emotional support.

The Young Women's Christian Association (YWCA), knowing the difficulties that women faced at university, tried to recruit university graduates for their Student Department, which helped female students adapt to university life.[20] However, female students and graduates seemed to prefer to get support and friendship from their peers and began to form first alumnae associations and then later, university women's clubs. In Toronto, each of the separate colleges formed associations, many of which worked to establish badly needed women's residences. They in turn came together to form the United Alumnae Association of the University of Toronto and, in April 1903, twenty-two of them met at Trinity's St. Hilda's College to form the University Women's Club of Toronto. The initial impulse of the club was to be largely social; its stated goals were "to unite university women for social, educational, or any other work they may undertake."[21] They elected young Mabel Chown as their founding president. More than fifty women representing nine universities attended the inaugural meeting that welcomed graduates from any recognized university, thus broadening the scope of membership considerably from that of the alumnae associations.

Helping to extend the idea westward, Acadia graduate Evlyn Farris established a university women's club in Vancouver in 1907 when she found herself transplanted from her native Maritimes. Having recently married her college sweetheart, J. Wallace de Becque Farris, a lawyer and politician, she was struggling with her new role as wife and mother. With her experience from the Propylaeum Society at Acadia and an American Association of University Women (AAUW) club in Middletown, Connecticut where she taught, she hoped to make friends and to become active in reform initiatives.[22] Farris served as the club's first president from 1907 to 1910 and likely had a hand in spelling out its objectives: "to stimulate intellectual activity in college-bred women; to work for practical advancement of art, science, literature and civic reform; and to promote the social welfare of college-bred

Mabel Chown, first president of the University Women's Club of Toronto.

women."[23] The "college-bred" was later dropped. Farris focused on promoting the establishment of the University of British Columbia (UBC) in 1908 and ensuring women's status there. Helen Gregory MacGill joined a year later, bringing her own experience in social activism and legal reform. In 1908, the Vancouver women encouraged those in Victoria to establish a club under Rosalind Young, who worked with Farris to promote UBC.[24]

A Toronto graduate helped bring the idea to Winnipeg. On May 5, 1909, Dr. Mary Crawford, Margaret Johnson, and Lillian Beynon Thomas established another club in that city. Crawford was a physician, active with J. S. Woodsworth's All People's Mission in North End Winnipeg and the Political Equality League.[25] Lillian Beynon Thomas was a well-known journalist, author, suffragist, and member of the Canadian Women's Press Club. Margaret McWilliams joined the club soon after. After graduating from the University of Toronto, she had worked as a journalist in the United States, then married Roland McWilliams in 1903. The first woman to study political economy at University College, her classmates included Roland and future prime minister William Lyon Mackenzie King. Like many early leaders, she had a stellar academic record—she was a star pupil at Harbord Collegiate; associate editor of the *Harbord Collegiate Review*; treasurer of the Literary Society; and president of the Girls' Debating Society before studying at the University of Toronto.[26]

An Edmonton club was founded in 1910, two years after the establishment of the University of Alberta, and accepted graduates, faculty wives, and women whose husbands were in the educational sector. Their goals were to give women students of the university a social life that would be both cultural and wholesome, and to offer a scholarship of $50 to the woman in the freshman year who achieved the highest record of scholarship.[27] In the same year, eight women graduates of the University of New Brunswick, led by Annie Chestnut, formerly Annie Tibbets, came together in the Ladies Reading Room—their assigned room as female students—to form an alumnae association, later accepted as a member of the federation.

From that point on, university women's clubs grew like mushrooms. In Ottawa, on April 14, 1910, fifty-four women gathered at Carnegie Public Library, many of them former members of the Toronto, Edmonton, and Victoria clubs. After some discussion they decided that their goals would be "to keep members in touch with one another; to incite members to continue to be students; and to promote a feeling of responsibility of women for women."[28]

Five years later, Mrs. W. E. Stapleton brought together sixteen university graduates to form a club in Regina. She was the wife of the president of the Methodist Regina College founded in 1911, which affiliated with the University of Saskatchewan in 1925 and later became the independent University of Regina. Mrs. W. W. Andrews, the former Nellie Greenwood, first female student at Victoria University, and wife of Regina College's first president was elected club president.[29] In Saskatoon, on May 18, 1918, fifteen university graduates met at the city's first high school to form the University Women's Club of Saskatoon.[30] Grace Swanson was elected president, and Christina Murray was honorary president. The latter made her home available to graduates to discuss what she called progressive ideas and encouraged activities that would provide intellectual stimulation through the study of relevant issues of benefit to the community. The Murrays often invited female students, a minority on campus, to their home for luncheons, a practice that was particularly common on small campuses where student numbers were low.[31] This club had close ties with campus personnel but still welcomed women from all recognized universities.

Historians know more about the Women's University Club of Ottawa (UWCO) than many others, thanks to a thesis written on it. The Roman Catholic University of Ottawa did not yet accept women and some of the club members came from McGill, Queen's, or the University of Toronto. Most were under the age of forty and two-thirds of the women who joined between 1910 and 1920 were single. Of them, only 48 per cent were in paid employment. By the 1930s, however, that number had increased to 87 per cent.[32] Of those who were working, approximately two-thirds were in the civil service, and the remaining third were teachers. The civil servants were predominantly clerks and stenographers, overqualified in most cases, but there was also an assistant botanist, an assistant geologist, a librarian, an editor, two practising physicians, and the secretary of the Ottawa Welfare Bureau, Charlotte Whitton.[33] It appears that the married women were the most mobile, most having relocated with their husbands.

Given the centrality of university education to their identity, it is not surprising that University women's clubs gravitated, for the most part, to a membership of graduates only. In Ottawa, the club initially accepted undergraduates with second-year standing, but in 1917 voted to restrict membership to those who had graduated from an accredited university. New members had to be approved by the board.[34] In Vancouver, after careful thought and discussion it was decided to keep the club for graduates only, and not to extend membership to a woman with an honorary degree.[35]

The Edmonton University Women's Club did accept non-graduates as members and the McGill Alumnae Association also had associate members, but as Catherine J. Mackenzie noted in 1924, "they really have no business in an Alumnae Society or University Women's Club at all, so we have refused to take them in anymore."[36] Edmonton retained its non-voting members until the 1960s, as many believed that they were "some of our most valuable members." Often married to deans, faculty members, or captains of industry, such members sometimes helped build women's residences by providing access to funds and the corridors of power. At Victoria College, for example, Margaret Proctor Burwash, the wife of Chancellor Nathaniel Burwash, and society women Lillian Treble Massey and Margaret Eaton served on the Victoria Education Residence Association that ultimately built and managed Annesley Hall for female students.[37] The Ottawa Club records noted each woman's alma mater, along with her name and marital prefix.[38] But even among this group of pioneering women, the documents followed the naming conventions of the period, with women using their husband's names or initials rather than their own, although sometimes both were used.

The Edmonton club's records identified one of its raisons d'être as helping women to attend university and they channelled their fundraising efforts into scholarships. In doing so, they did not explicitly tie their efforts to existing formal discrimination against women in the awarding of scholarships such as the Rhodes Scholarship, for which women were not eligible. Still, women were conscious of informal exclusion of women in academic awards, the lack of priority they received, and the prejudices against women scholars. There are anecdotal references to female students earning but being denied scholarships. At UNB, for example, the L. A. Wilmot Scholarship was initially granted to any deserving matriculant, but, at the request of Mr. E. H. Wilmot, was later restricted to men.[39] In the pre-admittance era, women who had won entrance scholarships through outstanding results in matriculation exams were unable to use them.

Socializing continued to be a focus of the early clubs. In a March 1913 special "Women's Edition" of the *Vancouver Sun,* the Vancouver club's second president, Annie B. Jamieson, a teacher and vice-principal of King Edward School, member of the library board, school trustee, and member of UBC senate, stressed the importance of socializing, although she conceded that "being conscientious women, the club very early lent itself to all kinds of social service." She went on:

> At first the big world about us did not seem to attract us strongly. Our own little world was so delightful; getting acquainted with women from so many colleges; finding a bond of union so strong and so delightful; rejoicing in the thought that the best things pertaining to college life were not hopelessly past and gone, but renewed in a larger life. All of these seemed legitimate and very much worthwhile.

Maintaining a balance between sociability and more serious matters was occasionally a struggle. In Toronto, Mabel Cartwright, club president from 1906 to 1908, expressed the opinion that "the Club more than justified its existence by the pleasure it gave valuable members of the community whose lives were already active enough." Further, she added, with so many members of such different opinions, "this craving for activity" led to division.[40] Cartwright, Lady Principal of St. Hilda's College, Trinity clearly felt she was busy enough.[41]

Teas, Christmas parties, luncheons, and dinners, sometimes with national and international speakers, were the order of the day. The Toronto Club, which often met at Annesley Hall, had a yearly luncheon complete with toasts to the king, to the country, to English universities, to American universities, to the University of Toronto, and to Queen's, often followed by replies to the toasts. Some dinners were held in honour of prominent individuals, often in the field of education. In 1913, the Winnipeg club co-sponsored a formal dinner with a men's university club at the Royal Alexandra Hotel to celebrate the reorganization of the University of Manitoba and the appointment of its first president, Dr. James A. MacLean. The evening featured distinguished guests Dr. Robert Falconer, president of the University of Toronto, and the president of the University of Washington. One newspaper source noted that "To add a cosmopolitan touch cigars and cigarettes were served at the head table." The next day, however, the women were shocked to read newspaper reports describing the "party of the intellectual elite at which tobaccos and PERHAPS intoxicants had appeared." While the club was not officially prohibitionist, many members were sympathetic to the cause, and the women "seethed with indignation at this implication that our beautiful party had been a drunken orgy."[42]

Other events were geared toward attracting new members as many clubs took both a maternal and recruiting interest in girls and women presently studying at university or even thinking about doing so.[43] As the Winnipeg club noted:

> They were the "little sisters" soon to join us. Their numbers were still small enough to make contact possible and some of the happiest memories of the early days are of those contacts. For some years a rather formal luncheon, with toasts, was given each spring at one of the big hotels to do honour to the girls of that graduating class.[44]

Meetings also featured discussions, debates, and performances. Members themselves often gave talks on a topic they had researched that was of interest to the group or on a trip they had taken. Such experiences offered women a valuable opportunity to research, to write, and, at a time when women were discouraged from public speaking, provided an entrée—for women who wanted to pursue it—into the world of politics and feminism.[45] Debates were particularly popular. In Ottawa, a formal debate was held on "whether the young woman whose parents can afford to keep her at home should not compete with other young women for paid employment." This provoked considerable discussion and the no forces won.[46]

Club lectures included everything from international affairs to the latest popular book, interior decorating, and even bridge. In their efforts to raise scholarship money, some clubs tried to attract notable speakers and opened the lectures to the public. Some of the lectures organized by the Ottawa club and held at the YWCA featured reviews of such contemporary feminist works as Olive Schreiner's *Woman and Labour* (1912) and Charlotte Perkins Gilman's *Herland* and *The Yellow Wallpaper*. From the outset, clubs also gave special recognition to accomplished women, some of them their own members. The Regina Club invited Dr. Augusta Stowe-Gullen from Toronto to speak on the challenges of practising medicine in Canada, and Judge Ethel McLachlan to speak about her experiences as the first female justice of the peace and juvenile court judge in Saskatchewan.[47] Other lectures were geared toward reform. In Winnipeg, Methodist preacher and social reformer J. S. Woodsworth spoke on "Responsibility Toward the Immigrant."[48] Evidently, some lecturers arranged something of a "club circuit"— Woodsworth spoke in both Toronto and Winnipeg and American author and political activist Helen Keller spoke in Ottawa and Winnipeg. The latter speaker earned the Winnipeg club an impressive $672.

Some clubs established study groups for the arts—music and drama as well as literature. Opportunities to perform in plays, play readings, and concerts were plentiful as a program of monthly meetings had to be filled up. Sometimes these homemade productions became public events with a political message. In Victoria and Vancouver, the clubs presented a one-act play called "How the Vote Was Won," its advertisements claiming that it had first been produced in the Royalty Theatre in London in April 1909.[49] This may have been the production that Lillian Beynon Thomas was referring to when she returned to Winnipeg and urged the Political Equality League to mount a production similar to the one that she attended in Vancouver in 1913. The resulting 1914 production of a mock Parliament, starring Nellie McClung, may not have been the first such production, but it is certainly the most famous. Immortalized in one of Historica Canada's "Heritage Minutes," it will forever be associated in the popular imagination with the achievement of women's suffrage in Manitoba, the first province to grant this feminist goal. Such productions, which blended humour with political mockery, had a long history—the first was produced in Winnipeg in

1893 by Dr. Amelia Yeomans and the Woman's Christian Temperance Union (WCTU). As Joan Sangster writes, such plays "were fairly safe, genteel forms of protest, but they undoubtedly empowered women, some of whom were apprehensive about speaking out or performing in public."[50] They also raised money for the cause.

Handicapped by their exclusion from full citizenship and political participation, many of the university women's clubs lent support to the suffrage movement in the hopes of gaining the vote for women. The next chapter examines the involvement of the university women's clubs in social issues, legislative reform, and the suffrage movement, particularly among those members active in the women's movement.

Footnotes for this chapter can be found online at:
http://secondstorypress.ca/resources

Chapter 2
REFORM, SUFFRAGE, WAR, AND A NEW FEDERATION

Mrs. Pankhurst herself proved to be a lady of dignity and charm, of the type to meet in any English drawing room.
—Elsie Moore and Avis Clark McWilliams, 1909–1959,
University Women's Club, Winnipeg[1]

To their surprise, Winnipeg university graduates in 1911 found that their controversial dinner guest was in reality quite "charming" despite her reputation as a suffragette, or radical advocate for votes for women. Clearly, though, not all of the university women's clubs fully embraced the suffrage movement. This chapter explores the clubs—particularly in the larger cities—that were active in various social reform activities and community service, occasionally doing research into social issues and advocating for political change. Many university women in this decade promoted women's appointment to boards and commissions, especially in universities and an innovative group of British Columbia club women did make the link between the campaigns for suffrage and for legislative reforms. Combined with their undeniable contribution to the war effort, the university women's push for legislative changes contributed to winning the vote for Canadian women of European descent.

In the years 1880 to 1920, Canada experienced social dislocations caused by rapid economic growth, urbanization, and immigration. Middle-class women responded in a myriad of ways to help those most adversely affected. The newly organized university women's clubs often worked with other women's organizations such as the Young Women's Christian Association (YWCA), the Woman's Christian Temperance Union (WCTU), the Imperial Order Daughters of the Empire (IODE), and the Local Councils of Women (LCW), which was federated at the national level into the National Council of Women of Canada (NCWC) in 1893. While university women were fewer in number, they often had better access to the channels of power. Many women's organizations, frustrated in their ability to affect reforms due to political powerlessness, decided to advocate for the vote for women. The earliest example is the WCTU—founded in Canada in 1874 to advocate for temperance and other reforms affecting women and children. In 1910, it became the first women's organization to officially endorse suffrage.[2]

Through much of the nineteenth century in Canada, as in other liberal democracies, the right to vote had been extended first to property-owning men of European descent and later came to include working-class men. This has been called universal manhood suffrage but, in fact, Indigenous, Chinese, Black, and other minority men were still excluded. Almost all women—with the exception of a few unmarried female property owners who voted at the municipal level—were also excluded. The official justification for denying women the vote was that married women were by law subordinate to their husbands and were represented by them in the political arena.

Women began to demand suffrage in the late nineteenth century, both in the name of political equality—that is, as a right in and of itself—and, especially in this period, in the name of motherhood. Many women believed that, as mothers, they should have the power to influence society for the good of all, drawing on the stereotypes of women as more maternal and moral than men. The prevalence of racist views in this period even led many white, middle-class women to assert that their votes were worth more than those of the immigrant, working-class men who had just recently been given the right to vote. Margaret McWilliams from the Winnipeg Club believed that, as a Christian, it was "her duty to help in the moral regeneration of this present world." She unquestioningly held, as a feminist, the conviction that women should have equal rights and equal opportunities with men, yet she also maintained that women's particular responsibilities for nurturing children and creating homes "should also be acknowledged with commensurate right," and that women's homemaking skills could be transferred to the public realm.[3]

University women's clubs were not founded as part of the women's suffrage movement—although many of their members were suffragists—and the right of access to education and the professions was a central tenet of the women's movement. More commonly, the university women's clubs, especially in larger cities such as Vancouver and Toronto, were involved in social reform initiatives. Members of the University Women's Club of Toronto were particularly active with two settlement houses, as the institutions were known at the time: the Evangelia Settlement House, founded in 1902, and the University Settlement House, founded at the University of Toronto in 1910.[4] Located in poorer neighbourhoods, they allowed university women to live and work among impoverished and immigrant communities, offering them health, educational, and other services. An Evangelia representative spoke at the Toronto Club's first meeting and recruited volunteers to teach English classes for immigrants.[5] About a year later, the club paid $25 to become a member of Evangelia—a hefty sum for the period—and contributed annually for the life of the settlement. The club also maintained ties with University Settlement and had a seat on its board until 1973.[6] Settlement work was closely tied to the emerging field of social work. In 1914, the Toronto Club sponsored a round-table conference on social work and appeared to play a minor role in the founding of the University of Toronto's School of Social Work later that year. According to the club's history, this was made possible by a generous gift from a "public spirited citizen" who had attended their conference at the club's invitation. While the school does not credit the club, it does acknowledge Sarah Warren, widow of rubber and tire magnate Harold D. Warren, who gave the new school three years of financial backing. Her ties with the club are not well-documented but she was a member of two short-lived groups, the Social Workers Club (1912) and the Club for the Study of Social Sciences (1911).[7]

At the same time, many of the clubs were forming civic groups or committees. In 1912, the Toronto Club's Civic Betterment

Committee was one of its most active groups, although it also had committees devoted to industrial, social, and educational themes. Maternal issues were often central to reform efforts since motherhood was important to many members' identities. In Vancouver, Mary Bollert, who later became dean of women at the University of British Columbia (UBC), worked with Evlyn Farris to create a Parent-Teacher Federation. The Toronto Club worked with the Local Council of Women to campaign for supervised playgrounds (an early form of daycare for the poor). Toronto also sought to raise the standards of domestic service—a perennial concern—through education, partnering with Central Technical School to create courses in domestic skills. In the words of one member, "What we want is someone to do for housework what Florence Nightingale did for nursing."[8]

University women's clubs also tried to help women working in industrial and commercial employment. As educated women, they felt particularly well placed to conduct research that they could then use as a prelude to advocacy. The Toronto Club launched a two-year program to investigate the position of women in industry.[9] However, club women were not always sensitive to the economic realities of working-class women. In Winnipeg, Margaret McWilliams led a study on "The work of women and girls in department stores of Winnipeg" that concluded that the wages and hours were fair. Other contemporary observers such as Carrie Derrick at McGill University, and reformer/politician J. S. Woodsworth came to a less positive conclusion. As historian Mary Kinnear notes, the club women had "sympathy for women who had to stand up all day, in draughts and sometimes evil-smelling air, who had to dry their hands on unclean linen, who had to write a myriad of sales slips and receipts, who had to search for cheap living accommodation, and who were concerned about their moral reputation," but the report was "eloquent in its silences," failing to mention unions, health and safety concerns (except for seats for workers), or demands for fewer hours or for wage increases.[10] Still, the report was widely distributed and helped to change public opinion in favour of the appointment of women factory inspectors and the passage of a minimum wage law, which occurred in 1918. The Vancouver Club proposed a Maternity Protection Act, prohibiting new mothers from returning to work until six weeks after their confinement. It also prohibited night work for women and youth. Some working women resented the restrictions such "protections" placed on their employment options.[11]

The early university women's clubs had their greatest successes in defending professional women and in securing appointments for their members to various public boards and commissions. They believed that capable women would prove their worth in the civic sphere and erode the prejudice against all women. Sometimes this strategy promoted the careers of their own members—and so much the better. From 1911 to 1913, the Vancouver Club backed women candidates for the school board. And they were not content with mere scraps from the men's table. After some initial successes, they complained that women were being passed over for board chair duties and began to advocate for these. The Toronto Club worked with the Local Councils of Women to obtain the appointment of a woman inspector of public schools, Aletta Marty, who happened to be a club member.[12]

The Vancouver Club advocated on behalf of New Brunswick-trained lawyer Mabel French, who moved to Vancouver in 1910 but was denied admittance to the British Columbia bar. The same thing had happened to her in New Brunswick, where she fought the exclusion and won.[13] Evlyn Farris convened a university women's club committee to deal with the issue and got an interview with W. J. Bowser, the attorney general. Appealing to him as a fellow Maritimer, Farris was persuasive and persistent—when Bowser tried to stall, she refused to leave his office. She secured quick passage of Bill 45 in February 1912, and French was called to the bar on April 1—a significant victory for the new club.[14]

Most of the clubs were supportive of women teachers, who made up approximately one-third of their members. In Vancouver in 1918, the club passed a resolution calling for "equal privileges and salary for men and women teachers in practice as well as in theory, and that all positions including principalships and inspectorships be open to women."[15] Nowhere were teachers as poorly positioned as at the university level. Some faculty heads actually took pride in excluding women, believing they would lower the academic standards at their institutions. At most universities, female professors were congregated at the lowest end of the pay scale, largely in part-time positions and in female subject areas such as English and modern languages. When female enrolment significantly increased in those subjects, and when many men went overseas during World War I, some universities hired female assistants to teach women—in separate classes at a reduced salary with limited faculty privileges. Later, when the universities established nursing, home economics, and social work programs, female faculty began to congregate there.

The university women's clubs did make a few inroads into university governance. Having experienced discrimination at university as students, and as teachers in the school system, women realized the importance of representation in getting women accepted into all programs, including professional programs, and helping women make inroads into faculty teaching. They achieved some success in gaining women's appointment to university boards, although their impact was initially quite limited.

When Evlyn Farris came to Vancouver in 1905, the University of British Columbia (UBC) existed only on paper, and she set to work helping to realize its foundation. The province had passed the necessary legislation, but progress was stalled by arguments as to where the new university would be located—Vancouver or Victoria—and political inertia. Farris is among the leaders of British Columbia club women whom historian Lee Stewart credits with promoting and upholding women's place at UBC. An effective speaker, writer, and lobbyist, Farris reminded both the public and the government that UBC "must accommodate women's interests in higher education, beyond the mere fact of their admission."[16] Rosalind Young, whom Farris had convinced to take on the presidency of the Victoria University Women's Club, was married to BC's provincial secretary, H. E. Young, who introduced the act to establish the university in 1908. Rosalind Young had drafted the legislation, ensuring that (at least on paper) women would have equal privileges with men and that women would be eligible for appointment to the university senate. In 1915, when classes finally began, Farris was appointed to it, but she found that it actually had little power and in 1917, after helping the Liberals win the election, she was rewarded with an appointment to the more effective board of governors. During her tenure on the board, she supported extra-curricular teaching to spread education across the province.[17] Employing her skills as hostess and unofficial public relations officer, she enhanced the institution's prestige and longevity. Nonetheless, despite her hard work, Evlyn Farris could do little to stop the use of "assistant" English professors in separate female classes during the war years.

University women did not always agree on how to represent women's interests. Farris parted company with many of her fellow club members on the introduction of programs such as nursing and home economics at UBC. She was a strong believer in liberal arts and fought programs geared specifically toward women, even though she

Evlyn Farris, founder of University Women's Club of Vancouver.

believed that married women should devote their full attention to homemaking. She believed that "women's programs" would lead to the segregation of women into "feminized" areas of work and study. But the majority of university women's clubs adopted them as a strategy to "upgrade" work that women were already doing. Nursing was introduced to UBC in 1919, although Farris did win one concession—nursing students were required to take two years of general arts along with their practical training.

Margaret McWilliams was appointed to the Council of the University of Manitoba in 1917, yet she felt she was unsuccessful, resigning in 1933 over the lack of women appointed to university government and the low numbers and slow careers of faculty women at the university.[18] The Alumnae Association at the University of New Brunswick (UNB) fought for representation on their university's senate. When they were initially refused, the women hired a lawyer, incorporated, and had an amendment to the University Act introduced into the legislature. In 1919, the amendment granted two places on the senate to alumnae (the Alumni Association for male graduates of the university already had two places).[19] At Dalhousie University, Eliza Ritchie, a suffragist, early graduate, and active club woman became the first female member of the board of governors, serving from 1919 to 1925. The youngest of three daughters to attend Dalhousie, and the only one to graduate (1888), she completed a PhD at Cornell in 1889 and taught at Wellesley for ten years before returning to Halifax. With an independent income, she devoted her life to lecturing, promoting the advancement of women, and supporting a women's residence, Forrest Hall, at which she served one year as "warden."[20]

The United Alumnae Association at the University of Toronto and the University Women's Club (whose membership overlapped considerably) successfully campaigned for the appointment of three women to the university's senate in 1911. They were Gertrude Lawler, head of the English department at Harbord Collegiate and Charlotte Ross, a University College graduate who taught at Margaret Eaton School and later served as head of English at Havergal College. A little later, physician and suffragist Dr. Augusta Stowe-Gullen was also appointed.

These concessions came out of a 1908 controversy at the University of Toronto over the proposed establishment of a separate college for women, which illustrates the divisions among university women themselves.[21] In response to a substantial increase in female enrolment, particularly at University College, historian George Wrong convinced the university to explore the possibility of establishing a separate women's college, an idea that had been floated much earlier when women were first admitted to the college. Wrong's committee included no women, met in secret, and accepted no briefs or submissions from outside groups, yet it concluded that a separate women's college was "both feasible and advisable."[22] In response to this, university women met with the new president of the university, Robert Falconer, arranged through his secretary, Annie Patterson (BA 1899), an Alumnae Association member. Female students then waged an effective protest against the Wrong report, ensuring that the idea was never implemented.

It does not appear that the protest against a women's college was unanimous. Initially at least, the University Women's Club, then under the presidency of Dr. Helen MacMurchy, a controversial and conservative feminist, supported the Wrong report.[23] In Anne Rochon Ford's history of women at the University of Toronto, she notes that the University Women's Club approved of the idea of a separate college because it "might encourage women to begin to think of themselves more as individuals in their own right and less in their relation to men."[24] This sounded like a tepid endorsement of separate education. They added, however, that "it would be better to see the results of the remedies now being tried to overcome the evils of co-education than risk others that would be inevitable with the establishment of a new college." Another source later noted that this consensus remained unchanged despite a series of meetings where "prominent speakers addressed the club on the pros and cons of co-education."[25] That sounded like a tepid endorsement of the status quo. University women undoubtedly remembered that the university administration had used the prospect of a separate women's college to keep women out of University College until 1884. Some female academics were sympathetic to separate colleges, which were prevalent in Britain and the United States; if they were well-funded, such institutions could offer excellent education and freedom from the competition and hostility women often experienced in co-ed schools. They also provided faculty positions for female academics. In reality, though, separate colleges for women had a poor history in Canada—early ladies' academies had been financially precarious and were short-lived. Many female educationalists believed that as long as only women attended, that would remain the case. The university administration knew that separate colleges were expensive, but had apparently been hoping for a wealthy benefactor like the one who had helped at McGill. But such a donor never materialized in Toronto and the women—having demonstrated that they could exert effective influence—were conceded representation on the university senate.

There may also have been some confusion regarding separate colleges as distinct from women's residences. Universities, forced to admit women, did try to create separate spaces for men and women. Early examples of separate colleges—St. Hilda's, for example, affiliated with Trinity College—continued to exist as women's residences after hopes for separate colleges faded. Alumnae Associations were certainly in favour of residences for women.[26] Margaret Addison, dean of Annesley Hall, one of the first residences for women at the university, envisioned it as a much-needed place to provide a warm and inviting atmosphere for women students.[27] An early University of Toronto graduate and mathematics professor, Alice Cummings, noted, "Years of residence at Bryn Mawr and at Vassar have impressed on me how great a deprivation it was to the students of my day to have no residence for women." The lack of such a residence, she added, "deprived me of one of the great benefits of a college training, namely the opportunity of becoming better acquainted with the many earnest and scholarly women who were fellow students with me at the University twenty five years ago."[28] Still, the protest against the Wrong report indicates that after several decades of co-education, some female students felt that competition with men at school was not such a bad idea because it would better prepare them for the work world.

University club women joined thousands of Canadian women in support of World War I (1914–1918), work that was often highly publicized. In Winnipeg, "instead of literary or academic discussions our regular sessions now took the form of sewing meetings when we worked twice each week on dressing gowns for hospitalized soldiers."[29] In Toronto, war work included the preparation of surgical dressings and hospital supplies for the Red Cross and the University of Toronto Hospital, one of several university-equipped overseas military hospitals. In British Columbia, several clubs took on the processing and collection of sphagnum moss used for dressings when cotton was in short supply. It was particularly abundant on Lulu Island, a little south of Vancouver.[30]

Shortages of food and other commodities imposed restrictions on social events, but educational lectures did not stop entirely. People were hungry for war news and some clubs secured war correspondents for very popular lectures, usually donating the money raised to war charities. Winnipeg's Civic Committee began to investigate increases in food prices and looked into whether some goods could be produced at home. In December 1916, Margaret McWilliams addressed the club on the issue and took it upon herself to monitor wartime food prices. This led to her appointment to the provincial government food board in 1917.[31]

Although some historians and many popular writers have suggested that this work led to the granting of women's suffrage at the end of the war, this popular myth gives too little credit to the long years of struggle that women had put into the suffrage campaign. It might be fairer to say that politicians used war work as a justification for reversing their previous hardline positions against suffrage. The war did, however, have an impact on the social reforms that university women championed, slowing down legislative reforms because many women felt that it was unseemly to demand political rights when the country was at war. But as it dragged on, many felt that the huge sacrifices being made both overseas and at home warranted a better Canada. Thus suffrage, as well as prohibition, two campaigns that were closely linked, achieved success in the war's aftermath. The war also enhanced women's educational gains as more women attended university when men went off to war and a few faculty positions even opened up to women. But like most war opportunities in this and the next war, the gains disappeared once peace was made.

Toronto UWC volunteers in the physics building, University of Toronto, making sphagnum moss dressings for wounded soldiers overseas.

Some club members were reluctant to endorse suffrage, feeling that an educated woman had to behave in an exemplary fashion, or she would bring shame on all of them. In Ottawa, the club debated the suffrage issue in 1913. Conversations heard on the sidelines indicated that while the majority was in favour of enfranchisement, "not so many approved of immediate steps being taken to gain that end."[32] As noted above, similar sentiments were expressed in Winnipeg when British suffragist Emmeline Pankhurst was invited as a guest lecturer in 1911. One club history indicated that some women feared the controversy she would bring:

> A few of the members opposed the undertaking, but some felt that there was a distinct difference between a proper academic interest in a movement advancing the right of women to share in the government and personal association with the leader of its campaign of violence; who had fought with policemen, set fire to His Majesty's mailboxes, chained herself to lamp posts so that she could not be removed from a vantage point from which to shout her message to members of the government; who, to sum it up had become only too familiar with jails from the inside.[33]

In protest, some women refused to sit with the executive on the platform but later regretted it when "we took our inconspicuous seats in the audience, practically incognito" and "had an uneasy feeling that we were traitors to our group and to our cause" as Pankhurst proved herself dignified and charming.[34]

Prominent women, especially those married to public figures, appear to have been protecting their husbands' reputations. Margaret McWilliams in Winnipeg never came out publicly in favour of suffrage, although she actively promoted women's participation in politics after it was won. Farris supported it only when her husband's party did so, and did so then to gain legislative improvements.

Many club members, however, were well-known suffragists such as Helen Gregory MacGill in Vancouver, and Lillian Beynon Thomas and Dr. Mary Crawford in Winnipeg. They organized much of their suffrage activity through other organizations. The Vancouver Club illustrates how university club women gradually

learned that it was difficult to effect change in society without political power. They had forged a particularly successful partnership with

Helen Gregory MacGill, legal reformer and member of UWC of Vancouver.

the Local Council of Women in a program of legislative reform in 1911, when a joint Laws Committee was formed under the leadership of Helen MacGill. This followed lectures by legal experts who surveyed the field.[35] Indeed, dower laws could leave widows destitute, married women's property laws did not allow them to own their own wages, custodianship laws recognized only the father, and estate laws failed to recognize women's familial contributions.[36] The committee went to work petitioning the government and watched for opportunities to push their agenda to reform these injustices. Little progress was made under the ruling Conservative government led by Richard McBride, and the committee decided to concentrate their efforts on legislation regarding the guardianship of children.

By 1915, the club decided that "these reforms might take forever to materialize as long as women had no power to elect or defeat the lawmakers."[37] During the presidency of Laura Jamison from 1915–1917, the club unanimously passed a resolution supporting the franchise for women. The Vancouver Club then allied with British Columbia suffragists and supported the opposition Liberals, who took a position in favour of suffrage. In May 1915, MacGill and Farris helped establish the Women's Liberal Association (WLA), electing Mrs. W. H. Griffin, a former president of the Local Council of Women as president of the new organization, with Mary Ellen Spear Smith as vice president. They campaigned actively, helping the Liberals to win a convincing victory in September 1916, taking thirty-seven seats to the Conservatives' ten. Wallace Farris and Ralph Smith (husband of Mary Ellen) were both elected and Premier Harlan Carey Brewster publicly acknowledged the support of the WLA. Farris and MacGill were among those women invited to sit in the provincial legislature for third reading of the suffrage bill in 1917, and to a celebratory dinner afterward. Both women also received political rewards: MacGill was appointed juvenile court judge and Farris was named to the UBC board of governors. MacGill used her appointment to create an innovative family court system within the newly created juvenile court, while Farris looked out for the rights of women at UBC.

Over the next ten years, a program of innovative legislation was passed. In 1916–1917, the Vancouver Club secretary reported that "The Laws Committee is gloating over the satisfactory attainment of women suffrage in British Columbia, the Equal Guardianship Act, and the Deserted Wives Act. For years the club has been striving for this consummation and views the result happily."[38] In January 1918, the club recommended that the government establish pensions for mothers having dependent children left without sufficient means of support and the act passed in 1920. In the same year, a minimum wage for women was passed as well as amendments to inheritance laws.[39] Many of these changes were copied in other provinces, with BC legislation serving as a model.

Historians credit MacGill for this legislative revolution. A self-taught expert on family law who did her own research, in 1913, she published the book *Daughters, Wives and Mothers* in which she outlined all the British Columbia laws that she felt needed changing.

She revised the work several times as the laws changed; the last version, called *Laws for Women and Children in British Columbia*, appeared in 1935.[40] Evlyn Farris also contributed to this work. She had been interested in law in university, seeing it as a way to give direction to society. She would not practise law, given her views that married women should devote their full attention to homemaking, but she believed that she could influence her husband to promote the views that they both shared.[41] MacGill certainly credited Farris's political influence on Wallace Farris, who was BC attorney general from 1917 to 1922, for their successes. Evlyn Farris would notify women's groups whenever legislation began to stall so that they could send a delegation to Victoria. Once her husband was in office, Farris deliberately maintained a low profile, appearing only as a supportive wife and elegant hostess who whispered in the right ears. Farris had great intellect and organizational skills, and inexhaustible drive, but she believed that to achieve reforms she had to work through men. As her biographer, Susan McClean, explains, "She had lived in their world at home and at university. She understood the way they thought. She knew how to approach them, to make them feel needed and important, to challenge them intellectually, to bring them to her side."[42]

Farris's relationship with female politicians such as Mary Ellen Spear Smith also reflects her belief in indirect influence. Following the death of her husband, Ralph, Smith won a by-election in January 1918, on a platform of "women and children first."[43] Farris feared that Smith's approach would lead to the formation of a separatist, women-only party and even tried to block Smith's endorsement by the Liberals.[44] Still, Smith, one of the more successful of the suffragists-turned-politicians of the post-suffrage era, played a considerable role, along with MacGill, Farris, and the Vancouver University Women's Club, in legal reforms and in improving women's place in mainstream political parties through the creation of the Women's Liberal Association. Although the CFUW would sometimes emulate Farris's strategy of behind-the-scenes influence, not all would have agreed with Farris's notion that certain causes should be avoided "because it would divide the members and taint the Club's impartiality in the eyes of men in power, thereby destroying the Club's effectiveness."[45]

THE CANADIAN FEDERATION OF UNIVERSITY WOMEN

With the crisis of war over, and the dawning of a sense of nation-hood and internationalism, the ideal of forming a federation seemed appropriate. Margaret McWilliams, the organization's first president, credited the federation's "birth" to British professor Winnifred Cullis, who had been active in the British Federation of University Women (BFUW),[46] and was planning to form an international association. Cullis had lectured at the University of Toronto and had Canadian connections.[47]

In 1917, following the American Association of University Women (AAUW)[48] proposal that the Canadian clubs affiliate with them, Toronto's May Skinner was appointed to the International Relations Committee and attended the AAUW's Chicago convention in 1918. In the fall of that year, the Americans invited a British Mission on Education that included Rose Sidgwick and Caroline Spurgeon, both active in BFUW, to visit the United States. When the mission came to Toronto, they no doubt discussed their plans to form an International Federation of University Women. Winnifred Cullis suggested that the "Canadians should organize at once in order to be among the first members of the international body."[49] The founding meeting was held in London in July 1919, at which British delegates met with Virginia Gildersleeve, dean of Barnard College and a representative of the American association. The goals they agreed on were strongly influenced by the war, and the new organization sought to prevent a similar conflict by fostering friendship and understanding among a worldwide, united body of university women. The Canadians joined soon afterward.

The formation of the CFUW also had roots in local initiatives. A 1912 letter from a Miss Little to the Toronto Club asked them to correspond with other Canadian clubs to find out what was being done to form a Canada-wide group. The club minutes record them as being in favour of forming such a union, asking the incoming executive to draft a constitution and send it to other clubs.[50] This was done, and the Toronto Club received replies from Winnipeg, Saint John, Vancouver, and Ottawa. There is little documentation on what happened next, except for a few notes in club histories speculating that the war had intervened. Likely it had.

In telling her particular version of the creation story, McWilliams chose British over American influence and peace and international-ism over the Canadian group's core social and educational mandate. We do not really know why—perhaps she simply preferred Cullis as a "co-founder." An expert in physiology, graduate of Newnham College, Cambridge, and the University of London, Cullis was the first woman in the United Kingdom to serve as a professor. She certainly had solid credentials. But then, so did Dean Virginia Gildersleeve of Barnard College. Like most Canadian organizations, the CFUW took inspiration from both the British and American groups, although the British were clearly favoured.

In Winnipeg, in June 1918, a committee was organized to draw up a provisional constitution and plans were made to invite clubs to a meeting in Winnipeg. McWilliams then travelled to Toronto to confer with Mrs. John Cooper, May Skinner, and Laila Scott. Together they drafted a constitution, which articulated the follow-ing purposes:

a) to stimulate the interest of University women in public affairs, and to afford an opportunity for the expression of united opinion;

b) to promote the higher education of women, and especially to encourage research work;

c) to facilitate social intercourse and co-operation between the women of different universities.[51]

According to the 1919 constitution, the university women's clubs and alumnae associations, rather than individuals, would form the membership of the federation.[52] The clubs paid fees to the feder-ation at a rate of $5 per twenty-five members. Voting for officers was to be held by ballot at a triennial meeting, with executive or council meetings in intervening years. Any member could attend a general meeting and take part in discussions, but only those elected by clubs as delegates would have a vote.

McWilliams favoured a decentralized structure, as she was anx-ious to avoid what she viewed as the autocracy and central-Canadian bias of the National Council of Women of Canada (NCWC), which had led to disaffection from the western provinces. McWilliams had

CFUW organizational meeting in Winnipeg, 1919.
Back row, left to right: Mrs. C. Wiley (Ottawa), Mrs.
E. Smith (Victoria), Mrs. Sadler (Winnipeg), Jessie
Dykes (Toronto), and Kathleen Teskey (Edmonton);
front row, left to right: Lexa Denne (Victoria), May
H. Skinner (Toronto), Dr. Margaret McWilliams
(Winnipeg), Mrs. G. L. Lennox (Winnipeg), and
Dr. Geneva Misener (Edmonton).

chaired a subcommittee to revise the latter organization's constitution, and she ensured that reforms rejected by NCWC were enshrined in the CFUW's new constitution. Meetings were to be triennial rather than annual and any club member could attend them—measures intended to reduce the influence of the richer, more populous regions of Canada.[53] Clubs were fairly autonomous in pursuing their own activities and an effort was made to disperse triennial meetings across the country. Similarly, the president was expected to visit all the clubs during her three-year tenure and often travelled at her own expense, although the federation did assume some costs.[54]

The CFUW constitution stipulated that club or alumnae association members were to be graduates of recognized universities or academic equivalent, the latter to be determined by the Executive Committee. In fact, it was found in 1919 that some clubs, such as the Edmonton Club and the McGill Alumnae Association, included non-graduates, and "a compromise was reached in which two types of membership were instituted: federation (voting) and associate (non-voting)."[55] Some clubs wanted to include non-graduates so that they could participate in study groups, or to extend membership to a woman of high academic standing who did not have a degree.[56] Although the federation generally discouraged associate members, the final decision on membership was left up to the clubs.

Despite the disruption of the Winnipeg General Strike in May and June, which received barely a mention in the minutes, the founding meeting went off as planned in August 1919. Forty-one delegates attended from seven clubs[57] and McWilliams was elected president, May Skinner was elected first vice president, and Mrs. Douglas Thom, the former Mabel Chown, was elected second vice president. The delegates set up committees on education and vocations, and made plans for a scholarship, a publication to be called *Chronicle*, and surveys on education and vocations.[58] The Travelling Scholarship, meant to be an equivalent to the Rhodes Scholarships, for which women were ineligible, was to be financed through lecture series and tours.

These plans were ratified at the first triennial meeting in August 1920, held in Toronto. The formation of the new federation brought the work of the early clubs into a more structured format that would allow it to take on new directions. The early club women brought with them some of the philosophical underpinnings of the CFUW: the efficacy of quiet influence and a determination to use their education in the service of society rather than for their own gain.

In the 1920s the federation worked on building clubhouses, established a scholarship, and put their own stamp on issues relating to education, libraries, peace, and professions for women.

Footnotes for this chapter can be found online at:
http://secondstorypress.ca/resources

Chapter 3
THE 1920S: FINDING THEIR PLACE

The reminiscences of these women whose ambition, perseverance
and devotion to high ideals opened the way for all those of us who
followed and so made possible our own Federation, have given
us a record of notable achievement that cannot but inspire us to
greater things.

—Elinore Wheeler, federation archivist[1]

Elinore Wheeler reported on a survey into the experiences and
careers of early women university graduates at the federation's
second biennial meeting in 1923. There were plans to publish a
collective biography of these educational pioneers and inspirational
founders of the organizations, but these were never realized.[2]

In 1919, the federation was brand new and unsure of itself, but
by the end of the 1920s, it had consolidated and grown, and had
begun to advocate for women. The organization had inherited from
the clubs a focus on providing friendship and networking opportunities for university-educated women, and community improvement
initiatives in education, the arts, and social welfare. To expand on
these, the federation established committees on education, libraries, and vocations. Resolutions began to take a prominent place
in the machinery of governance as a means of establishing policy.
The federation would later put in place a more formal machinery to
influence legislative changes based on those resolutions, but for the
time being their advocacy was fairly informal. Clubs were largely

autonomous and could send voting delegates to the triennial meetings on the basis of one per twenty-five members up to a total of twenty-five, and then one per fifty after that. They organized their own programming, such as lectures, social events, fundraising, and often had parallel committees with the federation. They could also pass local resolutions and act on them without federation interference. The federation launched the *Chronicle* to keep members in touch with one another and to allow the executive to keep members informed of decisions on the national level. One of the federation's first projects was to introduce the Travelling Scholarship, which made a significant contribution to advanced study by women and assisted some of them to gain academic appointments.

These early ventures were based on a philosophy, which Kinnear called a "meritocratic vision tinged with a sense of obligation,"[3] that was articulated by the national organization's first president, Margaret McWilliams. McWilliams had studied political science with future Prime Minister Mackenzie King, worked as a journalist, and had led numerous organizations. She was an orator with "great stamina, energy and an unusually fine mind," and was able "to endow whatever she was doing with a special value, a worthwhileness, which brought forth in those who worked with her powers they did not know they possessed."[4] As leader of the new federation, she asserted that education was a privilege that necessitated giving back to society. The university was expected to inculcate in all students a deep sense of social obligation and leadership. For example, Reverend H. J. Cody, 1930s president of the University of Toronto, defined the educated man as one who was able to use "the mother tongue correctly and precisely" and to demonstrate a "refinement of manners…and the power to do or earn money in the workaday world."[5] Like men, university women were also expected to reflect middle-class respectability, but there was an added emphasis on their "natural" role as nurturers both in the community and in the home. The earliest women university graduates strove for exemplary behaviour, fearing that any misstep would put the entire group into disrepute. McWilliams further stressed that women's community service should demonstrate the worth and competence of the educated woman and gradually erode the prejudices against them. For the most part, federation members were liberal or moderate feminists whose main goal was to allow women to take a larger share in the leadership of Canadian society through improved access to the professions, business, and academia.

The federation's first triennial meeting in Toronto in August 1920 set a tone that reflected the importance of friendship. In her remarks, McWilliams expressed her hope that the new organization would offer "an unrivalled chance to revive old college friendships and to create new ones in that spirit of comradeship which is the fine flower of college life."[6] The elegant social events reflected university-educated women's better-than-average financial security and ethnic privilege; they were women who shared common values and social connections with the ruling elite. At one such event, delegates spent a "delightful" evening being escorted through Hart House—which was ironic given that female students wouldn't be able to use the facility until 1972. They were also entertained at a tea party at the Royal Canadian Yacht Club in Toronto and had dinner at the elegant Sunnyside Pavilion on Lake Shore Boulevard.[7]

Subsequent triennial meetings were often held in or near the president's hometown, although intervening executive meetings—called council meetings—were more often held in central Canada. The 1923 triennial meeting, under McWilliams, was held at Minaki, just north of Kenora. The 1926 triennial was in Montréal, at McGill's Royal Victoria College, during President Susan Vaughn's tenure, and the 1929 triennial was held in Vancouver and presided over by Mary Bollert. Meetings always included locally arranged entertainments. At a 1924 council meeting, a luncheon at the Château Laurier was attended by two hundred Ottawa Club members. In Vancouver, Evlyn Farris hosted a tea at her home and meeting attendees enjoyed dinner at the Shaughnessy Golf Club.

The organization grew steadily, if not spectacularly, throughout the 1920s. By 1923, there were sixteen clubs in the federation with 1,280 members from seventy-five universities. Eighty-one per cent of the members held bachelor's degrees and 8 per cent held master's degrees. Reflecting the newness of women's education in Canada, a minority (fifteen) had graduated from Canadian universities, while forty-four were educated at American institutions, and thirteen at British schools. Reflecting the youth of the organization, only 12 per cent of its members had graduated in the 1890s, while 71 per cent had graduated between 1900 and 1920, and 15 per cent in the last three years. Teachers represented 36 per cent of members, homemakers 40 per cent, and 8 per cent were engaged in commercial work, mostly secretarial. Teachers ranged from elementary to university level, but only 4 per cent of them taught at a university. The rest were doctors, missionaries, social workers, librarians, dentists, lawyers, judges, nurses, and dieticians.[8] Figures from the Ottawa University Women's Club membership in this period show a large number of civil servants, apparently most of them underemployed in clerical jobs.[9] It also appears that, at least among the Ottawa Club, women followed the social customs of their era, identifying as Miss or Mrs., with married women using their husbands' names or initials rather than their own. In the early part of this period, social conventions dictated that most of the single members who lived at home were not employed. This soon changed, however, and single women joined the burgeoning job market, largely in sales and clerical work, for at least a few years before marriage.[10]

By 1927, the federation included twenty-three associations and 1,863 members, welcoming the University of New Brunswick Alumnae Association as well as new clubs in St. Catharines, Niagara Falls, Hamilton, and Montréal.[11] The organization did express concerns that the membership numbers were not keeping up with the increased enrolment of women in universities; the number of women undergraduates grew from 16.3 per cent of all students in 1920, to 23.3 per cent in 1940. Still, in 1929, the federation was attracting an impressive 60 per cent of new graduates.[12] Some historians have credited this loss in membership to a decline in all-female social networks in the 1920s,[13] although women's culture was still important, particularly among single, professional women whose emotional and social support usually came from other like-minded women.

Clubs responded to members' interests and local conditions, which led to a variety of programming that combined socializing with educational activities and grew in breadth and diversity throughout the decade. Interest groups and study groups, for example, proved to be quite popular. A typical annual club program might include monthly meetings with a fall tea, a Christmas party or concert, and an annual dinner meeting in May or June. Vancouver's

1922 Christmas party featured a doll-dressing event "accompanied by much merriment," with the dolls later donated to the Victorian Order of Nurses to be distributed to needy girls.[14] Other social events were designed to recruit new members, such as Saskatoon's receptions for women graduates that were held in association with the annual teachers' convention. Regular meetings usually had a business component, followed by some type of entertainment, lecture, or discussion. The Toronto Club's music group, for example, provided concerts, one of them held at the Heliconian Club, a social and intellectual meeting space devoted to women in the arts. Clubs in smaller towns were modest in their expectations. In Niagara Falls, the club selected speakers who were ideally "endowed with missionary zeal and no craving for financial success."[15] In 1919–1920, the Saskatoon Club chose drama as a program theme, while Edmonton members debated the value of intelligence testing.

Sponsoring public lectures was a popular way to raise money. Edmonton invited their own members, such as Mrs. E. T. Bishop, the first woman elected chairman of the Edmonton Public School Board, and curriculum specialist Donalda Dickie, to speak.[16] In one case, the importance of making money seemed to overshadow club women's own interests. Ottawa's 1928 lecture series, which featured University of Toronto professors, included a talk by classicist Maurice Hutton, who spoke on the evils of co-education! He could not have received a warm welcome, although his denunciation of the modern craze for dancing must have caused a few chuckles. Surprisingly, he was invited back a year later to give an immensely popular talk on ancient Greek philosophy.[17]

Many of the lectures honoured outstanding women. For example, the federation collaborated with the American Association of University Women (AAUW) in hosting Marie Curie's visit to Niagara Falls on her 1921 American tour. The two organizations jointly contributed $100,000 toward the purchase of radium for her research. The Ottawa Club invited McGill academic and activist Carrie Derick and agrarian feminist Violet McNaughton from Saskatchewan. In the early years, many clubs had given some of these women the position of honorary president, but this became less popular by the 1940s and 1950s.[18]

Study groups, particularly in some of the smaller centres, often

CFUW and AAUW women meet
Madame Curie, Niagara Falls, 1921.

emphasized cultural subjects such as poetry, literature, drama or play-reading, art, and music. Regina organized an art exhibition and Winnipeg's drama group put on plays. Other study groups tackled subjects as diverse as child study, education, the law as it pertained to women and children, and conversational French. Indeed, the possibilities were as limitless as the imagination of the women creating them.

Many of the clubs held classes on current events. Margaret McWilliams herself began conducting bi-weekly lectures and discussions on current events in 1915. For a time, the Winnipeg University Women's Club sponsored these talks, and in other cities, local clubs' held lectures and discussion groups on civic engagement.[19] McWilliams' lectures grew into an institution and when Roland McWilliams became Manitoba's lieutenant governor in 1940, they were moved into the ballroom of Government House. These talks were popular and influential, and many political leaders and journalists wanted to know what McWilliams had said on a given topic.[20] Current event discussions taught women how to exercise their newly won voting rights in the post-suffrage era, and to hone their own research, writing, debating, and presentation skills. The federation, like so many other women's groups, ultimately served to train women for political activities should they later decide to pursue them. Participation taught them rules of order, how to run meetings, and gave women practice—and confidence—in public speaking. McWilliams, who believed that women's managerial skills as homemakers qualified them for political leadership and that education made them capable and insightful critics of civic institutions, herself ran for city government in the 1930s.

As mentioned, the federation sometimes branched into political advocacy as issues arose. In 1921, it joined other women's groups in calling for the appointment of a woman senator, a move that eventually propelled five Alberta women to challenge the Canadian government's assertion that the constitution barred women from the Senate.[21] Similarly, the federation and many local clubs encouraged women to run for school and library boards, city government, and other political offices.

As the clubs grew, they needed venues in which to hold meetings, concerts, dinners, and entertainments. Alumnae Clubs often had access to university buildings, but the larger urban clubs began to search for permanent clubhouses to provide women with attractive meeting spaces, meals, living quarters for single, professional women and hospitality for visitors. Elite men have a long tradition of establishing clubhouses where they can network and that highlight their status in the community. University women, anxious to play a broader social and political role in society, also found it appealing to acquire large, elegant, older homes in desirable districts. CFUW, even before a clubhouse existed in a Canadian city, made a pledge of £1,000 toward a Canada Room in the planned British clubhouse, Crosby Hall. There was considerable excitement about the establishment of international clubhouses—in the United States, the AAUW purchased a clubhouse near the White House in 1921, and there were similar spaces in Paris, Rome, Athens, Brussels, New York, and Baltimore. Now, when federation members visited London and other cities, they would have a women's space where they could stay.

Being part of this international network of women was a point of pride and was seen as a way to encourage membership.

Canada soon joined the trend. When the Montréal University Women's Club was opened in 1928, "the first and only University Women's Club in the Dominion,"[22] the CFUW president warmly congratulated the group. Their clubhouse would allow Canada to reciprocate the hospitality of friends from other national affiliates of the International Federation of University Women (IFUW). The creation of a clubhouse had been the founding goal of the Montréal alumnae associations when it re-established itself as the University Women's Club of Montréal. Built in 1908 by noted domestic architects Edward and William Sutherland Maxwell, it was one of four houses in pairs of two that sat at right angles to Peel Street and faced each other across a common driveway.[23] Various alumnae groups furnished the common areas of the house that members could reserve for private parties. There was a card room and a handsomely paneled dining room that opened onto a garden with wide elms and slender poplars, twelve airy bedrooms, and two bathrooms on each floor. Although it was acquired at below-market value, the $45,000 cost was a major financial commitment—the terms required $10,000 in cash as a down payment with the balance to be paid by February 1932 in annual instalments of not less than $1,500. The club charged an entrance fee of $25 plus a $15 annual fee, and offered bonds up to $10,000 to members and friends, but the hefty dues led to a membership shortfall. The club attracted 257 charter members, less than the hoped-for three hundred and the house was later sold.[24]

Toronto and Winnipeg would also establish their own clubhouses. In Toronto, alumnae member Annie Patterson had investigated the possibility as early as 1910, but, unable to raise enough money, the club had to rely on various other venues such as Annesley Hall on the University of Toronto campus, local restaurants, and the Women's Art Association.[25] The Toronto Club, which hosted executive meetings of the federation in 1925 and 1927 as well as the 1926 triennial meeting, reported difficulty in securing a permanent space, opting instead for the costly alternative of renting a small room as headquarters and larger rooms for entertaining. In 1928, with a membership of 250 graduates, the club decided to acquire its own headquarters. In order to legally transact business,

Fourth Triennial Conference, Canadian Federation of University Women, Vancouver BC, August 21–23, 1928.

they created a holding company, University Women's Graduates Limited, which raised money by issuing stock. The club purchased a house at 162 St. George Street at a cost of $45,000.[26] The alumnae associations donated much of the furnishings and the clubhouse opened in November 1929, offering bed-and-breakfast accommodations, meals, and even a venue for wedding receptions.[27] Having the clubhouse allowed the club to hold more frequent meetings along with Monday teas, luncheons, and dinners. The Toronto Clubhouse played host to a CFUW meeting in 1929.

Several clubs tried to acquire a clubhouse but were unsuccessful. The Ottawa Club raised money and negotiated with the Women's Canadian Club to share what would become the Chelsea Club in downtown Ottawa. There was even optimistic speculation that it could be used as an Ottawa branch of a still-only-dreamt-of National Vocations Bureau. Unfortunately, however, disagreements over privileges led the club to withdraw. During the presidency of the irascible future Ottawa mayor Charlotte Whitton, the Ottawa Club even tried to take over the Chelsea Club's board, although nothing came of this.[28] Relations later improved, and the club used the facility from time to time.

Clubhouses held another attraction for university women. In Montréal, for example, the clubhouse filled the accommodation needs of professional women and those attending the university. In an era when a woman living alone was still frowned upon, single, professional women who could not live with relatives experimented with living together at settlement houses where they could provide each other with social, material, and emotional support. Women students congregated in nurses' residences and university residences for similar reasons. The Toronto clubhouse also offered accommodation to single women.

After the initial excitement wore off, clubs soon realized that owning and maintaining a clubhouse was a drain on their financial and human resources. Toronto was particularly unfortunate in having purchased their clubhouse on the eve of the Depression. The club's new financial obligations gave them less time and energy for participating in the welfare programs of the community.[29] Still, the appeal of property ownership was persistent. Even among relatively wealthy women, their exclusion from financial and property management meant that they took great pride in being able to form companies, issue stocks and bonds, and run a clubhouse.

The federation also found that not all members shared the enthusiasm for a British clubhouse—many members resented the special one-dollar levy on each member to pay for it. Fundraising to meet this large pledge to the IFUW took up much of Susan Vaughn's presidency from 1923 to 1926 and had to be supplemented by private donations and local efforts. To raise more funds, Vaughn also conducted a national lecture tour on literature, her academic specialization.[30]

As discussed, socializing was far from the only focus of the clubs. There was also an impetus to provide service to the community. In 1926, retiring president Susan Vaughn remarked that there was room in the federation's broad design for a vast array of interests including humanitarian work.[31] She noted that where intellectual workers gathered, schemes for human betterment and the improvement of living conditions were certain to flourish. Prior to the 1920s, which was an active period of social reform in Canada, many disparate women's groups came together to campaign for women's suffrage. After they achieved the vote, these groups all went their separate ways. Working-class and socialist feminists dedicated themselves to changing the economic and political systems to ensure greater equality

not just for women, but for all, especially workers. Middle-class feminist reformers, like university club members, pursued goals especially geared toward university women graduates. Nonetheless, they

The Toronto clubhouse, 162 St. George Street, Toronto, Ontario.

continued to seek ameliorative reforms, often aimed at women and children. Prominent Vancouver member Helen Gregory MacGill, for example, founded a branch of the Business and Professional Women (BPW) in Vancouver in 1923 to assist the growing number of women working in sales and clerical jobs. The Canadian Federation of Business and Professional Women (CFBPW) emerged seven years later. British Columbia legislative reforms on the legal standing of women and children continued into the 1920s, as did the crèche (daycare centre) housed in the Women's Building, a cooperative venture that provided space to women's organizations.[32]

While the federation and clubs in larger cities were more pre-occupied with such initiatives than clubs in smaller towns, they all made contributions. In 1924, Moose Jaw made a $50 donation to a hospital for tubercular mothers, while other clubs contributed books to libraries, toys for Christmas hampers, and donations to the Salvation Army. Montréal and Toronto both undertook settlement work. May Skinner served as the Toronto Club's representative to the University Settlement and organized the collection of books for the library, sewing classes, and baby clinics.[33] Over the years, Edmonton Club members taught English to "foreign" girls and staffed kindergarten classes and story hours at local hospitals.

It was not unusual for smaller clubs to do advocacy work of short duration and local scope. Such efforts sometimes emerged out of a study group or lecture. For example, the Ottawa Child Study Group lobbied the local board of education to change school hours for Grades 1 and 2 after hearing a lecture on the importance of sunlight to young children.[34] They also joined the Local Council of Women in an initiative to lobby for the medical inspection of schools, a popular public health reform of the period. But they declined to lobby the federal government for women's access to the civil service when asked by the federation, thinking that they were too small to take on such an ambitious project.

The CFUW, confident in the research abilities of its members, started to increase its capacity for developing expertise in specific areas. The earliest Education, Vocations, and Libraries Committees, for example, turned their energies to researching topics relevant to women and children, which in turn prompted the women to use their political influence to lobby various levels of government on social, political, and/or legislative issues.

Education, in particular, was a natural fit given the members' high educational attainment and a membership made up of one-third teachers and a great many more mothers. The Education Committee was convened by Geneva Misener, a classics professor at the University of Alberta from 1912 to 1945, an advisor to women students, and a member of the university senate.[35] The committee recommended improvements that would increase the low level of high school attendance, then only 6.2 per cent. The report concluded that 80 per cent of the school population in Canada was enrolled in elementary schools—compared with only 56.20 per cent in the United States—but pointed to the slow progress of students in rural schools due to irregular attendance and over-worked teachers in the primary grades.[36] It recommended more uniform attendance laws from one province to the next, and an increased expenditure per child on education. As noted, committees at the federation level were often mirrored in clubs—indeed the national committees sometimes emerged out of the local ones. Edmonton's Education Committee helped organize Girls Conferences with the YWCA and other groups to provide education, vocational guidance, and recreational activities to young women in the city. This idea had originated in a 1917 provincial committee chaired by Geneva Misener. The committee also lobbied for English as a second language classes, and increased provincial educational standards. By 1925, the requirement for a passing grade had been raised to 50 per cent from the previous 30 per cent.[37]

Library reform also appealed to university club women. At a time when funding from philanthropist Andrew Carnegie was helping to build community libraries across Canada and the United States, progressives viewed the library as an important educational institution, one that would foster good citizenship values among both adults and children. A report by the federation's 1923 Library Committee, convened by Jessie Montgomery, provided a thorough survey of library conditions, legislation, and policy in Canada, and stressed the importance of access to libraries, especially for children in rural communities.[38] Later in the decade, the committee's reports detailed some improvements they had helped bring about, including increased expenditures on juvenile literature, the opening of children's rooms, and the institution of story hours in libraries across the country. Montgomery, who was very active in this field in her home club of Edmonton, was educated in Scotland and had taught school in rural Alberta before obtaining a BA in 1914 and Bachelor of Library Studies at the University of Wisconsin in 1915. Her employment as an organizer of travelling libraries for the University of Alberta's Department of Extension no doubt influenced her activism. The Edmonton Library Committee also studied legislation in British Columbia and Ontario in anticipation of redrafting Alberta's library legislation, investigated local school libraries, and asked the provincial government for an increase in grants.[39]

The federation library report also encouraged the appointment of women to local library boards and the improvement of standards, training, pay, and working conditions for librarians. Frustration at the lack of both a national library association—the Canadian Library Association was not established until 1946—and a Canadian-based library school would appear as a constant refrain in the national committee's reports. Two Toronto Club members, Winnifred Barnstead and Bertha Bassam, later helped found a library school at the University of Toronto and pioneered in the standardization of library procedures in Canada.

The federation's Vocations Committee was established to help university-educated women obtain employment that was appropriate to their education. The committee members chose to use the term vocations to evoke the notion of a calling, rather than a job or profession, and, presumably, to allow them to include the volunteer work that many married women did. Convenor Elsinore Macpherson outlined the great and increasing opportunities for university-educated women in her 1920 report. She optimistically outlined opportunities in the fields of law—which were very few— social work, business, and industry, although she acknowledged that "there is still, apparently, a certain suspicion of the college woman in business."[40] At the same time, she identified a potential new field that mixed social work with business, the field that we would now call human resources.

Macpherson recommended that women act as trailblazers, encouraged women to seek employment opportunities in all fields, and encouraged potential employers to hire them. Some of the women graduates who did not wish to teach were exploring such jobs. All was not rosy, however, as the discrepancy between salaries for men and women tended to stratify the job market. So did some of the new educational programs being introduced, such as nursing and home economics and the University of Western Ontario's degree course in secretarial science.

To remedy gender stratification in the workplace, Macpherson recommended an equal pay policy. She also recommended the establishment of a central employment bureau for professional women that would do research into vocations for women, promote university-educated women to employers, and conduct placements. She pointed to the formation in 1920 of the US Women's Bureau, which promoted the rights and welfare of working women. The new Canadian federation, however, worried that they did not have the capacity for such an endeavour, and the committee's recommendations were revised at the next triennial. That report encouraged women to use existing government agencies, although, in fact, there were no such agencies in Canada at that time. Three years later, in 1923, when the Vocations Committee made a similar recommendation, the federation was still not in a position to undertake it, and the 1926 report asked clubs to appoint local vocation officers and work through universities. The federation, with no administrative staff and run entirely by volunteers, was not in a position to help.[41]

Nonetheless, the federation clearly saw the need and in 1928, it and a few clubs joined forces with two women who were already in the process of establishing such a bureau in Toronto. Mrs. N. A. M. MacKenzie served as chair, and Jean Gertrude (True) Davidson, a graduate of Victoria College at the University of Toronto, was director. They set up an office on Bloor Street West and began research into what occupations were open to women and to inform qualified women of available positions. The story of this bureau is best told in the context of the Depression years and will be explored in the next chapter.

In 1930, the federation asked Alice E. Wilson, a 1926 scholarship winner, to help the Vocations Committee promote the advancement of women in the civil service. It was Wilson's own case that prompted the CFUW to actively advocate for more senior jobs for women in government. When her employer, the Geological Survey, blocked her efforts to pursue a PhD, the federation went to work on a full-scale lobbying effort: Susan Vaughan sent a telegram to the president of the University of Toronto; Mabel Thom wrote to Charles Dunning, MP; Geneva Misener contacted Charles Stewart, minister of mines; and Rosalind Young consulted the University of British Columbia's dean of arts Reginald Brock, who also happened to be a geologist. Stewart agreed to provide Wilson's replacement —a condition of her leave—and granted her six month's leave *without* pay. Wilson told the committee that this was a ruse to diffuse embarrassing publicity and to prevent her being granted leave *with* pay.[42] Still, Wilson believed that her limited success set a precedent for women in the civil service. Wilson's story is explored in more detail in Chapter 13.

In relation to employment, the club's focus was often directed toward teachers since teaching was one of the few professions open to educated women and they were well-represented in federation membership. In 1920, Jessie Muir, an Ottawa Collegiate Institute teacher, alerted her club to a pay disparity between male and female teachers. The club then passed a resolution endorsing the principle of equal pay for teachers and sent it to the school board.[43] The club's records indicate that the board rectified the situation. However, they offered no further details on the scope of the disparity. Nonetheless, the Ottawa Club counted this as a victory. Muir, described as a feisty champion of women's rights, helped found the Ontario Secondary School Teachers' Federation (OSSTF) in 1919.[44] In 1928, the Vancouver Club declared support for equal privileges and pay for male and female teachers, including access to principalships and inspectorships.[45] The federation continued to use Geneva Misener's education report to lobby on behalf of female teachers, asking for enhanced teacher training and gender equality.

Academic appointments were a major area of concern for the federation—small wonder as so many of the early leaders were academic women, including the three CFUW presidents who followed Margaret McWilliams. Susan Vaughn, federation president from 1923 to 1926, was a McGill University "Donalda"—the name given to McGill's early women graduates in honour of their benefactor Donald A. Smith, later Lord Strathcona. Vaughn completed her MA in 1899, became a lecturer in the English department at McGill, and, by 1918, had achieved the position of assistant professor of English. Mary Bollert, federation president from 1926 to 1928, was the dean of women at the University of British Columbia (UBC) from 1922 to 1941. Laila Scott, president from 1928 to 1931 had studied modern languages at St. Hilda's (Trinity College); finished her master's degree two years later in Germany; joined the Trinity staff in 1917; and then became an associate professor in 1924. She also had a seat on St. Hilda's Council and was a founding member of both the University Women's Club of Toronto and of the federation.

In her 1923 education report, Misener noted that fifty years had passed since women were first admitted to Canadian universities, and that women now formed nearly half of the student body in the faculty of arts. Yet only one woman to every fourteen men advanced beyond the undergraduate level. As well, while one-third of female university graduates become teachers—and 85 per cent of Canadian elementary and secondary teachers were women—only five or six per cent taught at universities. To make matters worse, if nursing and household science were excluded, women made up only 1 per cent of the teaching faculty at Canadian universities.[46]

The biographies of the early presidents show the extent to which academic women were expected to supervise female students in an atmosphere that blended elements of separate education within co-education and were able to achieve only marginal academic status. Laila Scott and Susan Vaughn, respectively, functioned as matrons of women's residences at St. Hilda's at Trinity College and Royal Victoria College at McGill. Both of these institutions had begun as separate women's colleges. Laila Scott never became a full professor despite her master's degree and long years of teaching at Trinity; Mary Bollert was placed at the lowest professorial rank in UBC's English department, and was never made an ex-officio member of the university senate, as were other deans. Despite expectations that she would do public speaking, attend conferences, and perform duties similar to other deans, she was never given an expense account.[47] Fortunately for her students, she was "a kindly generous person, luckily possessed of private means,"[48] who seems to have embraced the maternal role expected of her.

Women continued to search for ways to surmount academic barriers. Elinore Wheeler's 1923 survey of educational pioneers asked participants to comment on why there were so few women at the executive levels of secondary schools and in university positions. Many pointed to the fact that women were expected to marry, and that a woman "must be far superior to the men with whom she competes to be appointed to such posts." As well, the prevalence of co-education in Canada, in contrast to women's colleges in the US and Britain, made the outlook even less promising. Women teaching at universities knew that they were being paid less than men and were promoted less often despite being better qualified. Many had master's and doctoral degrees at a time when male professors often did not. But, like the early educational pioneers, they were careful not to make waves. As historian Mary Kinnear found in her examination of university teachers in Manitoba during this period, most were acquiescent; they were sometimes resentful but rarely rebellious. Doris Saunders, who won a federation scholarship in 1925, taught for many years at the University of Manitoba, noting that she "felt privileged to be there."[49] Still, women knew they were blazing trails, and organizations such as the Canadian Federation of University Women slowly began to demand more and better seats at the academic table.

The marriage bar was one of the handicaps that women often discussed, highlighting the absurdity of keeping educated women from using their knowledge in all but volunteer roles. Although marriage conventions were sacrosanct and club women usually shunned controversy, some, especially single professional women began to question them. Geneva Misener, for example, argued that "marriage and a profession may go hand in hand for a woman as for a man."[50] Elsinore Macpherson, who had chaired the national body's Vocations Committee, had written her 1920 thesis on "Careers of Canadian University Women." She spoke more bluntly than most, noting that "women who gave up careers for marriage hindered the professional development of all women." She believed that doing so reinforced employers' belief that female employees were temporary, forcing women's salaries down and limiting their access to promotions.[51] Not everyone agreed, however. Even some single women like Charlotte Whitton—child welfare advocate, hockey player, and later mayor of Ottawa—insisted that women must choose between motherhood and a profession.

The work of the Vocations Committees also encompassed young women and, at the club level, members often reached out to local schools to tell female high school students about possible careers and encourage them to attend university. In Vancouver, Evlyn Farris was a guest speaker in Annie B. Jamieson's class at King Edward High School and one young woman, Marjory Martin (Mrs. Gosford) remembered the impression that Farris made, remarking on "her lovely fairness set off by an apricot taffeta suit."[52] Responding to Farris's charm, she resolved to go to university and, at the same time, to follow some rather more conventional advice to help her mother and always throw out dead flowers. The positive voices of club women urging young women to attend university and consider unconventional careers may have been the only encouragement that many of them heard.

As one of the major disincentives to women attending university was cost, CFUW and individual clubs showed a constant commitment to providing scholarships for them. The Edmonton Club's founding objectives included the establishment of a $50 scholarship for the freshman woman with the highest academic achievement. By 1920, they were awarding $100 to the Grade 11 female student with the highest standing in English, Latin, French, and history. This club did not restrict its largesse to women and girls: one gold medal ($30) for the student with an 85 per cent standing in third and fourth years was awarded to Roland Mitchener, future governor general of Canada.[53] The scholarships were primarily financed through members' fees and by 1929, the Vancouver Club members paid a then-princely $5 membership fee ($3 for women who were one year past graduation).[54] Some clubs also set up student loan or donation programs. At UBC, Mary Bollert worked with the university women's club to pass donations to needy students through her office and the Queen's University Alumnae raised $200,000 for a women's residence. When it was built, one of its members, Annie Laird, was appointed dean.

While local clubs helped high school students get to university and undergraduates to stay there, the federation established its $1,000 Travelling Scholarship to encourage advanced study for women. Believing that the most convincing argument for women's academic appointments was productive scholarship, the federation devoted resources to cultivating academic women qualified to take up teaching and research posts in Canadian universities.

The federation scholarship was funded, not through endowment, but by a levy based on the membership size of each club.[55] Although they were by and large committed to supporting women's education, clubs occasionally complained about contributing their share. The Ottawa Club, for example, debated whether this should be the club's primary goal as opposed to fostering fellowship among women.[56] To supplement the scholarship funding, the federation secured the services of Canadian poet Bliss Carman in 1921 and American poet Vachel Lindsay in 1922 for nation-wide lecture tours. Unfortunately, though, because of the tremendous distances and related travel costs, these projects were less than stellar financial successes and were not continued. When the matter later came up for discussion in 1929, the majority of clubs also expressed opposition to national lecture tours as scholarship fundraisers.[57]

While the founders of the Travelling Scholarship may have underestimated the persistent, systemic nature of discrimination against women in academe and placed a lot of responsibility on the shoulders of individual women, the goal of enhancing women's advanced education came to define the organization, give it purpose, and unite its members. The successes of the phenomenal group of academic achievers who won the Travelling Scholarship—worthy of greater attention in its own right—will be explored in Chapter 13. The next chapter takes us into the 1930s, when the worldwide economic Depression introduced a whole new set of challenges to women trying to find their place in the community and in the working world. The period forced the CFUW into a defensive posture and the organization was able to realize little in the way of real progress.

Footnotes for this chapter can be found online at:
http://secondstorypress.ca/resources

Chapter 4
THE DEPRESSION:
DEFENDING WOMEN'S RIGHT TO WORK

...quietly with increasing definiteness in Britain, the United States and Canada there is a drive to get women out of business positions and the professions. The exclusion of married women from employment in many large businesses is now quite general. The railways for some years now have definitely set a limit to the positions women may be allowed to fill.

—Cora Hind, Winnipeg Club member and feminist[1]

The Depression that began in the autumn of 1929 and continued with varying intensity throughout most of the decade had a devastating impact on Canada. Farmers, the poor, and unskilled workers were hardest hit as businesses failed, and unemployment rose to unprecedented heights. In the west, depressed prices for farm products coincided with a terrible drought and many farms had to be abandoned. The resulting exodus to towns and cities, particularly in British Columbia and Ontario, found municipalities overburdened and unprepared to provide for the destitute. Minimal relief was doled out on the principle of "less eligibility"—a meagre and humiliating amount meant to preserve the work ethic.[2] For most of this period, little help came from the provinces or federal government. Young men (and a few women) rode the rails looking for work and the federal government even resorted to establishing military-style work camps to quell potential unrest. The cost of living dropped, making life more comfortable for those securely employed or well

off, but many people lost their jobs outright, while the more mar-
ginally employed lived in fear of being dismissed and/or having their
wages cut. Birth and marriage rates fell, a back-to-the-land movement emerged, immigration ground to a halt, and there was a rise in
both deportations and racism.

Relatively well-off federation members were sheltered from the
worst, but they were not exempt from suffering. Teachers found
it difficult to secure or keep employment as cash-strapped school
boards cut back and male teachers returned to the profession after
shunning its low salaries in the 1920s. Single women employed in
the new sales and clerical jobs that had opened up before and during
the 1920s found themselves unemployed. Women carried the heavier
domestic burden of having to make do, stretch meagre budgets,
provide extra emotional support to husbands and children suffering
unemployment, and care for the elderly at a time when few social
services were available. Some families doubled up their residences
with another family or took in boarders; those women who could
find it did formal or informal wage labour, but were often criticized
for "taking jobs away from men." Faced with unprecedented levels
of unemployment many Canadians blamed working women.

Growth slowed for CFUW in this decade—few new clubs were
formed, and there was a slight decline in female university attendance compared with men in the 1930s.[3] Membership remained
fairly static. In 1937, the membership secretary reported 2,251 members, compared with 2,125 in 1934–1935. Some women were unable
to afford the fees and there were a few anecdotal references to unemployed club members, although the topic was seldom discussed.
The 1932 Vancouver Club minutes note that the $10 Christmas
donation has been "expended in hampers for former Club members who gratefully acknowledge their receipt."[4] True Davidson, a
single woman who was trying to forge a new career through hard
times, was understandably angry when the Toronto Club cancelled
her membership due to unpaid fees in 1931.[5] At the time, she was
working free of charge to keep the federation's struggling Vocations
Bureau afloat. Undoubtedly, there were many others like her. The
membership did increase to 2,678 by 1938 but in 1939 the numbers
were down to 2,593. From 1933 to 1937, the number of affiliated clubs
remained at thirty-two. Late in the decade, however, the federation

welcomed new clubs from St. Catharines, Hamilton, Peterborough, Swift Current, Brandon, Thunder Bay, and Belleville.[6] And it seems that Ottawa, St. John's, and Sarnia nearly doubled their membership.

The federation, like many women's organizations, worked on a shoestring budget, moving administrative headquarters from one kitchen table to another with changes in executive officers, all volunteers. In 1939, they hired the first paid staff member—a permanent national secretary who worked from home for $400 per year, plus $100 for equipment. An Academic Appointments Committee, founded in 1934 to find jobs for the federation's scholarship winners, remained inactive for the rest of the 1930s. The minutes of 1938 record that the organization asked Dr. Margaret Cameron to convene a Resolutions Committee. Resolutions were used to express CFUW policy on political and social issues and would later guide the organization's advocacy. A resolution could originate with the executive or the clubs, after which they were circulated, sometimes edited, discussed, amended, and voted upon at triennial meetings. Clubs were well represented in the voting body, minutes recorded decisions taken at meetings, and the *Chronicle* kept members informed.

The kind of members in both the rank and file and the leadership was beginning to shift by the 1930s; there were fewer single, academic, or professional women, and more homemakers and volunteers. Membership figures from the Ottawa University Women's Club, for example, show that in the 1920s, 75 per cent of applicants were single and 25 per cent were married; in the 1930s, 59 per cent were single and 41 per cent were married.[7] This may be a function of an aging population—there was a recorded influx of older women in the late 1930s—but it also appears to reflect changing demographics within the group. There was also a slight increase in the number of women with graduate degrees and a greater specialization in subject area trends with the university-wide introduction of home economics, social work, and nursing. The federation reported in the 1930s that 31.4 per cent of its members were teachers, 5.3 per cent were in business, 3 per cent were librarians, 5.3 per cent did not report, and 8.4 per cent were in other professions such as medicine, nursing, dietetics, civil service, social work, journalism, farming, and the ministry. The remaining 46.6 per cent described themselves as housewives although the committee secretary was quick to add, they were "actually occupied with all the vocations included in the foregoing list."[8] The *Chronicle* continued to be published through these bleak years despite threats to discontinue it if members did not show greater interest. Although an abbreviated version was issued for 1935 and 1936, it remained a reliable record of what the organization was doing throughout the decade.

The women in leadership roles followed this trend as well. The federation's presidents were more likely to occupy conventional roles such as teachers, mothers, wives, and philanthropists than the academic leaders of the 1920s. Mabel Thom, for example, who served as president from 1931 to 1934, had, as Mabel Chown, founded the University Women's Club of Toronto in 1903. After marrying law student Douglas John Thom, she moved to Regina and became active in the Red Cross, the Women's Missionary Society, the Women's Canadian Club, and the peace movement as well as the University Women's Club of Regina. Laura Newman, president from 1934 to 1937, was a University of Toronto graduate in modern languages and a woman of independent means who performed the philanthropic role expected of women of her class. She helped found the St. Catharines University Women's Club in 1921 and worked with the Canadian Red Cross Society, the Young Women's Christian Association (YWCA), and the St. Catharines General Hospital. Charlotte Melrose from Edmonton was president from 1937 to 1940 and was likely an early member of the Edmonton Club before becoming its president in 1929. A McGill graduate, teacher, mother, and voluntary sector leader, she was widowed in 1920 at the age of forty-five. She taught school from World War I until her retirement in 1934 and volunteered for the Church of England, the Canadian Bible Society, the McGill Alumnae, and a women teachers club.

Fundraising was also affected by the depressed economic conditions. There were complaints in Toronto that the members were finding it hard to sell tickets to lectures, a staple fundraiser. Things were worse in the west. The Edmonton Club had great difficulty coming up with funds to send voting delegates to executive and triennial meetings.[9] The Regina Club had to discontinue its scholarship for several years after deciding in 1930, to grant scholarships to male and female students on the basis of scholastic proficiency, leadership, and citizenship.[10]

The Depression was particularly difficult for clubs that had just entered into property ownership. The Montréal Club's history records that, despite lowering its rates, its clubhouse nearly floundered when the stock market crashed in 1929:

> ...even professional people had their salaries cut and women graduates from colleges and universities were faced with unemployment. No women were being taken on in industry or business and many who had held responsible positions were let out because men with family responsibilities had to have any available work—and the married women members were wives of men who in their own businesses were faced with reduced profits and more and more retrenchments. A luxury like a social Club membership was the first economy to be exercised.[11]

Because of this, and the federation's interests in having a clubhouse for executive and out-of-country visitors, Montréal was allowed to pay the lower fees of an Alumnae Association.[12] Still, clubhouses were important for fostering fellowship among women from different countries, a primary focus of IFUW.[13] In 1937, the first hospitality scholarship was awarded to Phyllis Marjorie Gill, an honours graduate in natural science from Cambridge. She stayed at the Montréal clubhouse and the federation even supplemented her year with a trip across Canada.

The Toronto clubhouse, established in the 1920s, had some lean years too. By 1933 the club had lost one hundred of its members—down to 306—and had to reduce room rental rates and meal prices. Even so, many of the members shared Davidson's sentiment when she complained that she could not afford to eat there.[14] Until 1936, when conditions improved, the house was often empty.[15]

Although it was not a CFUW project, the Vancouver Women's Building, formerly Tait House at 752 Thurlow, was a product of Helen MacGill's initiative in 1911 and it provided space for many women's groups that helped to purchase and repair it. By 1913, five thousand women belonging to twenty-two organizations shared the facility. Reflecting the optimism of the 1920s, the groups acquired a new, larger building in 1926 that housed meeting space and social services such as the club's nursery. During the Depression, free classes were held there to train unemployed women as waitresses and sales clerks.[16] In 1935, difficulties in meeting the mortgage payments led to the painful decision to sell the building, and the Salvation Army purchased it in 1940.

Despite the economic downturn, the dream of having a clubhouse hadn't died. As early as 1911, the Winnipeg Club began to investigate the possibility of sharing one with other women's groups. In 1919, they received an offer from the American Women's Club of Winnipeg to share rooms in the Scott Block[17] and established a House Fund, with thirty-five members paying a fee of $3—later increased to $5—and funds began to accumulate. In 1938, an opportunity arose to view a house at 54 West Gate, the former home of author Ralph Connor, as a possible clubhouse. For reasons that are not recorded, the club rejected the idea of a cooperative women's building and decided instead to create their own clubhouse. They began renting it in 1939 and spent five months on renovations and furnishings. They were able to take advantage of Depression conditions that led to large homes being dismantled and "fine pieces of furniture less suitable for smaller quarters than for ours became available at prices ridiculously low, even in those times."[18] As their history notes, both the club and the city benefitted—instead of the historic building being demolished, the city received rent equivalent to the original taxes.

During the Depression years, many women's clubs focused on helping women in need, especially single women who were denied relief. Women at the Vancouver Club, cognizant of the plight of cash-strapped municipalities, hesitated to lobby for measures that would require public expenditures.[19] Nor did they want to be labelled radical. So they focused on charitable initiatives that often aimed at helping children. In 1931, the Vancouver Club's social service section established a work party at King Edward High School to repair children's clothing, with sewing groups and clothing depots continuing throughout the Depression years.[20] The Toronto Club had a morning study group that produced and donated quilts to the University Settlement and knitting to the Little Trinity Housekeeping Centre.[21] The remaking of clothes and bedding helped many Depression-era women, especially those in the hardest hit families of unskilled workers and immigrants.[22] The Toronto Club's civic recreation group established six centres with a trained person to lead children

Ralph Connor House, Winnipeg.

in games, songs, and dancing, thus helping overworked mothers with childcare.[23] Members of the Niagara Falls Club volunteered at a well-baby clinic and in Moose Jaw, members contributed to relief funds. The Regina Club held a bridge tournament to help the Welfare Bureau hire a social worker for families on relief. The Winnipeg Club's dietician-members conducted demonstrations of food values to representatives of sixty-five organizations, and distributed menus and food charts.[24]

Some of the clubs focused on helping needy students. The Saskatoon Club decided to donate the $250 they had saved for a clubhouse to the University's Bateman Fund for students. They noted that, as the plight of so many needy students came to their attention, "the concept of a Clubhouse Fund seemed less important."[25] Canadian campuses were also hard hit by the Depression and universities were forced to raise tuition fees substantially and, sometimes, make drastic program cuts. As a result, the number of female students, approximately 25 per cent of the student body in the 1930s, declined relative to males. Women from struggling families often had to drop out and take whatever employment they could find—sometimes in order to keep their brothers in school. Female students who did manage to continue their education found it hard to secure summer or part-time employment. Mary Bollert, dean of women at the University of British Columbia (UBC), remarked that families who normally hired students to work as domestics in exchange for room and board were now able to employ full-time maids for as little as $8 a month.

Some clubs that had not done so previously established local scholarships and bursaries in the 1930s. In 1931, the Victoria Club issued its first loan from a fund set up to help undergraduate students, later re-activated as the club's Diamond Jubilee Bursary, awarded annually to a mature student who was studying part- or full-time.[26] The Ottawa Club launched its first scholarship in 1935,[27] and Queen's Alumnae Association in Kingston established the Marty Memorial Scholarship in 1936, named for Dr. Aletta Marty (MA 1894), Canada's first female school inspector, and her sister Sophie, head of modern languages at Stratford Collegiate.[28] Some Alumnae Associations also worked toward establishing women's residences.

With grim conditions all around them, many clubs turned inward. The Toronto Club's history records, for example, "it is rather surprising to read in the Minutes that a debate was held on the subject, 'Resolved, that the primary aim of a women's Club should be social relaxation.'" Twenty-four speakers took part in a spirited discussion and a standing vote gave a large majority to the affirmative.[29] Middle-class standards were not sacrificed in entertainments either. In May 1934, the Vancouver Club held a carnival-themed dinner at which women dressed in costume. The Regina Club put on a Barnum and Bailey circus at the college to raise funds, thinking that would spread some joy amid the gloom.[30] At the 1937 federation meeting in Toronto, members had dinner at the Royal Canadian Yacht Club and watched the lowering of the colours at sundown, a longstanding naval tradition.

Public lectures continued to be important for fundraising, and some of the topics reflected the times. The Brandon Club, for example, sponsored talks on *Capitalism and the Five-Year Plan*, *Unemployment*, *The Gold Standard*, and *Business Depression*.[31] Saskatoon was one of many clubs to deal with cultural topics and in 1932 they cooperated with the Art Association of Saskatoon to bring in Arthur Lismer to speak on Canadian art.

Study groups also grew in popularity across the country and in some cities they were even linked to an increase in membership. Many clubs formed groups devoted to social exchange, creativity, and self-improvement; the Vancouver Club, for example, held discussions on social service, books, international relations, French, drama, education, science, transportation, and music.[32] In Hamilton, one of the newer clubs in 1930, Dr. Elizabeth Bagshaw, who was also the medical director of an early birth control clinic, started a child study and mental health interest group for members to study new developments in child care.[33] Other newer clubs, including those in Calgary, Saint John, Prince Albert, and Moose Jaw, had groups on mental hygiene, current events, the study of Russian geography, history, Canadian social problems, modern psychology, and arts and crafts.[34] Some of Ottawa's discussion groups—such as those on writers of the Irish Renaissance; short story techniques; drama (play-reading and play-production); music appreciation; and a writers' workshop—even had waiting lists.

The study of social and economic conditions in some clubs led their initiatives on public service and reform. The Vancouver Club added an International Relations Group as a successor to the old Laws Committee that had initiated the impressive British Columbia legislative reforms, which it called a "truly grand and historic old committee."[35] While some clubs declined to make financial demands of governments during the Depression, others became more activist. The Vancouver Club joined angry students in protesting draconian cuts at UBC. New political parties such as the Social Credit in Alberta and the Cooperative Commonwealth Federation emerged in this decade, accompanied by labour strikes and protests. The increasing evasion of minimum wage and other labour laws in the clothing and textile industries where many women were employed resulted in wages and working conditions worthy of "emphatic condemnation," as reported by the 1935 Royal Commission on Price Spreads.[36] When Toronto garment workers went on strike and made a direct appeal to the university women's club for support, the club recommended an enhanced system of inspection and pledged to purchase products with government-approved labels. In 1939, the Ottawa Club organized a roundtable conference on municipal affairs that generated a document calling for emergency relief and low-cost housing.[37]

By contrast, the clubs that were reluctant to seek public funding found they could do very little. For example, the Library Committee noted that "the financial stress of the times" had made it impossible to carry out many suggested reforms and improvements.[38] Still, it did lend its support to the Radio League's campaign for public broadcasting in Canada and, when the Canadian Broadcasting Corporation (CBC) was formed in 1935, it pressed for educational and children's programming.

In contrast, the Edmonton Club had a more active Education Committee that lobbied for publicly funded kindergarten and protested a school board motion banning women from serving as principals of schools with more than five rooms.[39] At the federation level, the Education Committee investigated the scarcity of positions for women in universities and in school administration. In 1937, although the committee reported that Canada was behind England and Scotland in hiring women as educational administrators, it occasionally veered toward blaming women for not being "aggressive enough in preparing themselves for and seeking higher positions in education."[40]

No one exemplifies the restrictions on women in educational administration better than Edmonton's Donalda Dickie. Despite her leadership and talent, she never held an administrative position in the Alberta Department of Education where she was employed as a normal school teacher, a position for which she was clearly overqualified. Born in 1883 to Scottish parents, Dickie was orphaned

Donalda Dickie, Alberta normal school instructor, author, and influential educational reformer.

Gertrude (True) Davidson, co-founder
of the Vocations Bureau and later mayor
of East York.

and raised by a grandmother who provided a strong role model. She was a brilliant student and, after winning medals in English and history, was awarded an MA at Queens in 1910. Dickie later attended Somerville College at Oxford, where World War I interrupted her studies. After transferring to the University of Toronto, she defended her thesis in 1929.[41] It is unclear whether she tried to secure an academic post in the Depression years, but she did contribute substantially to curriculum development and is widely recognized as an educational innovator. The textbooks she wrote featured positive portrayals of women and Indigenous peoples that were well ahead of her time, and her history of Canada, *The Great Adventure*, won the Governor-General's award in 1950. Dickie was an advocate for progressive pedagogy based on John Dewey's theories that stressed shifting the educational focus from subject matter to problem-solving. She pressured the United Farmers and later the Social Credit governments of Alberta for educational reforms.[42]

In other ways, CFUW, as the federation was coming to be called, asserted and supported women's right to work under equitable terms in an era when work was widely perceived as a male prerogative. They did this through practical initiatives such as the Vocations Bureau, and by responding to attacks on married women at universities and in the civil service. As noted in the previous chapter, at the end of the 1920s, the federation supported the Vocations Bureau, an experimental placement service for university-educated women. Meant to help them find suitable employment, it was a joint project between the federation and the team of Mrs. Norman (Margaret) MacKenzie and Gertrude (True) Davidson to provide a service to senior women students at the University of Toronto. In May 1930, Jean McRae, convener of the Vocations Committee, which had long advocated such a bureau, sent out an appeal to all the clubs that resulted in $435 being raised for operational costs. Davidson established the Vocations Bureau and began making placements.[43] Her goal was to place competent women in new roles to prove their worth and to offer women career counselling and training for interview skills.

In 1931, the value of the service was showcased in a *Chronicle* article.[44] One woman with postgraduate experience in English was placed in a bookstore, although this was followed by a position as head of a large circulating library. The bureau also found work for another woman as a researcher for a commercial company and she later secured a civil service position more in keeping with her skills. Reading between the lines, the casebook reveals the bleak prospects faced by women whose talents and education were frequently and chronically underused. One applicant was advised to stay in a dead-end job in the advertising department of a large store and to work off her frustrations by writing in her spare time, while waiting for conditions to improve. Another woman, placed with a new company, found that hard times were making her overworked bosses cross and overbearing but was advised to stick with the new business for a year or two until she became indispensable. Efforts to find university teaching positions for four winners of CFUW scholarships failed. Over its short duration, the bureau served a clientele that included recent graduates, women in unsatisfactory jobs, women seeking to change professions, and women returning to work after an absence.[45] In its first year, the bureau served 180 women who paid a placement fee of two dollars plus their first week's pay. Of eighty-seven requests from employers, the bureau was able to fill forty-eight.

Despite a few successes, the Vocations Committee concluded that what made other agencies of this nature in other countries work was access to external sources of revenue through government or universities. These were not available to the bureau and it could not survive as a self-supporting institution.[46] By July 1930, the funds were exhausted. Another appeal went out to the clubs and there were several schemes to find wealthy patrons, with no success. A search for sixty sustaining members, for example, produced only two. Indeed, the scheme based in Toronto was out of character for the federation, which did not usually support programs that were only available in one area of the country. Efforts to decentralize it—to get clubs to affiliate with local universities to provide the service—did not come to fruition. In the meantime, as MacKenzie reported:

> Miss Davidson has been running the bureau since November by herself, and at times has scarcely made enough to pay the rent let alone a salary for herself. She is totally dependent on her own efforts, and has managed to get along by writing and

doing odd editorial jobs. Obviously we cannot ask her to carry on like that for the next year.[47]

No wonder Davidson could not afford club membership or to eat at the Toronto clubhouse! After the failure of the Vocations Bureau, both Davidson and MacKenzie expressed disillusionment. Davidson said privately that college girls were finicky and disloyal and would quit a job in the summer to take vacation, then come back in the fall looking for another. Or they would just quit to get married.[48] Such remarks undoubtedly spoke as much to her disappointment as a true assessment of the bureau's results.

On a smaller scale, the Vocations Committee carried on the bureau's work, placing candidates and undertaking summaries of professional options for women. Some of the clubs in larger cities also had Vocations Committees. In 1935, the National Committee reported that it was difficult to do placement work under the current business conditions; they had only secured two part-time positions and one temporary one. They were, however, cooperating with the newly formed Ontario Vocational Guidance Association and later reached out to the federal Unemployment Insurance Commission, founded in 1940, and the Ontario Department of Labour, laying the groundwork for future cooperation.[49] The Vocations Committee also published a series of career advice articles in the *Chronicle*, including one by Kenneth Haige on newspaper work, another by A. Vibert Douglas on research, and a piece by Winnifred Barnstead on librarianship. They continued to search for sustaining members to finance a re-opening of the Vocations Bureau.

The federation also defended women who came under attack for working—especially married women—and tried to help unemployed women workers. In a 1936 issue of the *Vancouver Province*, Laura Jamieson, a Vancouver juvenile court judge, highlighted the plight of the unemployed woman, asserting that women were in business out of necessity and always earned a smaller income than men. In an era when unprecedented unemployment was causing major social and political disruptions, many men and women held the simplistic notion that women had caused the high rates of unemployment. Such views have been attributed to a working-class belief in a fair distribution of jobs and income, but they were also predicated on the belief that only the male breadwinner had a "right" to work. These views led to political pressures that hurt women. The Ontario civil service, for example, was pressured to purge married women from its ranks. But after a 1931 investigation into 269 married women on their payrolls, their findings did not confirm popular prejudice. They found that the women had disabled husbands, husbands with low paying jobs, or were widowed with children or elderly parents to support. Jamieson argued that as long as they were not overworked, employment served as a broadening experience for women,[50] and others asserted that women had a right to work for self-fulfillment and autonomy.[51]

The reality of women's employment was complex and the ideal of the male breadwinner/female homemaker did not stand up to the vagaries of a changing economy. Even in good times, women had to supplement the family income due to illness, death, poverty, or uncertainty. But with unemployment in the 1930s rising to more than 30 per cent, and families forced onto relief, the low wages women earned in sex-segregated job markets might keep a family afloat. Women in paid employment rose steadily throughout the century. Although the figures do not include informal work such as babysitting and domestic labour, in 1921, they show that 17.7 per cent of women were gainfully employed; in 1931 the number was 19.4 per cent; in 1941, 22.9 per cent; and in 1951 the figure was 24.4 per cent. Women were clustered in sex-segregated pockets of the labour market—in Canada, 84 per cent of women workers were in the clerical, service, and textile industries and they made up 94.8 per cent of stenographers, 96 per cent of housekeepers, and 100 per cent of nurses.[52] During the Depression, these sectors of the job market were not hit as hard as those occupied by men, so women's unemployment was less severe. If you were willing to work as a domestic, you could get a job in the 1930s, and as a result, it was not uncommon for a woman to be the only wage earner in a family. This created a moral panic that played upon fears of women usurping the male breadwinner role and emasculating men. It spoke more to the politics of gender than to economics.

While massive unemployment generated great sympathy for young men whose desolation and hopelessness was viewed as a major social problem, young women were virtually ignored.

Young, single club members were probably the hardest hit by unemployment and their problems were further hidden by census takers who did not count them as unemployed but as dependents.[53] Single women were not even eligible for relief and, if they found themselves jobless, were thus forced to rely on family or the largesse of private charity. Historian Margaret Hobbs notes that Canada's solution to (male) unemployment was women's unemployment, and that even women who defended women's rights in other areas still believed women should leave the jobs for men.[54] Sadly, we do not know how many unemployed club members or former club members there were—most of them likely let their memberships lapse. Teachers, who made up one-third of club membership, were sometimes turned out of jobs in favour of men and, with a shrinking pool of jobs and an oversupply of teachers, they underbid each other. School boards, starved for revenue, threatened wage cuts and school and/or program closures.[55] By 1935, according to one Ontario survey, 61 per cent of new graduates from normal schools could not find work. Indeed, the proportion of female teachers in Canada fell from 78 per cent in 1931 to 75 per cent in 1941.[56] Wage cuts were also targeted specifically at women. Evelyn McDonald, a Toronto English teacher complained that the Toronto Board of Education, in trying "to reduce the tax rate to meet the demands of city council, suggested a reduction in the women's teachers' salaries."[57]

The first blatant case of discrimination that the federation and Toronto Club responded to was the University of Toronto's attempt to remove married women from its payroll. In October 1931, in response to pressure from the premier of Ontario, President Robert Falconer submitted to its board of governors a list of married women employed by the university, resolving that "it was undesirable to employ married women in the University unless the Board are satisfied in individual cases that such persons require to earn money for the support of their family."[58] Mossie May Kirkwood, dean of women and professor of English at Trinity College, who was married to a University of Toronto professor, remembered being called to Falconer's office on this account. Federation President Mabel Thom, the University Women's Club of Toronto, the alumnae associations, and the faculty of medicine all protested. Whether the university intended to act on the resolution or not, or whether it caved to women's pressure, Kirkwood and others kept their jobs. In their letter to Falconer, the federation referred to the "generally accepted principle of equality of opportunity for men and women," and the "tremendous economic wastage…in the training, at great expense by the State, of women who would be compelled upon marriage to discontinue the work in preparation for which they have spent years and made many sacrifices." The letter also appealed to self-interest, pointing out that such a ban would undermine the objectives of the federation's scholarship, which had benefitted the university. Thom also implored the president not to "add celibacy to the conditions under which women could obtain scholarships."[59] Toronto was not an isolated case. The Regina Club protested to its provincial government when an extended leave of absence was forced upon Dr. Alice Wells, a staff member at Weyburn Mental Hospital. Asking for her reinstatement, the club noted that, "since no reason has been stated, the public is forced to conclude that it was because of her married status."[60]

It was not enough to react to specific incidents, and the federation began to be pro-active, working with the IFUW on research into the issue of job discrimination. Early in the decade, the IFUW's Committee on the Status of Women asked member associations for lists of women employed on the teaching staff of Canadian universities, along with their rank and salary. Margaret McWilliams tried to obtain this information from the University of Manitoba but came up against President MacLean's refusal. This contributed to her decision to resign from the university council in 1933.[61] The information that was more readily obtained through publicly funded high schools, however, illustrated what women already knew—that female teachers were paid significantly less than their male counterparts. While many women privately admitted to having experienced discrimination, most were reluctant to state it publicly for fear of repercussions. One teacher cited the example of a school in which a male teacher was allowed days off each year for curling activities, without loss of salary, while the principal and other teachers filled in for him, but "a woman in the same school asked for a half day off to attend the funeral of a relative and was compelled to pay for a substitute."[62] The results of a 1936 IFUW study showed that among the Canadian club members more than half were teachers and among them, 60 per cent reported discrimination. Among the non-teachers, it was an even fifty-fifty split. Out of 178 who replied to the survey, 171 were single, three were married, and four were widowed, separated, or divorced. The survey also found that 60 per cent of the respondents lived alone, 5 per cent lived with their parents but made no contribution to the family income, and 35 per cent lived with parents and made contributions up to $1,500 per year.[63]

Discussion of the issue often focused on the civil service—not just in Canada but in Europe and Britain as well—perhaps because governments were more sensitive to political pressure. The IFUW raised the subject as early as 1930 at a Geneva meeting. Alice Wilson's scholarship experience first prompted the Canadian federation to look into it and, in 1933, it urged the government of Canada to appoint a qualified woman as a civil service commissioner. One year later, the organization protested discrimination against women in the service. Mora Guthrie, an Ottawa-based civil servant, conducted a survey that was published in the 1939 *Chronicle*. She found that only 18 per cent of the approximately 35,000 positions in the federal civil service were held by women and most of these were junior positions such as stenographer, typist, and charwoman. The majority of senior positions that women wanted access to was restricted to men, particularly the Grade IV appointments—that required a university degree.

Reforms to the civil service began in 1908 with the appointment of Adam Shortt, husband of member Elizabeth Smith Shortt and early Queen's medical student, as first chair of the Canadian Civil Service Commission. He began to put in place measures to eliminate patronage appointments in favour of a merit-based system that—technically at least—gave women the same rights as men. In practice, however, there were restrictions based on social perceptions that only men could handle administrative problems requiring initiative, judgment, and policy formulation. The Commission's thirteenth annual report found that out of 460 competitive examinations advertised in 1938, 412 were open only to men, thirty-nine were open to both sexes, and nine were available to women alone. Guthrie also determined that it was not unusual to find women with university training employed in the higher ranks of such areas as accounting, clerical, statistical, personnel, and administration, but they had entered through competitive examinations at lower grades and waited years for a promotion. In fact, many university-educated women were doing secretarial work.

While Guthrie did cite examples of exceptional women in the civil service, including federation stalwarts Alice Wilson and astronomer A. Vibert Douglas, she cautioned that they were the exceptions. Salaries reflected the real story. Of 6,300 positions occupied by women, 2 per cent received annual salaries of $2,000 to $3,000, and fewer than 1 per cent were making between $3,000 and $4,000. On the other hand, 54 per cent were paid between $1,000 and $2,000 a year and 43 per cent were making less than $1,000. Guthrie's concluding remarks asserted that "each individual comprising the State should be permitted to compete for employment in the Public Service on an equal competitive basis, and when employed should be paid, without discrimination, on the basis of the work done."[64]

For its part, the government of Canada denied that there was any discrimination against women and passed the blame onto the various departments over whom they claimed to have no influence. In 1939, the assistant secretary of the Civil Service Commission insisted that they "must furnish the departments with the class of help for which they make application."[65] The letter referred to the case of Marion Belyea, a Dalhousie graduate who applied for an assistant geology position but was told that she must apply as a student assistant. The letter acknowledged that women may in some cases fill positions such as chemist and geologist, however "the geology work as a rule involves a considerable amount of field work with rough life in the open and, whether rightly or wrongly, this is not considered to be suitable work for a female appointee."[66] Alice Wilson did this type of work despite a physical disability.

While the federation took the lead in lobbying on issues relating to the status of women, clubs were sometimes reluctant to join them. Ottawa, for example, despite having members who worked for the federal government, refused a 1934 request to use its influence to have Dr. Helen MacMurchy, newly retired from the Department of Health, named to the Senate. Jessie Muir reminded Ottawa Club members that "this was a big question and one which should be given careful thought...we are a small minority of women and

...a question of this nature should be left to a more representative body."[67]

Muir, who was vocal in the teachers' union, may have been unsympathetic to the elitist Senate, or to MacMurchy herself, or the Ottawa Club may have not been ready to lobby on such major issues. In acknowledging their failure, the CFUW executive noted that letters on this matter were "not encouraging reading for those who believe that women should take a larger part in national affairs."[68] However, as the Ottawa Club grew in confidence and financial security, it shifted ground.[69] In 1938, the club agreed to work toward improving access for women to the civil service and recommend methods of approaching the House of Commons committee that was investigating it.[70] The club also added its voice to the protest led by the local women's council against the replacement of female welfare investigators with men.

CFUW was deeply interested in making legislative changes through careful research and public policy formation. Women who were willing to move into the larger sphere were supported and encouraged, and the federation heartily congratulated Senator Cairine Wilson, the first female senator, on her 1930 appointment. CFUW leaders and presidents often encouraged women to engage in politics, arguing that women who stayed at home should take their places on school boards, municipal councils, and then, with the experience gained, go on to larger spheres.[71] Men sometimes challenged women's groups on their lack of representation. J. S. Woodsworth, for example, remarked that, "Until the women are well represented in the House, can they hope to have any real influence in the direction of political policies?"[72]

CFUW did naturally attract aspiring political women and over the years welcomed those from all political parties. Margaret McWilliams served four consecutive terms on the Winnipeg city council from 1933 to 1940, chairing two committees, one on health and another on unemployment; on the latter committee she helped reorganize the municipal relief department. She also promoted mothers' pensions, or mothers' allowances as well as other state-sponsored welfare benefits, to provide for needy single mothers and their children.[73] Vancouver juvenile court judge Laura Jamieson, moved by the stories of deprivation that she heard from women in her courtroom, joined the Co-operative Commonwealth Federation (CCF) and was elected to the provincial legislature in the spring of 1939 and re-elected in 1941. Jamieson's views were considerably to the left of many club women. She stated, for example, that, "So far as women putting men out of employment is concerned, men could change present conditions so that there is work for everybody." She believed that women's alleged conservatism was based on the fear of losing very necessary jobs and, less supportively, as "a pathetic desire for respectability."[74]

In contrast to Jamieson, Evlyn Farris, founder of the Vancouver Club, became increasingly conservative during this decade and retreated into her family and her work with UBC.[75] Less is known about the political views of Regina's first female alderman, Mrs. Ashley (Helena) Walker, except that she resigned her job as a high school math teacher when she married, and that her given name, Helena, was not widely known until after her death. She used her husband's name. She was elected in 1932, having already served on the school board since 1925 and becoming its chair in 1927. In 1932, the Regina University Women's Club gave her an honorary life membership in their club and she later served a term as president.[76]

As mentioned, the federation deliberately adopted a non-partisan policy. Nor did CFUW officially endorse candidates, although many women received support, encouragement, and training that helped them in future political roles, particularly at the club level.

By the late 1930s, CFUW could take pride in having survived the bad times. They had managed to award the Travelling Scholarship without interruption, had begun to use the *Chronicle* to highlight the talents, achievements, and obstacles that women encountered, and they did their best to protect the rights of women in the workplace. They also listened with dismay to the ominous sounds coming from fascists in Europe. Although some club members took part in peace activities, women would soon have to take up war work yet again. In the next decade they did their part to help exiled European women and postwar refugees, and took on leadership roles in guiding both the war effort and the transition into a new postwar Canada.

Footnotes for this chapter can be found online at:
http://secondstorypress.ca/resources

Chapter 5
THE WAR YEARS

From last September when the crushing of Poland took that country, so recently the scene of one of our international conferences, out of our world, through the virtual absorption — now completed — of the Baltic States into Russia, through the Finnish disaster in February — the Norwegian catastrophe in the early summer, to the final tragedy of France, happy and fruitful associations among women of these countries and ourselves have been rudely, and for the time being definitely cut off.[1]

—Report of the International Relations Committee,
Chronicle, 1940

Margaret McWilliams summed up the gloomy news from overseas in 1940 with a reference to the 1939 conference of the International Federation of University Women (IFUW) in Stockholm. The Canadian Federation of University Women (CFUW), like the rest of the country was in shock. Women had just emerged from the "making-do" days of the Great Depression and the attacks on wage-earning women only to face their second world war in a quarter-century, bringing with it worry, mourning, separation, and rationing. CFUW members put in countless hours of volunteer war work while, at the same time, running their households and raising their children, often without husbands, brothers, fathers, and sons. Some women found work outside the home or assumed executive positions in charitable organizations. Others took leadership roles in the newly created women's auxiliary services and government bodies established to deal with the emergency.

During these dismal years, Dr. A. (Ada) Dorothy Turville presided over CFUW as president from 1940 to 1943. A professor of romance languages and dean of women at the University of Western Ontario, Turville was a delightful raconteur with a soft spot for beleaguered France. Before the war she had been a frequent traveller to both France and Italy, and she was able to bring international contacts to her work in organizing CFUW assistance to European women. She had also been a founding member of the Association of Women Deans in 1936 and president of Alliance Française.[2]

In the early part of the decade, when the world seemed to be tottering on the brink of destruction, CFUW membership rose only slightly from 2,934 in 1940 to 3,008 in 1943. In 1942, the membership secretary detected an encouraging sign, however, with increased membership in more than 60 per cent of the clubs.[3] Ottawa, for example, led the way with fifty-eight new members.[4] By the end of the decade, once the war was over, membership numbers exceeded five thousand and improved conditions led to more new clubs being formed in smaller centres such as Smiths Falls, Ontario and Sackville, New Brunswick. In 1945, former CFUW member Edith Creighton brought eighteen women together at Memorial University to form the University Women's Club of St. John's. Because Newfoundland was then a self-governing colony of Britain, the women had to obtain special permission from the British Federation of University Women (BFUW) to join CFUW. Newfoundland did not become part of Canada until 1949. The Club's first speaker was author Margaret Duley, who spoke on women's emancipation, and early lecture topics included the *Political and Financial Implications of Confederation with Canada.*[5] In the same year, thirteen women formed a club in Nanaimo, BC under President Marjorie Neave and began raising money for the Unitarian Service Committee in aid of displaced women in Europe.[6] Dartmouth, Nova Scotia, a town of some ten thousand people, formed its own Club in June 1949 because travel to nearby Halifax required a ferry and tramcar ride; there was no bridge across Halifax Harbour until 1955–1956.[7]

In the 1940s, a new Committee on the Status of Women was created to replace the older Academic Appointments Committee that had disbanded in the 1930s. As well, CFUW formed a War Guests Committee to co-ordinate aid to refugee women and another on the Rehabilitation of Women War Workers. After the war, the federation added a new Committee on Penal Reform. Longstanding committees, each with a convenor, remained to deal with education, library, vocations, international relations, and scholarships. Elected officers included the president, first and second vice-presidents, recording secretary, corresponding secretary, membership secretary, archives secretary, and treasurer. The Publications Committee convenor was responsible for producing the *Chronicle* and the Library Committee created a new reading stimulation grant to encourage reading in rural communities. Further, the congregation of numerous clubs in smaller geographic areas made possible the first regional conferences and, later, the creation of regional officer positions. Resolutions brought forward from clubs, committees, or CFUW officers, were debated and voted on at triennial meetings, established CFUW policy, and guided the organization's growing lobbying efforts.

To mark the first triennial conference since the outbreak of war, the women attending the Calgary meeting sang the national anthem and sent a message of greeting and sympathy to London, England, to the only IFUW officer who was still active.[8] The Vancouver Club reported being overwhelmed with war work, but the Saskatoon Club managed to maintain a nucleus of study groups. Most of the clubs adapted their programming by inviting war guests and refugees to speak at meetings. In Edmonton, these included Julie Matouskova from the World Council of the Young Women's Christian Association (YWCA) and a refugee from Prague, as well as Dr. Frances Moran of Dublin, a distinguished lawyer and later judge at the Nuremburg trials. In Ottawa, members heard economist Phyllis Turner's insights into methods of preventing inflation and Lester B. Pearson's description of wartime London.[9] In Moncton, one of the club's interest groups was studying European nations in an effort to understand the causes of the war.

The war inevitably brought disruptions. The Vancouver Club's Christmas party, scheduled for December 8, 1941, had to be postponed due to the attack on Pearl Harbor and the resulting blackout all along the West Coast. When the meeting was rescheduled a few days later, it turned into a sewing and knitting circle for the Red

Cross.[10] There was no issue of the *Chronicle* published in 1944, and the national executive could not hold its meeting in 1945 because of travel restrictions. Wartime rationing meant that refreshments had to be scaled back or eliminated at meetings. The Edmonton Club moved from serving sandwiches and iced cakes to cookies that were rationed to two per person.[11] The Saskatoon Club eliminated refreshments altogether and invested the savings in the Victory Loan Fund and other war charities. Rationing was particularly problematic at the Montréal clubhouse, where the allotment was based on meals served in July and August, when there were few events and "no representation as to the number of meals served in the winter months could persuade officials to increase the rations."[12] In Toronto, women "said goodbye to the houseman who had given our premises such an air of distinction," the dining-room door was closed after noonday dinner on Sunday, and "Monday teas were so simplified they became Club Mondays."[13]

As they had done in World War I, CFUW members put their own needs aside to support the war effort. In most of the clubs, members were encouraged to use their individual talents in whatever way they thought appropriate. In responding to local needs, clubs assisted naval organizations in port cities, dealt with the influx of war workers into central Canadian communities, and entertained men and women in the armed forces stationed nearby. Members knitted, sewed, and rolled bandages, often at the local Red Cross, or at an individual member's home or at the club quarters. The Toronto Club worked with the University of Toronto War Service Committee and the St. Catharines Club made hundreds of pounds of jam from local fruit. In many centres, CFUW women held classes in first aid, home nursing, and, in a few western cities, even taught English for war exiles.[14]

With more than sixty clubs and more than five thousand members by the end of the decade, the long hoped-for regional conferences became possible. The first was held in Vancouver in April 1944 for clubs in British Columbia, and a second was held in August of the same year in Ottawa for clubs in Eastern Ontario and Montréal. By 1949, there had been eight regional conferences and these meetings sparked enthusiasm among members and provided a forum to discuss program content, study groups, and

CFUW projects. The formats varied. The 1945 meeting in Montréal held discussions on several topics, including women in politics and how to spend the federation's scholarship surplus. A meeting of the Saskatchewan clubs discussed study groups, scholarships, war work, membership, and the importance of social events.[15] CFUW also introduced national membership cards in 1947 to replace the club cards.

Clubhouses held a continuing appeal across the country. In 1945, the Winnipeg Club purchased the clubhouse it had been renting since 1939, having found that the number of study groups increased and club membership grew from 194 to 344. Long a source of pride, it was later designated a national historic site for its association with Canadian author Ralph Connor. The library was named in honour of Margaret McWilliams and a drawing room was named for Doris Saunders, CFUW president from 1955 to 1958. Clubhouses were expensive to run, however, and clubs that had these facilities had to charge higher fees—as much as $20 per year. The Montréal club-house continued to have financial difficulties well into the postwar years despite some very capable business managers.[16] As Montréal lawyer and CFUW executive Elizabeth Monk explained privately, the small English-speaking population of university women in Montréal could barely afford the expensive property's heavy taxes.[17] Across the Atlantic, the London headquarters of the British Federation of University Women (BFUW) and the IFUW, Crosby Hall, which was used by IFUW travellers and women university students, sustained damage in wartime bombings and CFUW raised almost $4,000 to help with repairs.

One of the major contributions that CFUW made to the war was the role its members played in filling senior executive positions in voluntary and government agencies. The Red Cross, a voluntary organization in peacetime, became a quasi-official branch of the military and the government in wartime. Toronto Club member Adelaide Plumptre had organized the Red Cross's wartime relief efforts during World War I by serving as superintendent of supplies, and organizing women's knitting, sewing, and much more. She annoyed her male compatriots by insisting that women be represented at the decision-making levels of the Red Cross and in 1915 she herself became the first woman on the executive of the Canadian Red

Cross Society. Historian Sarah Glassford notes that "she brilliantly embodied the ways by which maternal feminism could be used to create a powerful, public, activist role for women in this era."[18] She continued to play a leadership role in the Red Cross through the interwar and World War II period, becoming the organization's vice-chair in charge of war activities. She also edited *Despatch*, a newsletter aimed at generating donations.

There were many other CFUW women who provided leadership in wartime. Dr. Marian Templin, for example, who received her medical degree from the University of Toronto in 1922, was appointed Lady Superintendent of the nursing division of the St. John Ambulance Brigade in Hamilton. In 1942, she became the first woman medical officer in the Canadian navy.[19] She was certainly not the only CFUW member to take a leadership position in women's auxiliary services, munitions, or government bodies. Even the scholarship winners chosen during the war period seemed to be doing war-related research.

Montréal's Florence Seymour Bell, former convener of CFUW's Status of Women Committee, became Commandant of the Women's Volunteer Reserve Corps in 1941. This unofficial women's corps operated in Eastern Canada while the Canadian Auxiliary Territorial Service was active in parts of Ontario and the Western provinces. Working at their own initiative and expense, these corps gave women volunteers a military-style training in Morse code, signalling, and map reading. British Columbian Joan Kennedy had begun this movement at the time of the Munich Accord in 1938, when she forecast the coming of war. While the army insisted that women were unsuitable for this kind of active war service, Kennedy amalgamated her own homegrown Women's Service Corps with the B.C. Red Cross Corps, some of whose female members were already engaged in drill, first aid, and driving trucks. Kennedy was named B.C. Commandant of the Canadian Red Cross.[20]

The Canadian government was forced to relent in the face of women's pressure, compounded by military labour shortages, and established three auxiliary women's forces: the Canadian Women's Army Corps (CWAC), which eventually came under Kennedy's command, and the Canadian Women's Auxiliary Air Force, both established in the summer of 1941; and the Women's Royal Canadian

Naval Service, or Wrens, established a year later. Before the end of the war, some 50,000 women had replaced men who were moved into combat duty. Although they did mostly routine work, women's acceptance into the forces represented a major step forward for women with military aspirations. Previously, only nurses had been allowed to serve. After CFUW was invited to Ottawa along with other national women's organizations for a CWAC recruiting conference in July 1942, the federation encouraged its members to join, and it appears that many did. As university-educated women, CFUW members were eligible for officer status. Although a few of them are mentioned in the *Chronicle*'s pages, there are no precise figures as to how many served.[21] Ruth Russell, a member of the Kitchener-Waterloo Club, wrote a book, *Proudly She Marched: Training Canada's World War II Women in Waterloo County Volume 1*, on the CWAC, whose training grounds were located near their city, and Anne Kallin wrote a second volume on the Women's Royal Canadian Naval Service.[22] Both volumes were published by CFUW Kitchener-Waterloo.

Economist and CFUW member Phyllis Turner assumed a leadership role on the Wartime Prices and Trade Board (WPTB) established in September 1939 to set price and production ceilings on many consumer goods in order to control inflation. Turner served as administrator of oils and fats, ensuring the supply, preservation, and collection of oils needed for glycerine, a key ingredient in the manufacture of explosives. In Québec, long-time suffrage leader and CFUW member Thérèse Casgrain worked for the board's Consumer Branch.[23] Part of a massive network of female volunteers keeping an eye on prices at their local stores that was so critical to the board's success, the federation set up its own Price Control Committee at the national level and most clubs had their own liaison officers. The WPTB also worked in conjunction with the Women's Voluntary Services Division, created by the federal government in 1941 under the Department of National War Services to recruit labour for war industries.[24]

In addition to assisting the government in its anti-inflation measures and auxiliary services, CFUW helped mobilize the Canadian work force. The National Selective Service (NSS), also established by Prime Minister Mackenzie King in 1941, began to regulate the recruitment of civilians by enlisting single women for wartime industries.[25] As labour demands grew, however, the government began to recruit married women with no children; by the fall of 1943, married women with children were being asked to work "3 or 4 hours a day, or 2 days a week."[26] Day nurseries were established to care for their children and income tax provisions put in place that doubled a husband's basic exemption and made it profitable for wives to work. The NSS's Women's Division was headed by Fraudena Eaton, a Vancouver Club member.[27] Dr. Mary Salter at the Department of Labour and Dr. Olive Ruth Russell at the Department of National Defence also helped to organize women's labour.

One of the federation's unique contributions during the war was their assistance to university-educated women, especially Jewish academic women from areas of Europe under Nazi control. This topic will be dealt with more fully in Chapter 14. The leader of Canada's role in this was Dr. A. ("Allie") Vibert Douglas, who was well known internationally through her eighteen-year leadership of the IFUW Fellowships Committee and chair of CFUW's special War Guest Committee. An accomplished astrophysicist, Dr. Vibert Douglas was much loved and respected by her students and colleagues.[28] During World War I she interrupted her education at McGill University in mathematics and physics and, accompanied by two aunts, followed her enlisted brother to London, England. There she worked as a statistician in the London War Office and for this work was awarded the Order of the British Empire (OBE) in 1918 at the age of twenty-three.

Dr. Vibert Douglas returned to Montréal, and received her doctorate from McGill in 1926. She also did postgraduate work at the Cavendish Laboratory of Cambridge University with Ernest Rutherford and at Cambridge with Arthur Eddington, whose biography she later wrote. Her great-niece later noted that Vibert Douglas did not believe that she would ever progress beyond the position of lecturer at McGill, and in 1939 she accepted a position at Queen's University as dean of women. She held that position until 1958, drawing attention to the restrictions against women at Queen's—particularly in medicine and engineering—and became a fierce advocate for women in professional programs.[29] She was appointed a lecturer at Queen's in 1943 but was not promoted to

Dr. Alice (Allie) Vibert Douglas,
President, IFUW (1947–1950).

a professorship of astronomy until 1946, a position she held until her retirement in 1964. Together with Stuart Foster, she "investigated the spectra of A- and B-type stars and the Stark effect with the 72-inch telescope of the Dominion Astrophysical Observatory."[30] In 1943–1944, she became the first female president of the prestigious Royal Astronomical Society of Canada.[31] Following her death in 1988, Asteroid 3269 was renamed Vibert-Douglas in her honour and there is a crater on Venus that also bears her name.

Not all of the federation's efforts to assist war refugees met with unqualified success. CFUW members volunteered their homes to give temporary shelter to 308 children of BFUW members, but the British government later decided that the evacuations would be too dangerous.[32] And although restrictive Canadian immigration policies left the federation unable to bring many refugee university women from Europe, CFUW did help European women who found themselves stranded in Canada because of the war. In this, they were assisted by three donations from the American Association of University Women (AAUW) of $1,000 each.[33] As will be discussed in greater detail in Chapter 14, by 1944, AAUW donations, supplemented by CFUW funds, had helped twenty-three war guests in Canada from Oxford, London, Dublin, Bristol, Kraków, Paris, and Petrograd.[34]

Ursula Macdonnell, CFUW's second wartime president (1943–1946), was a professor of history (and dean of women) at the University of Manitoba from 1920 to 1944. As CFUW president she channelled donations of money and clothing to IFUW, as well as to newly formed agencies such as the United Nations Relief and Rehabilitation Agency and the Unitarian Service Committee. The latter was founded by Dr. Lotta Hitschmanova (1909–1990), a Czech refugee who did manage to escape war-torn Europe and became a CFUW member.[35] Through a special war fund, CFUW had been collecting money and clothing to send to exiled or displaced university women in Europe, although shipping and currency restrictions prohibited transport during the war. Canadian clubs received lists of university women in displaced persons camps and many clubs "adopted" some of them.[36] After the war, the St. John's Club, for example, wrote letters and sent gifts of clothing and food, including ingredients for Christmas cakes.[37] Macdonnell also encouraged local clubs to help replace books and scientific equipment in European universities that had been destroyed during the war.

The federation and the clubs also asked the government to allow more refugees and displaced persons to come to Canada. Vibert Douglas suggested that the "burden which Great Britain is carrying in giving haven to European refugees is something so tremendous as to challenge Canada to…deal more generously with applications for admission to residence in Canada."[38] At its 1943 triennial meeting in Québec City, the club suggested that the federation form a committee to work with the Canadian National Committee on Refugees in an effort to educate public opinion about admitting larger numbers of people displaced by the war.[39] Cairine Wilson, the first female senator appointed after the 1929 Persons Case, chaired that committee as well as a Senate Standing Committee on Immigration and Labour. She had begun promoting a more humanitarian approach to immigration in the 1930s, at a time when it was immensely unpopular. After being awarded an honorary degree in 1943, Wilson became eligible for membership in the Ottawa Club and quickly became active. Along with Constance Hayward, CFUW's international relations convenor, she made a pitch to the 1949 triennial for the federation to sponsor displaced persons.[40]

There had been a great deal of inflation, unemployment, and unrest following World War I, and to prevent a recurrence of that instability, in March 1941 the Canadian government established an Advisory Committee on Reconstruction chaired by McGill University principal F. Cyril James. Women's organizations protested when no women were appointed to the committee and no women's issues were addressed in any of the subcommittee themes. Margaret Wherry, president of the Canadian Federation of Business and Professional Women's Clubs (CFBPW) spearheaded a campaign to alter the terms of the advisory committee and it picked up steam with support from the Québec-based Ligue des droits de la femme (League for Women's Rights).[41] In April 1943, women succeeded in having the terms of reference for the James Committee extended to include a study of postwar problems relating to women. Mackenzie King's choice of chair for the new subcommittee was perhaps not surprising—Margaret McWilliams and her husband, then lieutenant governor of Manitoba, were personal friends of his dating back to their University of Toronto days. A prominent array of club women joined McWilliams on the government-appointed committee, including Dr. Vibert Douglas and two Vancouver Club members, Evelyn Lett and Grace MacInnis.[42] CFUW offered its assistance by conducting local surveys of women workers who had replaced men in banks, offices, and schools during the war.

The resulting McWilliams subcommittee report was unique in many ways. In a period when most people assumed that women would return to the home after their wartime jobs, McWilliams stated categorically that women had proven themselves in wartime employment; whether married or single, they had the right to determine for themselves whether they would work outside the home for pay. Further, the report insisted that women receive equal pay.[43] In other respects, however, the report was more conventional and emphasized traditional areas of women's work such as social work, nursing, domestic service, and personnel work.

Domestic work remained the largest area of employment for women until 1951. In 1911, 37.6 per cent of employed women worked in this sector and, although the number fell to 27.2 per cent in 1921, it rose to 34 per cent in 1931. To raise its status, the report suggested replacing the category "domestic service" on census forms with the less demeaning term "household workers."[44] Efforts to raise the status of domestic work were not new and certainly served the interests of middle-class women who employed servants. But McWilliams' recommendations that domestic workers be protected by written contracts and covered by the National Labour Code, minimum wage legislation, unemployment insurance, and "workmen's" compensation were novel. She also argued that raising the status of domestic work would benefit wives as well as household workers, that marriage should be recognized as a partnership between husband and wife, and that wives should be included in social security provisions and pensions.

The McWilliams subcommittee also called for the new family allowances—or baby bonuses, as they were known—to be payable directly to mothers, and for the creation of morning nursery schools. This last provision was particularly relevant to CFUW members because, as the report pointed out, it would help highly trained professional and businesswomen "make an adequate return to the state for their expensive education" and free women to do volunteer work in their communities.[45]

The report on postwar problems relating to women was a late addition to the Advisory Committee on Reconstruction and received little attention. The subcommittee had been appointed in the spring of 1943 and was originally given until the summer of 1944 to complete its work. With little notice, however, the women were suddenly asked to finish their report early and the result was that some issues—such as training programs and lack of security for older, self-supporting women—did not get the thorough consideration they deserved.[46] McWilliams put on a brave face in the 1943 *Chronicle*, noting that although the finished product was not as complete as they'd hoped, it required no apologies. James had been less than supportive, cancelling meetings and asking the women not to garner any publicity. As a consequence, national women's organizations were not consulted until the last minute; without their commitment and support, the government had less cause to take the report seriously.[47] The McWilliams subcommittee was also assigned the additional task of preparing a special report on how a new plan devised by Canadian economist Leonard Marsh's subcommittee would affect women. Presented in March 1943, the Marsh report—officially entitled *Social Insurance and Allied Services*—recommended expanded social programs and a Keynesian economic policy using state regulation of the economy to ensure prosperity. It effectively provided a blueprint for the postwar social welfare state.

When the McWilliams report was presented to the House of Commons in January 1944, it drew little comment and was quickly shelved.[48] McWilliams had optimistically assumed that women could not be ignored because of their wartime work and sacrifice, but that is exactly what happened. The government ignored survey results and some media coverage indicating that many women wanted to continue working after the war.[49] Fearful of male unemployment and social unrest, they launched propaganda campaigns thanking women for their service and asking them to give returning veterans priority in the job market. The 1942 Civil Employment Reinstatement Act, which made it mandatory for employers to rehire veterans first, then war widows, and, finally, single women who could not find husbands, kept many women out of the workforce. The only part of the McWilliams report to be embraced by the government was a short training program for domestic servants launched in 1945 by NSS called Home Aide.[50]

Despite its short-term failures, the McWilliams report made important recommendations. As historian Gail Cuthbert Brandt writes,

> A quarter of a century later, the Royal Commission on the Status of Women in Canada would restate many of the subcommittee's recommendations: more effective and accessible technical education for women, including training programmes for household workers; better educational and social services for rural women; the extension of unemployment insurance to include groups of women such as private duty nurses and household workers; and an adequate, federally supported daycare system.[51]

Many CFUW study groups examined the McWilliams report along with other postwar planning documents like the Marsh report as part of their study groups and discussions. They continued to debate the role of women in the workforce—married women in particular. CFUW study groups and standing committees offered women working in their homes the mental stimulation that domesticity lacked. The market-driven economy, however, accorded them scant recognition for their efforts in the voluntary sphere and clubs were soon passing resolutions to reform income tax legislation to encourage married women to work for a salary and other family law reforms.

At the CFUW's ninth triennial conference, held in Québec in August and September 1943, the federation welcomed its new francophone contingent, with outgoing President Dorothy Turville making some of her remarks in French and the conference making an effort to function in both languages.[52] There is no record of how successful that was. Within CFUW, the Association des femmes universitaires de Québec (later the Association des femmes diplomées des universités [AFDU]) was first organized in 1943 in Québec City as a bilingual club. In 1949, however, an entirely francophone section comprising seventy-five members was officially created under its first president, Madeleine Laliberté.[53] Among the leaders of the Québec group was Georgette LeMoyne, one of the first women to receive a university degree in French Canada who devoted her life to promoting women's education and employment. A CFUW fellowship for study in the French language was later named for her. An AFDU was also founded in Montréal in 1949 with goals similar to those of the English clubs.

Both of these early clubs, in the interest of promoting higher education among francophone women, held lectures, discussions, social events, and passed resolutions. The Québec City AFDU also succeeded in building a women's residence at Laval University. At its first meeting, the Montréal Club apparently also voted on whether to admit nuns to the organization, recognizing them as a well-educated group of leaders in education, culture, and health care in the province. Although history does not indicate the result of the vote, no religious orders seem to be represented on the executive. Montréal's first president, Florence Martel, was an American-born feminist who had studied French literature at Laval and worked with Thérèse Casgrain in the fight for women's rights.[54]

While the university graduates in Québec City clearly wanted to have a club for francophones, the demise of their short-lived bilingual club, which alternated English and French programs, was a disappointment to the national executive. In 1948, a split had emerged between the two language groups, apparently rooted in personality, language deficiencies—especially among the anglophone women—and differences in interests. The francophone group was younger, many of them Laval medical students who did not share the interests of older anglophone women. Although much effort was made to salvage the club, the federation was left with two separate clubs, one English and one French. CFUW executive members consoled themselves that two clubs could attract more members separately, but Ruth Harrap Crummy, CFUW president at the time, confided privately that she found the situation "sad" and thought it reflected poorly on university women who should try to carry out in their everyday lives the ideal of the "universal mind" that higher education was supposed to teach.[55] Crummy, CFUW president from 1946 to 1949, was a Queen's graduate in English and history from Vancouver who helped found the Vancouver Community Arts Council, was an active member of the Women's Musical Club, the Vancouver Art Gallery, and the Vancouver Symphony. She also chaired her club's child study group in 1935 and served on the boards of the Children's Aid Society and Community Chest.

The immediate postwar years must have been a disappointment to the federation. After cooperating with government and industry on the war effort, none of their own ambitions had been realized. McWilliams gave the situation a positive spin when she addressed the federation's 1946 Silver Jubilee triennial noting that women brought into the postwar world "new knowledge of their own capabilities, a new prestige derived from undertaking new tasks with better than expected results, a greater self-confidence and an acknowledgement of their right to work." She also predicted that equal pay was coming.[56] Individual women had certainly gained experience and confidence doing new types of work during the war, making decisions and handling the family finances in the absence of male breadwinners. But proving their abilities did not translate into an acceptance of their right to work outside the home or to get paid the same as men. Government and industry treated women as a reserve labour force to be called upon in times of need and dismissed when not needed, and thousands of women were forced to return to more traditional tasks or retreat into full-time homemaking.

The federal government implemented the 1944 Family Allowance Act in 1945 and—as the McWilliams report had called for—sent the "baby bonus" cheques directly to mothers, with the exception of a short period in Québec; Thérèse Casgrain protested the brief patriarchal concession to Québec anti-feminists and the decision was rescinded.[57] The amount was substantial in real dollars, much more so than it is today, but it was no substitute for a salary, even if it did make the lives of some mothers easier. Popular women's magazines put forward a powerful domestic ideology to address the pent-up demand for consumer goods. The level of female employment, which had risen to 33.5 per cent in 1944 from 24.4 per cent in 1939, fell dramatically after the war. By 1954, it had climbed back up to 23.6 per cent, but it was not until 1966 that it reached the 1945 level.[58] More women married and at a younger age and, along with increased postwar immigration, they fuelled the baby boom. Nonetheless, while the workforce participation of women declined, the proportion of married women in the workforce continued to rise.

CFUW continued to battle for civil service jobs for women—in 1946 the Ottawa Club protested the Civil Service Commission's practice of advertising positions to men only. The club also campaigned to have a woman appointed to the commission. Until 1954, married women were forced to leave the federal civil service—and, even later to leave school boards and provincial civil services[59]—a bar that had been temporarily lifted during the war. CFUW wrote letters to the Civil Service Commission, the CBC, and National Research Council, but they all replied that married women were not wanted. The CBC explained that its generous pension program was the reason for excluding married women, apparently believing that it was self-explanatory that married women did not need pensions. Employers made exceptions when it suited them, however, such as in isolated areas where certain skills were scarce. The CBC reserved the right to hire creative talent on a contractual basis regardless of marital status.[60]

In the aftermath of the war, CFUW gained international recognition. On a visit to Canada, treasurer J. M. (Marguerite) Bowie, who had held the fort in London through the dark war years, promised that the next IFUW meeting would be held in Canada because "the university women of Europe are so grateful for the assistance given them by Canadian university women during the war."[61] When Dr. Vibert Douglas's name came up as the appropriate woman to accept the honour of becoming the first Canadian president of IFUW, she initially deferred to Bowie but there were concerted efforts to convince her and, in the end, she was elected IFUW president at the 1947 meeting held in Toronto. Bowie became the first vice president.[62] Four other Canadians were elected to IFUW committees: Dr. Martha Law, Elizabeth Monk, Mrs. J. L. Savage, and Dr. Mabel Timlin.[63] Former CFUW presidents Laura Newman and Laila Scott organized the first IFUW meeting in Canada—and the first since the war—at Trinity College. CFUW assisted some sixty university women from war-ravaged countries with meals and accommodation so they could attend.[64] A message from Prime Minister Mackenzie King was read which stressed the furthering of international friendship and good will.

The weather in Toronto was oppressively hot and humid as it can be in August, but that did not stop an impressive round of entertaining, sightseeing, and guest lectures. Highlights of the meeting were widely reported in the newspapers, including discussions on maintaining the peace and ensuring equality for women. Many of the eastern clubs took advantage of the presence of visiting international delegates such as international legal expert Dr. Frances Moran, who spoke on international law and the Nuremberg Trials, and invited them to speak at their meetings.[65]

Although the Vocations Bureau had been abandoned, CFUW was still committed to the idea and called for the establishment of a Women's Bureau in the Department of Labour modelled on a comparable US Bureau established in 1920. They hoped such an office would make work placements and advocate for women in the workforce. Success would elude them in 1945, when they joined forces with the YWCA, the CFBPW, and the NCWC to pressure the federal government to establish such a bureau. They finally succeeded in 1954.[66] The CFUW Vocations Committee turned its attention to producing and distributing information leaflets on specific vocations. Nora Guthrie wrote one on the civil service; Dorothy Riches, director of Queen's school of nursing wrote on nursing; and Winnifred Rowles of the personnel department of the nylon plant of Canadian Industries Limited in Kingston wrote a pamphlet on personnel work. The committee produced others for librarianship, secretarial work, home economics, and social work.[67] The *Chronicle* also published articles on careers. Hazel Dorothy Burwash, PhD, reported on women in the Canadian diplomatic service, noting that during the war women were accepted into the Department of External Affairs as temporary assistants for diplomatic work and in 1947 were allowed to write the competitive entrance examinations. Twelve of them obtained the rank of officer.[68]

Throughout this decade CFUW generally had little success in obtaining academic appointments for its members, although, with most men overseas, a few women did find positions. During the war years, the Academic Appointments Committee re-emerged and compiled a register of qualified women, including refugee women, and sent them to university heads. They received answers described as sympathetic, especially to the plight of refugee women, but no

Dr. Marion Grant from Wolfville was
president of CFUW from 1949 to 1952.

offers. In 1942, the committee reported that two women in one university were promoted to the rank of assistant professor, "partly (as we are assured by a high official) in consequence of the stir we have made."[69] In 1943, the committee's work resulted in the appointment of Mary E. White, a federation scholarship winner, as associate professor of classics at Trinity College. She replaced an enlisted man. After the war, when veterans returned, the status quo re-asserted itself, although White retained her job. Edmonton club members felt that there was little chance of a woman getting a posting at the University of Alberta, but did recommend the appointment of Dr. Mary Winspear, who was already serving as women's advisor (1942–1945). They did not succeed and Winspear left for Queen's University; with no opportunities there either, this gifted teacher eventually established a private girls' school in Montréal where she developed innovative bilingual teaching methods.[70]

The scope of the Academic Appointments Committee was expanded during this period to include administrative appointments and in 1946 CFUW's president communicated with the Department of Labour and the Civil Service Commission to suggest candidates for vacant spots. It also collaborated with other organizations to create a list of available women for specific types of work. Former scholarship holder Dr. Dixie Pelluet of Dalhousie University convened the committee from 1947 to 1948, but was discouraged with the results.[71] Although the 1949 chair had success in one or two cases, incoming CFUW president Dr. Marion Grant from Acadia (1949–1952) mused privately that it might be better to merge the Academic Appointments Committee with the Status of Women Committee because the results to date hardly justified the effort.[72]

Other committees strove to place women in new roles. The federation's Education Committee pushed women to seek positions as vice principals of high schools, although it pessimistically noted they should only do so "if their qualifications are superior to those of male applicants."[73] By the end of the decade, the committees hoped to make a dent "in the armour of anti-feminist prejudice"— this was the first time that the *Chronicle* used the "f" word.[74] The federation's Library Committee, which had felt powerless to change the chaotic, underfunded state of libraries during the Depression, launched a reading stimulation grant in the 1940s to improve access to children's reading materials in rural areas where, they noted, 95 per cent of Canadians had no library service.[75] Brandon, Manitoba received the first grant of $350 in 1946. Many clubs also helped construct libraries in their communities, the Ottawa Club helped secure a building for the Ottawa Little Theatre, and the Vancouver Club lobbied for a provincial ministry of the arts in BC.

CFUW was an organization that took its governance very seriously—the constitution, articles, and bylaws were regularly discussed, debated, and voted on at their meetings.[76] This attracted more women interested in politics. At the 1945 regional conference in Montréal, in a debate on the issue, one woman expressed the view that it might be divisive if clubs backed a woman from a particular party. President Macdonnell thought it would be safer to place women in senior civil servant positions, as CFUW often tried to do.[77] However, in a later *Chronicle* article, Catherine MacKenzie, the CFUW vice president who chaired the discussion, challenged women to take to the hustings and chided them for their fear of criticism or of jeopardizing husbands' careers or business prospects.[78]

The municipal level seemed the best place for women to exercise political leadership and there was thus a concentration of female candidates for school and library boards and for municipal government. In 1945, Edmonton's Mary Butterworth ran successfully for the school board and became the second woman to chair it. The first, Mrs. E. T. (Thryza) Bishop, also a club member, had worked hard to win tenure for married women teachers. Elizabeth Monk of the Montréal Club became a city councillor after Québec finally allowed her to be called to the bar in 1941.[79] As women gained political confidence, a few took to a bigger stage, often through family connections. CFUW member Grace MacInnis, daughter of J. S. Woodsworth and wife of MP Angus MacInnis, was elected CCF MLA for Vancouver-Burrard in 1941, where she served until 1945, and later she was elected as a federal member of Parliament. Influential within provincial and national party circles, she worked for low-income housing, consumer rights, and women's equality.[80] The first university-educated woman to enter federal politics did so as a widow. Following the death of her husband, who had first held the seat, "Cora" Casselman was elected MP for Edmonton East in 1941. Before her defeat in 1945, she lobbied for mothers' allowances, better pensions, and health insurance.[81] Casselman served twice on the executive of the Edmonton Club and as vice president and convener of the Legal and Economic Status of Women Committee of the national federation. She was also part of the Canadian delegation at the founding of the United Nations and later ran unsuccessfully as an Alberta Liberal Party candidate in Edmonton in the 1955 provincial election.

Along with its wartime horrors, the 1940s did bring economic expansion and new roles for CFUW members. But after dutifully knitting socks and organizing volunteers, women were told to go home to soothe the furrowed brows of their war-weary menfolk. Despite the domestic ideology that descended on women in the 1950s, organizations like CFUW quietly began to learn the new language of human rights and to work toward a world in which women could reach their potential and gain greater recognition for all that they did.

Footnotes for this chapter can be found online at:
http://secondstorypress.ca/resources

Chapter 6
THE BABY BOOM,
DOMESTICITY, AND FEMINISM

*I was from a small town, and had found university life so stimu-
lating, so that when I found myself married and living outside
of Edmonton on an acreage, I thought the UWC would be a good
group to get into—it was quite exciting to come back and find all
these other [like-minded] people. The meetings were large and the
speakers interesting—there were lots of things going on.*
—An Edmonton member who joined in the 1950s[1]

The decade of the 1950s is popularly defined by the postwar baby
boom, which lasted from about 1946 until the early 1960s. After
the Depression, followed immediately by war, when unemployment
and separation disrupted families, Canada's birthrate jumped from
a low of 227,000 live births per year in the mid-1930s to 343,504
per year in 1946, and peaked in the late 1950s with 479,009 per
year.[2] National advertisers and governments sent a clear message
to women who had worked during the war—they should go home
and let returning servicemen rejoin the workforce. The effect of the
policy was to increase female unemployment.[3] Between 1944 and
1946 more than 300,000 women—25 per cent of the total female
workforce—left their jobs, some voluntarily, others involuntarily.[4]
Most Canadians still believed that the primary breadwinner should
be male and advertisers pushed the dream of home ownership, with
new cars and the latest domestic technology, in low-density residen-
tial communities in which married women were expected to devote

themselves to fulltime motherhood and homemaking.[5] During the Cold War, McCarthyism in the United States, along with its softer Canadian version and the very real threat of nuclear war, helped make the 1950s a somewhat conventional decade—at least on the surface. But gender stereotypes never reflect exactly what is happening in any society. There was simultaneously a growing trend toward married women in the paid job market, and a substantial number of women did participate in the workforce, even at the height of what has been known as the age of domesticity. At the same time, the number of girls finishing high school rose dramatically between 1945 and 1960, and from 1950 to 1963 the number of women attending university tripled.[6] The rise in men's attendance did not come close to matching this phenomenal growth. In educational terms, women were catching up.

The CFUW president who ushered in the decade was Dr. Marion Elder Grant, who served from 1949 to 1952. Clearly CFUW could still attract prominent academics to its leadership. Grant had a long association with Acadia University in Wolfville, Nova Scotia—her mother had been dean at Acadia Ladies Seminary and Marion had grown up in an academic world. She graduated from Acadia in 1921 and taught for a few years before completing a PhD at the University of Toronto. She taught at Baylor College for Women in Texas where she served as dean of women before attending University College, London. Grant then returned to Acadia University to attend to her ailing mother and eventually became dean from 1936 to 1960, head of the psychology department, and a member of the board of governors. She was widely published in the fields of early childhood education, learning disabilities, and the importance of children's play. She also founded both a university women's club in Wolfville, as well as the Fundy Mental Health Clinic, the first freestanding clinic of its type in the province. A woman of wide interests, Grant was active in the Baptist Church, the Imperial Order Daughters of the Empire (IODE), and various professional associations.[7]

During her presidency Dr. Grant tried to visit all of the new clubs, travelling by train and bus. She also welcomed the 1951 ground-breaking report of the Royal Commission on National Development in the Arts, Letters and Sciences (the Massey commission) and witnessed a major initiative in penal reform. Her term

Ribbon-cutting ceremony at the Art Exhibit, Château Laurier, Ottawa, August 18, 1952. Dr. Grant, President, is in the centre; Mrs. S. A. Quigg, Ottawa Convenor, is on the left; and Mrs. G. Ross Gibson, National Convenor, is on the right.

ended at the twelfth CFUW triennial conference held in Ottawa in 1952, where guests were entertained at the Dominion Experimental Farm with Ottawa Mayor Charlotte Whitton presiding,[8] and an art exhibit at the Château Laurier. The federation created a new fellowship to honour Margaret McWilliams, who had died suddenly in 1952, and commissioned a history of the organization's first thirty years for IFUW.

This era was also a period of growth for CFUW. By 1959, membership numbers had nearly doubled from those of 1940, to 9,445. This, in part, reflected the staggering growth in the number of women attending university. Many new clubs were formed in the 1950s, especially in the growing suburbs. When the first suburban club was formed in North York in 1951, CFUW tried to persuade the women to join the Toronto Club, but the women objected that it was too far away for young mothers and the fees needed to support the clubhouse were too high. The geographic restrictions that CFUW initially tried to impose did not make sense in the new city configurations and were eventually dropped.[9] Catherine Marcellus, historian of the new Abbotsford, British Columbia Club, remembers being recruited as club president. She recalls sitting in her kitchen surrounded by babies and exclaiming, "I could not possibly do that.... I've never done anything like that before," while the more experienced recruiter counters, "Cathy, you don't know what you can do until you try."[10] The story has a certain 1950s ring to it. She did become club president and the lesson stuck with her all her life, illustrating the important role that the clubs played in developing women's skills and encouraging them to look beyond their homes. This new club in Abbotsford decided to accept associate members, feeling that women who shared the club's spirit enriched their ranks even if they did not have degrees. Clubs were also formed in smaller towns such as Cornwall, where the wives of engineers working on the St. Lawrence Seaway, one of the biggest technological projects of this era, had relocated. Charlottetown, Prince Edward Island was the only provincial capital to form a new club in this decade.

Many longstanding clubs also ballooned in membership. The Edmonton Club peaked from 1959 to 1961 when the discovery of oil in Leduc, Alberta dramatically increased the province's population. The Ottawa Club expanded to four hundred members by 1959 and became increasingly active in advocacy.[11] President Doris Saunders reported in 1956 that "the file labeled 'Clubs' is positively bulging at the seams, and letters telling of the formation of serious groups on education, status of women, libraries and creative arts, etc. 'make music for our ears.'"[12] Never entirely satisfied, however, CFUW presidents bemoaned the fact that their membership was not keeping pace with the increase in university enrolment. As it became less of a novelty for women to go to university, women perhaps had less incentive to seek out a club of like-minded peers. To help counter these trends, the federation produced a recruitment leaflet in 1951, distributing 3,500 in English, and five hundred in French. Many clubs also did their own local recruiting through social events and scholarships.

The federation's structure and constitution also expanded. After Québec women won the vote in 1940, thanks to campaigns led by CFUW member Thérèse Casgrain and the fact that more and more francophone women were attending university, new French-speaking clubs were formed in Trois-Rivières and Ottawa-Hull; the latter had both an English and a French club. The number of vice presidents fluctuated between two and four, joining the president, past president, and various secretaries on the executive. The Academic Appointments Committee was disbanded in favour of a Status of Women Committee with a broader mandate. In 1958, CFUW created the first office of regional directors in Ontario to help organize regional conferences.[13]

CFUW further formalized its resolutions procedures, establishing committees on resolutions and administrative procedures and printed instructions to clubs on how to submit resolutions to the national office in the *Chronicle*: resolutions should "deal with public matters of sufficient importance to be brought to the attention of all members," i.e., of national concern,[14] be brief, well researched, propose some definite action, and indicate the individual, body, government department, or institution to which the resolution was directed. Once received, the national committee arranged for the resolutions to be voted on, first at the club level, and if passed, at the triennial meeting.[15]

Given Canada's murky jurisdictional divisions, there was often confusion as to who should take the lead in advocacy. The federation

At the back, left to right: Dorothy Flaherty,
Dr. Marguerite Ritchie, and unidentified
person; in front, left to right: Margaret E.
(Pegi) MacLellan and Margaret Gilleland.

would follow up on successful resolutions with letters and visits to the appropriate political leaders and incorporate them into CFUW policy. In some cases this happened at both levels—the local clubs would approach their member of Parliament while the federation wrote or visited a minister or federal department. Regional vice presidents and provincial directors followed up on resolutions that fell under provincial jurisdiction, especially in the case of education. One example of this process was the brief presented by the Alberta clubs to the Royal Commission on Education in 1958 chaired by Senator Donald Cameron that focused on improving academic standards in secondary schools, on library improvements, and on examining requirements for university entrance across the country.[16] Improvements to library facilities, bilingual programs, and programs for gifted children were also recommended.

Despite the growth in numbers and officers, CFUW did not achieve its goal of establishing a permanent head office in Ottawa, although the organization did decide in this decade that the paid executive secretary and volunteer president should live in the same city. In 1956, President Saunders described her office, with its typewriter, mimeographing machine, and filing cabinet, as "our little cubby-hole that serves as an Executive Office" from which letters were sent to prime ministers and ministers of finance on legislative matters.[17] In 1958, the head office moved with President Vivian Morton to a room in the University of Saskatchewan's School of Agriculture Building, where the university provided a telephone and access to its stenographic pool.[18]

The 1950s had begun auspiciously with the report of the Massey commission, a major articulation of cultural nationalism that recommended funding to the arts and sciences and the establishment of the National Library and Canada Council. Reflecting many interests dear to the organization, CFUW had submitted a brief to the commission in which it stressed scholarship and research in education.[19] The Massey commission reinforced work that clubs had quietly done in their own communities—sponsoring art exhibits and performances, funding libraries, managing festivals and exhibits, and encouraging members to sit on boards of arts and cultural organizations. The commission led to the establishment of new cultural institutions and the strengthening of existing ones, the latter including the Stratford

Dr. Hilda Neatby, CFUW member, historian and educator.

Shakespearian Festival founded in 1953, the National Film Board, and the Canadian Broadcasting Corporation (CBC). The establishment of the Canada Council for the Arts in 1957 is also linked to the Massey commission. The federation later lobbied for representation on the Canada Council's twenty-one-member board, managing to get four women appointed.

To cap it all off, the government had named long-time CFUW member and former Education Committee chairman Dr. Hilda Neatby as one of the commissioners; it was an immense source of pride for the federation. Neatby had been born into a genteel, poor, but learned family in Saskatchewan. She excelled academically and studied at the universities of Saskatchewan and Minnesota, becoming an expert in post-conquest Québec history. One of the few women who had managed to obtain an academic post during the Depression, Neatby eventually became head of the University of Saskatchewan's history department, a position she held from 1958 to 1969.

In 1953, Dr. Neatby sparked a national debate with her controversial publication, *So Little for the Mind*, in which she made an impassioned plea for the humanities in education. One of a number of leading public intellectuals who had been shaped by the experiences of two wars and the Depression, Neatby's views reflected the 1950s' distinctive cultural nationalism, a growing bureaucracy built around the social welfare state, and Canada's emergence as a "middle power."[20] Fearing that the growing emphasis on technical subjects in educational curricula—meant to prepare an ever-widening school population for twentieth-century jobs—would lead to a "dumbing down" of education, she rejected the idea that education should be useful and open to all.[21] She feared that Western civilization—as enshrined in the university—was at a crisis point and believed that her generation must provide leadership to restore excellence. Neatby had received funding and encouragement to write the book from Vincent Massey himself, who shared her alarm at the growing trend away from the humanities.

The topic was certainly within the purview of the CFUW, with its focus on education and stress on the humanities.[22] The organization actively participated in the debate triggered by *So Little for the Mind*. While many sympathized with the book's humanist critique of modern education, and members were proud of their intellectual "celebrity," progressives in their ranks such as Edmonton's Donalda Dickie must have taken strong exception to the book. Inspired by the theories of John Dewey, progressive educationalists proposed a child-centred theory of teaching that focused on learning by problem solving, with less emphasis on content. Driven by a belief that education must meet the needs of a democracy, this approach represented a dramatic departure from the traditional classical preparation for university. In the end, the Edmonton group took a diplomatic middle ground, asserting that "the needs of youth would probably be well served by incorporating the best procedures of both systems into the secondary school."[23]

Neatby's more vocal critics, both in the CFUW and more globally, labelled her a conservative and an elitist and some even zeroed in on her gender and accused her of emotionalism. Modern educational theorists, however, believe that Neatby's book remains a well-reasoned, insightful "liberal humanist critique of educational theory."[24] Whether one agreed with it or not, the book struck a chord, selling nearly 8,000 copies in its first year and going to four printings and a second edition. A regional CFUW conference in Hamilton in May, 1954 held a debate on the question, "Resolved, that *So Little for the Mind* is an unjust indictment of education in Ontario." While the always-polite *Chronicle* did not report on which side won, the article did note that the discussion led to a study on the issue of the "bright child"—what we would today call the gifted child—and led to a request that the minister of education in Ontario provide special training for teachers of these students.[25] Similarly the Regina Club studied programs for bright children and, in 1958, made a submission to their public school board that resulted in a pilot project in which children were offered instruction in French. All of this seemed to come out of a discussion of the Neatby critique of diminishing excellence in education.

Stemming from concerns raised before the war, several clubs persuaded the federation to pass resolutions on penal reform, pressing the government, for example, to implement the 1938 Archambault Commission report on federal prison conditions. That reform initiative had been launched by the House of Common's sole female MP, Agnes Macphail, in the 1920s and 1930s, but the issue had been shelved during the war. The issue was rekindled in 1947 when Major-General R. B. Gibson, appointed as commissioner of penitentiaries by the federal Justice Department, began to initiate reforms that focused on the rehabilitation of prisoners. In the early 1950s, CFUW's penal reform committee reported that they were pleased with these reforms, particularly with the grants given to the Elizabeth Fry and John Howard societies, and the training for staff and prisoners. Because the criminal justice system straddled federal, provincial, and even local jurisdictions, the federation executive asked the clubs with active study groups to alternate serving as the federation's penal reform committee. The Halifax Club formed the first such committee, followed by Edmonton and then Regina, the latter two studying the Saskatchewan and Alberta systems.[26] In June 1950, the Ottawa Club's committee formed the CFUW penal reform committee, where the club had helped found the Ottawa Elizabeth Fry Society and assisted the Ottawa Club with jail visits and rehabilitation work, both at the Prison for Women in Kingston and the Juvenile Court in Ottawa.[27] In 1952, a group of members from Québec and Montréal, chaired by Dr. P. Cazelais, completed a report on Québec prisons and in 1954, the committee moved back to the Atlantic region.

Based on this research, CFUW put forward various resolutions on their own, as well as in conjunction with the Elizabeth Fry Society, that called for pre-sentence reports on offenders and for more trained probation officers. On a different front, the New Westminster Club in British Columbia, which had conducted a study of emotionally disturbed children, promoted a home for them in Vancouver[28] and advocated the creation of family courts, training schools for juveniles, training programs for prisoners, and improved training for prison staff. After the 1956 Fauteux Report recommended that the old ticket of leave system be replaced with a national parole board, CFUW asked for a woman qualified in corrections to be appointed.[29] The organization felt strongly that it was important to have a woman's input to assess the post-release environment of former prisoners, and to have someone who could understand women prisoners, especially given that male prison officials acknowledged that they found women difficult to handle.[30] CFUW put forward four names, including that of Margaret MacLellan, and there were some small victories. The St. Thomas Club arranged an open meeting with Daniel Couglin, director of probation services for Ontario, in November 1953 that resulted in the establishment of a county juvenile court.[31] In Ottawa, lawyer Margaret Ferguson was appointed probation officer for the Ottawa magistrate's court and similar appointments were made in Toronto and Windsor. By the end of the decade, however, much of this penal reform work had shifted to the Elizabeth Fry Society and CFUW became less active in it.

The appointment of women to boards and commissions remained a predominant concern of CFUW. In 1951, the Academic Appointments Committee prepared its usual Register of Canadian Women Available for Academic Posts and distributed it to Canadian universities. The previous year, the committee had requested that the National Council of Canadian Universities form a committee to "compile a register listing names of men and women whose qualifications met the standards set by the committee." The answer they received suggests that most university appointments were still being decided upon by word of mouth or by promoting promising students:

> The committee regretfully decided that they could not at present undertake such a compilation.... However, the Conference expressed itself in favour of advertising academic posts and intends to use *Saturday Night* for this purpose so that men and women in Canada will have a better idea of the posts that are vacant, even if the universities have little previous knowledge of the likely applicants. This will, I hope, tend towards the aims, which your Federation has had in making its own lists.[32]

It is undoubtedly not a coincidence that the few women who did manage to gain long-term academic posts, such as Doris Saunders at the University of Manitoba, had been educated there. In 1952, the federation decided to disband the Academic Appointments Committee for at least a triennial period and assigned the Status of Women Committee the task of compiling a roster of outstanding women whom clubs considered suitable for public office at the municipal, provincial, and federal levels. Dubbed the "Best Dressed Minds" list, it was intended to provide names of potential candidates for appointment to senior government and other posts.[33] Thus began a new CFUW phase in promoting women to prominent positions in government, business, and academia.

In 1955, the federation sent briefs to Secretary of State Roch Pinard as well as to Prime Minister Louis St. Laurent, women senators, and members of Parliament, to urge the appointment of a woman to the "three-man" Civil Service Commission.[34] They suggested five qualified women, including long-time civil service personnel officer Nora Guthrie and Constance Hayward, a liaison officer in the Canadian citizenship branch who had experience with the League of Nations Society in Canada. Guthrie was a Queen's graduate who had studied public administration and took on increasing responsibilities in personnel work. Accepted for further study in public administration at the University of Chicago in 1947, her employer refused to grant her leave, informing her that as a senior official she was needed to direct work during the postwar rehabilitation period.[35] Neither of these candidates got the job, but in 1957, Ruth Addison was appointed to the rank of deputy minister. Margaret MacLellan congratulated her, noting that such an appointment had first been requested thirteen years earlier and expressing the hope that it would set a new precedent.[36] In a letter to then-federation president Doris Saunders, Addison acknowledged, "I am very much aware of the part that women's groups like the Canadian Federation of University Women have played in making my appointment possible." She had to distance herself from lobbying for women but hoped that "in the years ahead, greater recognition will be given to women's place in the civil service."[37]

The federation also sought Senate appointments for women. CFUW had asked the Canadian Federation of Business and

Professional Women (CFBPW) for its help in proposing a prominent Toronto woman for the Senate, and they in turn asked for CFUW help in proposing an equally prominent, Western woman. As a result, the slogan "a woman senator for every province" was adopted by both organizations.[38] In 1953, PM St. Laurent named the first French-Canadian woman, Mariana Beauchamp-Jodoin an honorary member of AFDU, to the Senate. Active in many organizations, she founded a women's Liberal club in Montréal named for Wilfrid Laurier.[39] Muriel McQueen Fergusson, a member and advisor to CFUW's Status of Women Committee, was also named that year. Trained in the law, McQueen had been New Brunswick's regional enforcement counsel for the Wartime Prices and Trade Board and later served as regional director for the family allowance and old age security programs.[40]

Some within CFUW called for women to run for political office. The Status of Women Committee, for example, saw political involvement as a means of achieving reforms, and women's groups often worked with sympathetic female MPs on some issues. Apparently, not everyone agreed, however as reflected in a 1951 Status of Women Committee report:

> Your committee feels that a great deal has been done to allay the fears of those who felt that the University Women's Club must not become politically embroiled. We feel that we have established a definite line of demarcation between the political affiliation of the group and the political support by individual club members of a suitable woman for office.[41]

Still, many clubs supported women at the non-partisan, municipal level, the 1951–1952 *Chronicle* reporting that twenty-four CFUW members were serving on municipal councils, boards of education, and hospital boards, most notably Charlotte Whitton, mayor of Ottawa.

The career of Whitton certainly illustrates the pitfalls of politics for female candidates. In 1950, she decided to run for city council, asking CFUW, the Ottawa Club, the local council of women and other organizations to support her. It is not clear how much money the Ottawa Club or the federation contributed, but Whitton reasoned that, unlike most men, she had no profession to return to after a defeat and thus needed support. She also felt that women would be more supportive if they had made a financial contribution. When Whitton became eligible to assume the mayor's chair after the sitting mayor's sudden death, because she had won the most votes, her male colleagues tried, unsuccessfully, to push her aside. She was a controversial mayor and much resented by those who thought women should be ladylike. But she was hardworking, had a legendary memory for detail, was prudent with city funds, and eliminated the forced early retirement of female city workers. But she was also a little too fond of the trappings of office, and in the end, was given to dramatics that sometimes made a laughingstock of city hall.

In 1958, Whitton set her sights on federal politics, but had to fight her own Conservative Party to gain the nomination in Ottawa West, a solidly Liberal riding. At that time, the party did not allow women to vote at conventions, but she mobilized the West Ottawa Women's PC Association and threatened to hold a separate convention. She gained the nomination and despite a Diefenbaker sweep, lost the seat with a much smaller-than-expected margin. She believed, quite legitimately, that she deserved a political reward. Sadly, Diefenbaker ignored her entreaties and she ended up going back to municipal politics. While the combative Whitton may have rubbed many people—male and female alike—the wrong way, she certainly did not deserve the shameful treatment she received.[42] Her story was a cautionary tale for women with political ambitions beyond the municipal realm.

As always, the local club remained an important social focus for university women hosting Christmas parties, annual dinners, teas and luncheons. Refreshments varied from club to club and adapted to the times. One club reported serving wine at its meetings, something that would have shocked earlier members. Other clubs brought potluck dinners at members' homes into their social orbit, a concession to the "servant-less era." The newly formed Abbotsford Club, suggesting a seriousness of purpose and repudiation of domesticity, decided not to "try to out-cook each other."[43] The Toronto Club, which then numbered more than eight hundred members, undertook an extensive renovation and enlargement of its clubhouse with architect Napier Simpson in 1958. They added an elegant foyer, a seventy-two-seat dining room, and an upstairs lounge with French windows facing a sundeck.[44] Once a staple of club events, the practice of inviting university students, in the hope that they would later become members, was becoming less common due to rising student enrolment. McGill Alumnae, however, sponsored a public-speaking contest for girls from high schools in Montréal.[45]

In the 1950s, the CFUW demographic was predominantly young married women with a smaller contingent of single professionals. In Ottawa, for example, 62 per cent of members were married, of which 13 per cent were gainfully employed.[46]

CFUW's study groups, lifelong education, social events, and fundraising for scholarships and community projects gave an outlet to those frustrated with domestic work and lack of recognition for volunteer work. Most worked locally, but some members became active on federation committees. These activities were always interwoven with "fun, sprightly conversation, relaxing social times and lasting friendships."[47] Outstanding speakers were often invited to give lectures that raised money as well as educating members. Fundraising was a big component of local club activities often directed toward scholarships. The Regina Club used magazine subscriptions to raise funds and in 1951–1952 awarded a total of $1,500.00, more than any other club in Canada.[48]

Among the more serious enterprises were the study groups and although the federation often suggested topics such as education, childcare, psychology, international affairs, status of women, and—new to this decade—human rights, ultimately, the local clubs chose the subject matter. Some of the clubs studied royal commission or government reports—the Edmonton Club, for example, followed the recommendations of the Massey commission all through its 1952–1953 season, as did the Abbotsford/Mission City Club. After the Canada Council was established to strengthen funding for the arts, clubs often invited its representatives to speak. Culturally oriented study groups often provided meeting entertainments, including travelogues by members, play or drama readings, musical entertainment, and even barbershop quartets by visiting husbands.

Other groups focused on recreation—hiking and short excursions, for example—and socializing. The St. Thomas' Jaunters Club went on outings to museums, the Windsor salt mines, the Hydro developments, and Fort George.[49] Cultural groups studied art, music, drama, literature, interior decorating, conversational French (or English), and crafts. The St. Thomas Club took advantage of its proximity to the new Shakespearean Festival in Stratford to attend and study the plays. The Vancouver Club, in celebration of the provincial centenary in 1958, brought in the National Ballet, a "glittering opportunity to sponsor this national jewel on a West Coast stage, to contribute to the UBC [University of British Columbia] development fund, and to add to the club's own building fund."[50]

The interest or study groups often generated resolutions of local significance and club members sometimes followed-up on them with great enthusiasm by writing to or visiting members of city council, the school board, or a Member of Parliament. When the Abbotsford Club historian looked back on resolutions the club had passed—such as one deploring nuclear explosions—she remarked, "I am amazed at how frequently we telegraphed or wrote the prime minister, the premier, cabinet ministers, or even on one occasion the president of the United States." This zeal, she believed, reflected a confidence, less common today, that leaders wanted to hear what they thought.[51]

Dr. Martha Law, who served as CFUW president from 1952 to 1955, had graduated in 1923 from the University of Toronto with a degree in dentistry, then worked as a dental officer for the Toronto Public Health Department. A financial wizard, she learned to invest through the Toronto Stock Exchange and kept CFUW books in good order during her years as treasurer and as president. Law outlined some of her goals at the thirteenth triennial meeting in Edmonton, Alberta in 1955. One of them was to increase the number of clubs by twenty, which she did achieve, and another goal was to establish a permanent office, which would have to wait. Law knew the importance of a strong volunteer core and praised, in particular, the married women who formed "the backbone of our society."[52] Martha Law also oversaw the creation in 1952 of the $1,500 Margaret McWilliams Fellowship and the CFUW/IFUW fellowship named for astronomer, Dr. A. Vibert Douglas.

During this decade, CFUW also joined the CFBPW, the Young Women's Christian Association (YWCA), and the National Council of Women of Canada (NCWC) in promoting the establishment of a Women's Bureau in the Department of Labour. Margaret Wherry

of the CFBPW had led the campaign that failed in 1945, but it succeeded in 1954. CFUW had suggested this idea as early as the 1920s,
inspired by the American model and its own Vocations Bureau, and
was delighted that the government appointed one of its members,
Marion Royce, as director of the new bureau. Royce had taught
history and English at Toronto's Moulton College for Girls for five
years, then in 1928, became executive secretary of the National Girls
Work Board of the Religious Education Council of Canada. In 1940,
she was named education secretary for the Montréal YWCA, and
from 1942 to 1954, she served as secretary for social and international
questions at the World YWCA in Geneva. Her sister, Jean Royce,
was registrar at Queen's University and had earlier presided over
CFUW's Vocations Committee. Initially the Women's Bureau had
a limited mandate of providing research into the needs of women
in the labour force, and it served the government's purpose in managing a growing economy in which employers increasingly looked
to women to fill labour shortages. Over time, the Women's Bureau
expanded its role to developing and advocating policies to facilitate
equal opportunity for women in the labour force, improving vocational training, and recommending revisions to legislation on equal
pay, maternity protection, and child care.[53]

The mid-1950s also saw some early developments in equal pay
legislation. CFUW had long complained about unequal wages paid
to women, especially teachers, and joined other women's organizations in formally protesting this injustice. In 1954, the Edmonton
Club protested an Alberta government proposal to address the
teacher shortage by lowering the entrance requirements for the
faculty of education at the University of Alberta and shortening
the training period for teachers. The same club petitioned for the
appointment of more women to the faculties of education in Calgary
and Edmonton.[54] Somewhat ironically, the teacher shortage created
by the baby boom led to the lifting of early postwar prohibitions on
the employment of married women.

The teacher shortages had little effect on pay rates, however, and
some women's groups were trying to have the standard of equal pay
codified in Canadian legislation. The CFBPW won a major victory
with the introduction of the Female Employees Fair Remuneration
Act in Ontario in 1951, and then established an Employment

Conditions Committee to approach the federal and provincial governments. Soon other provinces followed suit, and in 1953 the federal government passed the Canada Fair Employment Practices Act to eliminate gender discrimination in the civil service.[55] CFBPW also won a prolonged fight to remove the words "for men only" from job advertisements issued by the Civil Service Commission."[56] The federal government passed the Female Employees Equal Pay Act in 1956, making wage discrimination based on sex unlawful across the board. Unfortunately, passing legislation does not guarantee implementation and employers invariably found ways to differentiate between jobs performed by men and those done by women to justify wage differentials. But it was a beginning.

As had been the case with suffrage, CFUW was late to advocate anti-discrimination legislation. Following the Kingston conference in 1956, CFUW asked the minister of labour, Milton F. Gregg, to implement the principle of equal pay, and he sent them a copy of the bill when it passed.[57] At that meeting, some members criticized the legislation as an encroachment upon an employer's right to choose his or her staff, preferring a program of education and persuasion to the use of legislative force or the evocation of rights.

Local efforts were often instrumental in affecting change as well. For example, President Law praised the Ottawa Club for mounting an effective campaign to secure facilities for women barristers in the plans to remodel the Ottawa courthouse.[58] With persistence, solid research, and the creation of an inter-club council with other women's groups, the club threatened to bring the matter to the attention of the media, thus overcoming protests by the Carleton County Law Association. Despite having no authority in the matter, the latter tried to exclude female lawyers, present and future, from the new courthouse.[59] They did not succeed. Similarly, the club defended jury duty for women. In 1951, the Ontario government made women eligible for jury duty but allowed them to obtain easy exemptions; in 1956, both the Ottawa Club and the Elizabeth Fry Society asked that jury duty be made mandatory for women, as it was for men. When this was discussed at a regional meeting, one woman cited the example of a lawyer who insisted that women should not be allowed to serve in traffic cases because they are "bad drivers."[60]

In 1955, Doris Boyce Saunders became CFUW president and

served until 1958. An early scholarship winner and the first woman to
be appointed full professor at the
University of Manitoba, her career
matched the CFUW ideal. She was
finally awarded the title Dr. only when
UBC conferred an honorary doctorate on her in 1957, in conjunction
with the fiftieth anniversary of the
Vancouver University Women's Club.
Unable to pursue a PhD at Oxford
because it still did not admit women,
Saunders enrolled in the bachelor of
letters program in English in 1926,
although she did not receive her
degree until 1936, when Oxford finally
granted degrees to women. Saunders'
Oxford degree was finally upgraded
to a master's degree in 1979. Saunders
served as president of the women's
branches of the Canadian Institute for
International Affairs, the Humanities

Dr. Doris Saunders, CFUW President
1955–1958.

Association of Canada, and the Women's Canadian Club. She was
also president of the University Women's Club of Winnipeg from
1943 to 1945 and chaired the federation Scholarship Committee
before assuming the presidency.

In 1958, when Saunders presided over the fourteenth triennial meeting in Montréal, it was co-hosted by Yvonne Letellier
de Saint-Just, president of L'Association des femmes diplômées
des universités (AFDU). This meeting represented the first time
that French was officially recognized within the federation. Guest
speaker Cardinal Paul-Emile Léger, archbishop of Montréal and
president of the University of Montréal, gave the keynote address
on bilingualism and humanism. At that meeting, the Library and
Creative Arts Committee, home to many artistic women, arranged
an art show of members' works. A similar display of both paintings
and books was held at a regional conference at the University of
Saskatchewan in Saskatoon in 1958.[61]

Dr. Doris Saunders, President (seated), in the mayor's office
during the CFUW Triennial Conference 1958, Montréal.

Driven by international developments such as the UN adoption of the Universal Declaration of Human Rights in 1948, the concept of human rights was also beginning to have an impact on women.[62] The UN Declaration, which Canadian legal scholar, jurist, and human rights advocate John Peters Humphrey had a significant role in drafting, asserted that everyone was entitled to all the rights in the document "without distinction of any kind, such as race, colour, sex, language, religion, political or other opinion, national or social origin, property, birth, or other status."[63] Other events and court judgments were changing the way Canadians thought about the differential treatment of ethnic minorities in hiring, accommodation, and restaurant service upside down as well.[64] Nova Scotian entrepreneur and beautician Viola Desmond had protested racially segregated seating in a movie theatre in Nova Scotia in 1946 and, although she lost her court case, she spurred on a movement. Other cases were more successful. After the war, Japanese and Chinese Canadians protested their exclusion from voting rights, and in 1951, the Supreme Court of Canada overturned the legality of real estate covenants that had been used to exclude some ethnic groups from buying property in certain neighbourhoods. The logical extension—to include women in a discussion of human rights—did not follow immediately. In 1950, Constance Hayward, a member of the federation's International Committee wrote an article on human rights in Canada in which she interpreted it as protection of religious and ethnic minority rights. CFUW endorsed human rights in relation to education, particularly articles 26–28 of the declaration of rights that read, "all Canadian children should be entitled, without payment of fees, without regard to place of residence and without regard to race, creed, personal wealth, or social position, to an education to the limit of each child's ability."[65] Other documents included the 1953 UN Convention on the Political Rights of Women, which the Canadian government did not sign until 1957, perhaps due to its less than stellar record on women's rights.[66] Nonetheless becoming a signatory to this Convention allowed Canada a seat on the eighteen-member United Nations Commission on the Status of Women (UNCSW), and further linked human rights with women's rights.

Given the CFUW demographic, it is not surprising that much of their advocacy was centred on the women's homemaking role. While some women embraced it, others struggled. The Edmonton Club's president, Mrs. Margaret Greenhill, thought that many university graduates were "frustrated to think that they had spent all those years [studying] and were now changing diapers."[67] One Eastern Ontario regional conference held in Ottawa in 1959 had as its theme "The Educated Woman in the World Today" and included such topics as "Should a Woman's Talents be Confined to the Home?" and "Barriers of Tradition in Jobs and Careers."[68] Marion Royce, speaking at the 1955 triennial meeting, explained that the modern conjugal family had displaced large kinship groups that had been predominant in an earlier era. The home was no longer a centre of production [for consumer goods such as clothing] and there was a trend toward individualism, but culturally, women were not yet accepted into the workforce. She quoted an American sociologist who observed that women were qualified for most jobs but were excluded by "traditional inter-personal attitudes," such as the shame that many men felt on being subordinated to a woman boss and the assumption that the sexes should not mix in social groups. Royce politely declined to call it discrimination. Nonetheless, she insisted that "society needs a set of values which provide dignity and fulfill-ment for both men and women."[69]

Women began to seek remedies. The Vancouver Club's Status of Women Committee worked with the local council of women on a study of older women workers to help women return to the workforce after raising children. The London Club, guided by alderman Margaret Fullerton, successfully lobbied to have a bylaw that prohibited the employment of married women rescinded by the city. Among the CFUW resolutions passed in 1958 was one asking the Department of National Revenue to allow gainfully employed women to deduct expenses for a housekeeper or nurse from their income tax.

One of the major economic issues of concern to all women, whether they worked in the labour force or at home, was succession duties and estate taxes. Just as reformers such as Helen Gregory MacGill had sought to give women, especially married women, greater legal and financial autonomy, postwar women continued to argue for married women to have financial independence. Although the demeaning laws that granted a husband control over the family's finances, including the wages his wife earned by her own labour, had been changed, for the most part, whoever owned property had the power to dispose of it. As a result, a wife was not entitled to share in family property flowing from her marital status. The same was true of a widow. Money or property bequeathed to her would be subject to federal estate tax and provincial succession duties.

As early as 1948, NCWC had begun to bring this matter before the federal government. After two years studying their brief, CFUW's Status of Women Committee decided in 1953, to support the NCWC resolution rather than confuse the issue by saying the same thing in a different way. It sought to secure recognition that a widow was entitled to half of a deceased husband's estate and should therefore not be subject to estate taxes and succession duties. In effect, the resolution asked for recognition of the economic contribution to the family made by wives. As CFUW argued, "it is the wise, faithful, laborious work of wives which leaves the husband free in body and mind to work in office or factory to earn the money which in time becomes their joint estate."[70] Advocates of the reforms pointed out that charities, which contributed nothing to an estate, were entitled to receive unlimited funds tax free while survivors were not. In its public statements, CFUW also drew attention to the fact that other laws had made tentative steps in this direction, including the dower and homestead laws that permitted the surviving spouse a life estate in the home property, as well as the Veterans' Land Act, the War Veterans Allowance, and the National Housing Act.[71]

Margaret MacLellan, then convenor of the Status of Women Committee noted, in 1958, that the same recommendations had been made over the previous ten years by NCWC, CFUW, and other women's organizations. The federal government did eventually introduce a new Estates Tax Act in the dying moments of January 1958, but it failed to pass before a new election was called. Had the legislation been adopted, however, it still would not have met the federation's expectations. When the election was called, CFUW addressed the leaders of the four political parties and pointed out that the new bill required a wife to prove that the money she had used to acquire joint tenancy of the family home had not been received from her husband. Conservative opposition leader John Diefenbaker made sympathetic assurances and, once elected, had his new minister of finance discuss the CFUW's proposals with them. When the legislation was passed in 1959, the federation found an improvement but still did not consider it the recognition of partnership they sought.[72]

The federation asked Ontario Premier Leslie Frost, in September 1957, to amend the Ontario Succession Duty Act to bring it in line with federal legislation and to add brothers and sisters to the preferred class of relatives in order to recognize the economic contribution of a single woman who did housekeeping for a sibling.[73] On March 10, 1959, CFUW joined other major women's groups in a deputation to the provincial treasurer to discuss this change.[74] The premier noted that he was studying the federal legislation and would give due consideration to the women's submissions.

Finishing the decade and moving into the 1960s, Dr. Vivian Brown Morton was CFUW president from 1958 to 1962. The wife and former student of historian Arthur Silver Morton, she completed a BA in history, but did not pursue a career in that field. Instead she studied at the Royal Conservatory of Music. Dr. Morton was also president and program convenor for the Saskatoon Arts Centre and co-founded the Saskatchewan Arts and Crafts Society and organized many festivals and conferences. She also served with her local branch of the Canadian Institute of International Affairs. In the 1960s, Morton would lead CFUW's first delegation to a prime minister, Lester B. Pearson, to advocate on behalf of women. Later in the decade CFUW led a campaign to persuade Pearson to name a royal commission into the status of women. Turbulent days would be ahead as the organization adjusted to the emerging women's liberation movement.

Footnotes for this chapter can be found online at:
http://secondstorypress.ca/resources

Chapter 7

A ROYAL COMMISSION OF THEIR VERY OWN:
CFUW LEADS THE WAY

*...the increasing subtle prejudices, invisible barriers, discrimi-
natory laws, and practices, found in every facet of our society
against women's full participation in the political, economic, and
intellectual life of this country....*

—Laura Sabia[1]

These were some of the reasons Laura Sabia cited in trying to convince CFUW members to pressure the government to appoint a
royal commission on the status of women.

It is fitting that a president of CFUW, one of the women's organizations established early in the century, would lead the campaign
for this defining event of the second-wave feminist movement in
Canada, or, as it was called then, the women's liberation movement. It speaks to the strong and enduring connections between
the old and the new movements, the former having laid much of
the groundwork for the new movement. It was very much a product of the 1960s, which saw the American civil rights movement,
student activism, Québec's Quiet Revolution, and the Indigenous
Peoples' renaissance challenge established authority. The decade also
saw Canada celebrate one hundred years of Confederation with a
major world's fair, Expo 67, in Montréal. In 1959, Doris McCubbin
Anderson, the new editor of *Chatelaine* magazine, began making
waves with articles on previously taboo subjects such as pay equity,
birth control, and domestic violence. Women's participation rate

Laura Sabia, CFUW President 1964–1967.

in the labour force was on the rise—by 1967 it had reached and exceeded the previous 1944 peak. But the most dramatic change was in the number of married women in the workforce. While in 1941 only one in twenty-five working women was married, by 1961 the figure was one in five.[2]

The number of women attending university continued to rise—which in turn propelled growth in CFUW membership and the need for increased institutional complexity. By 1964, CFUW had 11,000 members and 115 clubs. Nevertheless, President Margaret MacLellan argued that a central office would only be possible if the organization could double its membership, noting, "Surely, from a potential of 85,000 university women graduates in Canada, we can attract and hold 20,000."[3] New clubs were added constantly. In 1960, the creation of the one-hundredth CFUW club in Sainte-Anne-de-Bellevue in the Montréal district of Pointe Claire was featured in the *Chronicle*, which described its lively French conversation groups,[4] the establishment of a bursary for local students, and the club's first guest speaker—CFUW executive member Mary Winspear. As noted in an earlier chapter, Winspear had established a bilingual high school in Montréal after failing to find an academic post.

The growth was also reflected in the structure of the organization. In 1960, CFUW officers included the president, three vice presidents (representing the Central, East, and West regions), a recording secretary, a membership secretary, and the treasurer. By 1964, another vice president (VP) position had been added, dividing Central Canada into Québec and Ontario regions. A major constitutional change occurred in 1965 with the creation of Provincial Council of University Women's Clubs-Province of Québec/ Conseilées provincial des associations des femmes diplômées des universitiés (AFDU)-Province de Québec.[5] The new council brought together eleven English and French clubs under director Kathleen B. Farmer, a graduate of the Université de Montréal.

As the Quiet Revolution began to generate many reforms in areas of concern to Québec women—such as education, family, and health—the clubs knew they needed the added clout of a provincial association to argue their case. The Québec clubs met in Montréal to pass the resolution to establish a council and sent Emilie Trahan and Suzanne Coallier to the Winnipeg triennial to present it. With the support of CFUW president (and former Montréaler) Laura Sabia, the resolution passed and the new council, incorporated into the revised CFUW constitution and bylaws, allowed CFUW to have a voice in the major changes occurring in Québec in this tumultuous period.[6] The council submitted briefs to the Royal Commission on Bilingualism and Biculturalism and to the Royal Commission on Education in the Province of Québec, better known as the Parent Commission.

The leaders of CFUW were no longer called officers—there were now thirteen provincial directors, three for Ontario, two for Québec and one for each of the remaining provinces. The organization formed a special committee to explore the establishment of a permanent office in Ottawa, but, for the moment, the volunteer president, part-time paid secretary, and new press secretary would rely on donated office space, and the office would continue to move every three years with the election of a new president.

The Publishing Committee also made efforts to brighten up the *Chronicle* by shortening the business reports and adding more feature articles on topics such as the woman offender, women at Expo 67, and women returning to work. One article explored the question of what attracted members to the clubs. Some members were apparently turned off by lectures and reading royal commission reports, although one woman said she had learned more from her current affairs study group than she had through years of reading *Time* magazine and the daily newspaper. Many women, such as the mother of three who was relieved to see no mention of babies in the program, were not interested in having conventional domestic activities in their club lives. Another woman was happy that no one ever asked her to bake.[7]

This decade's CFUW survey of university graduates, members and non-members alike, provides a snapshot of women who did become members.[8] Compared with non-members, CFUW women were more affluent, older, and more likely to live in urban areas. They were also less geographically mobile and less likely to be working outside the home if there were children in the household. More and more members were married, although slightly less than in the Canadian population as a whole. In 1961, a scant 14 per cent of Canadian women age twenty and over were single compared with 23 per cent of CFUW members over the age of twenty and 28 per cent of non-members.[9] CFUW membership included a sizable component of affluent, stay-at-home mothers who were often leaders in community volunteer work. This is reflected in changes in the CFUW leadership in this decade. Whereas previous presidents included many academic women, this was no longer the case. The founding of the Canadian Association of University Teachers (CAUT) in 1951, as well as other professional associations representing the interests of academic women, likely drew some women away from CFUW. The workload of executive members also discouraged leadership among professional women. With the exception of one civil servant, the CFUW presidents in this decade were married community leaders with children at home and were not in paid employment.

Social and learning experiences were the clubs' bread and butter and clubs continued to pursue a number of different interests. The Moncton Club, for example, attended city hall meetings, entertained new Canadians, and followed new educational trends such as team teaching and streaming. The club in Renfrew, Ontario sponsored a panel on the special education of the "mentally retarded," as intellectually disabled persons were called then. New interests were as wide-ranging as investments for women, comparative religions, philosophy, gourmet cooking, creative writing, and gardening.[10] There were also twenty-nine groups studying French across the country. Some clubs sponsored performances by the Manitoba Theatre Centre, Les Grand Ballet Canadiens, and the Stratford Festival that raised money and brought performances to communities that might have otherwise missed them. In St. John's, the club helped create the Art Association of Newfoundland and Labrador in 1960.[11] Many clubs donated prizes to, or sponsored, music festivals, literary, and public-speaking contests, as well as supporting libraries and theatres. The Edmonton, Calgary, Port Credit, and Montréal South Shore clubs all established study groups on the "Indian problem."

The centennial decade saw a renewed interest in Canadian history with several clubs contributing to preservation projects such as Upper Canada Village, a collection of heritage buildings rescued from villages flooded by the St. Lawrence Seaway construction.

Regional CFUW conferences, which were becoming more and more popular, brought women together to discuss programming ideas, attend workshops, and listen to speakers. They also relieved the pressure on presidents to visit every club during their tenure, which was becoming increasingly difficult as the number of clubs grew. Some of the visiting duties were delegated to the growing number of vice presidents and regional directors. As with clubs, there was considerable local autonomy in choosing the themes of the conferences. Laura Sabia organized a regional conference in central Canada with the theme "Parlons Français" that featured discussions on introducing French in elementary schools along with demonstrations of teaching methods. At a successful bilingual seminar in Montréal in November 1962, the clubs in Québec struck a provincial committee headed by lawyer Elizabeth Monk to prepare a brief to the Québec government's Civil Code Revision Office that was preparing to overhaul the Québec Civil Code. The *Chronicle* reported that representatives of all the clubs, French and English, were present and that "discussions were carried on in both languages with only an occasional translation being found necessary."[12]

NEWSLETTER
from the President of the
CANADIAN FEDERATION OF UNIVERSITY WOMEN

Vol. 10, No. 1   Ottawa, Canada   September, 1963

The CFUW executive at the Renfrew Regional Conference, as featured in the "President's Newsletter" of September 1963. The photo shows Laura Sabia seated on the left with President Margaret MacLellan beside her.

CFUW Executive Members at Renfrew Regional Conference

Seated, left to right: Mrs. M. J. Sabia, St. Catharines, vice-president, Central Canada; Miss M. E. MacLellan, Ottawa, president; Miss G. E. Shaw, St. Catharines, treasurer; *standing:* Mrs. J. F. Flaherty, Ottawa, press secretary; Mrs. R. H. McCreary, Arnprior, provincial director, Eastern Ontario; Mrs. G. E. Boyce, Trenton, *Chronicle* editor; Miss M. C. Guthrie, Ottawa, CIR; Miss Lillian Handford, Renfrew, chairman, administrative procedures committee.

Bolstered by growing membership in the early 1960s, the Toronto and Winnipeg Clubs continued to enjoy the benefits of a clubhouse, although the Montréal Club sold their Peel Street house and moved to the Themis Club on Sherbrooke Street in 1963. The Vancouver Club acquired Hycroft Manor in the Shaughnessy area in 1962. Standing on a hill overlooking the city and the mountains of the north shore, Hycroft was designed in 1911 by the renowned Western Canadian architect Thomas Hooper for businessman and politician Alexander Duncan McRae. During World War II, the stately home had been used as a veteran's hospital. In acquiring it, as the club observed, it was both saving a historic building and one of Vancouver's finest homes, and giving members a focal point for club activities. Some of the members feared that a clubhouse might drain members' energy away from other long-established projects, but the art group was delighted to have somewhere to paint "all day, every day, if we so wish."[13]

The club bought the house for $30,500 and the Hycroft Restoration and Development Committee improved the heating, plumbing, and electrical systems, repaired the roof and gutters, and brought the building up to modern fire codes. They did all this in the space of one year with the help of more than one hundred volunteers. Fundraising events for the renovations included an annual antiques fair, and by 1964, Hycroft Manor was buzzing with activity. The club found that its clubhouse brought in new members despite a rise in fees.[14] When the triennial was held in Vancouver in 1967, the club was proud to host a buffet at Hycroft.

During this decade the regular standing committees continued to do their work. The Library and Creative Arts Committee awarded its reading stimulation grant to a library in a rural or small-town community every year. Later it would only be awarded every second year.[15] The Education Committee, which in 1964 consisted of twenty-four members from ten provinces and two language groups, focused on bilingualism. While a resolution submitted by a club in Arvida, Québec sounded a warning by tying the lack of communication between French and English speakers to the separatist movement, English clubs were excited by new possibilities "that Canadians may become truly bilingual."[16] CFUW called for compulsory bilingualism among the higher ranks of the civil

Hycroft Manor, University Women's Club of Vancouver.

service and Canadian ambassadors,[17] and their brief to the Royal Commission on Bilingualism and Biculturalism (1963–1969) argued that "school boards or Provincial Departments of Education ought to be persuaded of the importance of introducing French or English as a second language in earlier grades, to be taught by qualified teachers."[18]

French-language schooling, which the organization had first embraced as a program for gifted children, was catching on at the club level as well. The Renfrew Club held Saturday-morning classes with five bilingual teachers while the Elliot Lake Club organized theirs as after-school classes. The Regina Club donated its book *It's Fun to Learn French* and a French dictionary to all fifty-seven public and elementary schools in the city.[19] Clubs also expressed interest in teaching children with special needs, such as those described then as "slow learners" or "emotionally disturbed." Clubs in BC, Saskatchewan, Ontario, and New Brunswick undertook studies of the counselling services available in their areas. The francophone club in Montréal organized "Rencontre-Orientation," a program that brought two thousand girls to the University of Montréal for the day to learn about various professions from specialists in the field. In 1960–1961, the committee also reported that thirty CFUW members were serving on local school boards and thirteen on university governing bodies.[20] Phyllis Ross Turner had been named UBC chancellor.

Many of the clubs made submissions to provincial studies such the Royal Commission on Education and Youth—also known as the Warren commission—in Newfoundland. The St. John's Club submitted a brief in 1965 that addressed a perceived problem with undertrained teachers by recommending improved training.[21] The *Chronicle* reported that Newfoundland's minister of education consulted Newfoundlander Edith Manuel from the federation's Education Committee in formulating the province's new educational policy.[22] In Québec, the AFDU submitted a brief to the Parent Commission, which led to sweeping changes in the Québec educational system. A new provincial government gradually moved the administration of schools and teacher training from the Catholic Church to secular authorities. The province also abolished classical colleges—unique to French Canada, the collèges classiques run by

Dr. Vivian Brown Morton,
CFUW President 1958–1961.

Roman Catholic clergy—and the proportion of people in Québec, including women, attending university and CEGEP, previously much lower than the rest of Canada, increased significantly.

In 1960, CFUW took its first delegation to a Canadian prime minister under President Vivian Morton. They met with Lester B. Pearson to request the appointment of a woman to the National Parole Board; an increase in the number of female senators appointed; the establishment of a national library and national gallery; and legislative reforms to estate taxes and succession duties. CFUW was initially modest in its expectations, acknowledging that compromise was in the best British tradition and adding, "So far we have a perfect record of leaving the Minister in good humour, even when he's been known to have had a bad day."[23] Indeed, there was cordiality all around as Pearson concluded the meeting by asking the women for their suggestions on the forthcoming centennial celebrations, presumably reasoning that women were good at organizing parties. In 1960–1961, another delegation met with Ellen Fairclough, minister of citizenship and immigration, to ask for an amendment to the Canadian Citizenship Act that would automatically restore Canadian citizenship to Canadian-born women who had married non-Canadians prior to 1947.[24]

Margaret "Pegi" MacLellan served as CFUW president from 1961 to 1964. She was born in a manse outside Dresden, Ontario, graduated from the University of Toronto in history, English, and philosophy, and taught secondary school before joining the civil service, first as a researcher and editorial writer with the Dominion Bureau of Statistics and later, as research librarian and supervisor with the combines investigation section of the Department of Justice. MacLellan, a single professional woman with a lifelong interest in advocacy, began visiting women in prisons in 1951, helped found Ottawa's Elizabeth Fry Society, and was president of the University Women's Club of Ottawa from 1952 to 1954. She chaired CFUW's Administrative Procedures/Resolutions Committee from 1954 to 1961 and became a self-taught legal expert.

As mentioned earlier, when the UN Declaration on Human Rights was first discussed, CFUW members did not initially make the link between human rights and the status of women, but Margaret MacLellan did. Influenced by her work on the IFUW

Status of Women Committee from 1959 to 1968, she thus laid much of the intellectual groundwork for CFUW's campaign for women. Although the Canadian government did not pass the Canadian Bill of Rights until 1960, in 1953, MacLellan produced a detailed study for the Royal Commission on the Status of Women called "A history of women's rights in Canada," a thoughtful summary of Canadian women's history from pioneer times to the present.[25] Some of the topics for the 1961 triennial reflected her interest in human rights and the rights of the child.

CFUW's Status of Women Committee reported on the increasing number of competent women who achieved prominent positions, citing examples such as Charlotte Whitton, who had just been elected mayor of Ottawa for her third term in 1960; Francis Goodspeed, the first woman president of the Professional Institute of the Public Service; and France Trepanier, who was appointed to the Canada Council. In 1962, Eleanor Milne of Winnipeg had been appointed to the Royal Commission on Taxation, known as the Carter commission, and Marie Kirkland-Casgrain, first elected to the Québec national assembly in 1961, sat in the Québec Cabinet, serving as minister in various portfolios.[26]

In 1960, Isabel Janet Macneill was named the first female prison warden and head of the federal prison for women in Kingston, Ontario.[27] Educated at Mount Saint Vincent University and the Heatherley School of Fine Art in London, England, during World War II, Macneill had been a commanding officer of the Women's Royal Canadian Naval Service. From 1948 to 1954, she served as superintendent of the Ontario Training School for Girls in Cobourg, Ontario. Macneill, as a long-time member of the Elizabeth Fry Society in Kingston, advocated for inmate rehabilitation, including help for women prisoners who were afflicted with alcohol and drug addiction. An Elizabeth Fry Society brief that recommended educational and training classes, increases in staff, and the expansion of recreational facilities served as her blueprint for reform at the Prison for Women.[28] Isabel Macneill was active in the federation and, in 1960, addressed a CFUW regional conference on her work. Another woman active in the corrections field, lawyer Mary Louise Lynch, was appointed to the National Parole Board in 1961. A 1933 graduate of the University of New Brunswick (UNB), Lynch had a long association with UNB as secretary and registrar of its law school and served on its board of governors. She was also a former president of the Saint John Club.

Areas in which women's interests intersected with those of governments were easier for CFUW to gain concessions and, in the 1960s, the federation could claim some limited legislative victories. In 1961 there was relief on the estates tax and succession duties issue, and on requests for income tax deductions for students and working wives. The organization also sought to address the growing skilled labour shortage. At the 1964 triennial meeting in London, a number of married members expressed their frustration with trying to re-enter the workforce and asked for refresher or credit courses to help them do so. The attendees passed a resolution stating that CFUW should provide leadership to encourage university women graduates to augment their qualifications and "promote the return of professional women whose careers were interrupted."[29] MacLellan suggested the creation of an ad hoc committee to conduct a survey on continuing education and passed the task of completing it on to the next president, Laura Sabia, who took "Continuing Education for Women" as her triennial theme. After her presidency, MacLellan remained active in IFUW and later worked with the National Council of Women (NCWC) and the National Action Committee on the Status of Women.[30]

Laura Sabia served as president from 1964 to 1967 and left an indelible mark on both CFUW and the second-wave feminist movement. Her parents were successful Italian immigrants who gave their daughter a talent for storytelling, an irreverence for organized religion, and a belief that women could do anything.[31] Laura graduated from McGill in 1938 with honours in languages, married a young surgeon, and moved to St. Catharines, Ontario, where she raised four children. She joined the university women's club there and became president in 1955. When the office of provincial director—later regional director—was instituted in 1958, Sabia was elected to represent Western Ontario. In 1961 she became CFUW vice president for Central Canada and, in 1962, won an IFUW bursary to attend a meeting of the UN Commission on the Status of Women (UNCSW).

Following the 1964 meeting, the CFUW ad hoc committee got to work on the continuing education survey, consulting the

American Association of University Women (AAUW) as it had done a similar study of their 140,000 members in 1957.[32] The Department of Labour Women's Bureau was enthusiastic to help,[33] as was the Dominion bureau of statistics. They offered technical assistance and suggested that the survey would be improved by using a "control group" of non-member graduates. These two departments provided $11,000 in financial support along with another $3,000 from the Ontario department of university affairs and $2,000 from the Québec government. With the economy booming, government and business were anxious to get started, Sabia reported in 1965 "a sense of urgency on part of government, the business world and even the universities to the need for highly developed brainpower among women."[34]

In January 1966, a volunteer brigade from the Ottawa Club directed by Marion Royce mailed out 16,000 questionnaires and the Montréal AFDU handled the French questionnaires. They derived the list of non-members from the alumnae records of eight English-speaking and two French-speaking universities. The return rate on members' questionnaires was a respectable 43 per cent and that of the control group was 37 per cent, which indicated a strong interest.[35] In 1967, the University of Toronto Press published the survey, *Women University Graduates in Continuing Education and Employment,* authored by Pat Cockburn, a consultant in economic, market, and opinion research, with the assistance of Yvonne Raymond. CFUW was pleased with the results. What had begun as a survey primarily of interest to CFUW members had become a professional work worthy of influencing policy-makers.[36] It was later submitted to the Royal Commission on the Status of Women (RCSW).

Not surprisingly, the survey found that the higher a respondent's education the more likely it was that she would be in the labour force—in fact, education exerted a more powerful influence than age. The results showed that 55 per cent of all graduates were working, the majority of them non-CFUW members, and they were more likely to be in the fields of health, education, library science, and social work than in the general arts or humanities.[37] A further 7 per cent had definite plans to return to work, but 38 per cent had indefinite or no plans to do so. The desire to go back to work was strongest among the youngest respondents.[38] Compared with non-members, working CFUW members were more often in part-time employment and were motivated by a desire to put their education to use. Club members who were studying were also more likely to be drawn to liberal arts and leisure-oriented education than to job-related training.

In a reflection of the recent dramatic increase in university attendance, the survey also showed that both the member and non-member groups were relatively young—in 1961, 40 per cent of all female graduates were under thirty-five and the majority were under fifty-five.[39] The conclusions were not as statistically significant among the French-speaking respondents for two reasons—the small sample size and the fact that the translated questionnaire did not fully reflect the differences between the two educational systems.[40] Government sponsors of the survey were particularly interested in the group of young, well-educated graduates who had educational and/or work plans. This is evident in the survey's recommendations, which included vocational counselling, income tax deductions for household expenses, and improved access to both part-time work and part-time study.[41] Many respondents mentioned their husbands' attitudes as an important factor in their decisions, but the survey's recommendations did not address it.

While work on the survey was being carried out, the federation also held conferences on continuing education at Hycroft Manor in Vancouver and at York University in northwest Toronto. Women attendees articulated a strong desire to achieve something in their own right and a sense of responsibility to use their education and abilities. They recommended childcare, scholarships, and the removal of age restrictions on educational programs. They also called for the federal government to hold a commission on the status of women, an idea that Sabia was actively promoting.[42]

Neither Laura Sabia nor Margaret MacLellan were happy with the "cup half-full" philosophy that some CFUW members adhered to. Sabia believed that women were too polite in dealing with politicians who invariably complimented them on their appearance and then ignored their requests. MacLellan complained that "amendments made to the Ontario Succession Duty Act in the last session did not include any of the proposals made in our six-point resolution presented to Premier Frost in 1959."[43] Amidst the encouraging government support for the continuing education survey and the increasingly noisy women's movement, Sabia wrote to the prime minister in January 1966 asking that Canada "press the United Nations for a seminar on women's rights to be held in Canada" in conjunction with the United Nations' International Year of Human Rights coming up in 1968. She promoted the idea as a golden opportunity for Canada to show its interest in human rights as they pertained to women by discussing topics such as marriage, divorce, abortion, birth control, income tax, succession duties, higher education, and the right for women to serve on criminal juries.[44] She added that CFUW had discovered through its continuing education conferences that prejudices against women in business and the professions were detrimental to the recruitment of Canada's much-needed brainpower.[45] When she wrote to External Affairs Minister Paul Martin, she stressed that women "would not accept a secondary and subservient role."[46] To Senator Muriel McQueen Fergusson, a CFUW member and ally, she expressed her general frustration with the government treatment of women:

> The Expo board was a brilliant example—an all-male board was appointed (they forgot women were part of the human race)— then when protests went in to the Government, they quickly appointed a Woman's Advisory Committee, gave them no budget but gave them the signal privilege of selling passports!![47]

Sabia decided that unified action was called for, a strategy she had earlier used as a CFUW vice president. Believing there was strength in numbers, she convinced the CFBPW, the Women's Institutes of Ontario, the Catholic Women's League, the Provincial Council of Women, the Council of Jewish Women, the Federation of Women Teachers of Ontario, and others to pool their resources to lobby the Ontario government on the issue of succession duties. Together they represented more than 150,000 women.[48] Sabia used the tactic again in May 1966, when she wrote to more than thirty women's organizations and proposed that they work together to pressure the government to appoint a royal commission on the status of women. Receiving a positive response, she organized a meeting at the Toronto CFUW clubhouse and the attendees formed a new organization, the Committee for the Equality of Women in

Canada (CEWC). By September, the group had decided that a royal commission was more likely to succeed than pressing for a human rights code or human rights commission, as had been done in Ontario in 1962.[49] In her president's report of 1966–1967, Sabia told CFUW members that they would present a brief to the government requesting a royal commission to inquire into the status of women in Canada and make recommendations that would enable Canadian women to achieve excellence in public and private life in accordance with the Universal Declaration of Human Rights.

Sabia pressed for change at the provincial level as well; she told Ontario Liberal leader Andrew Thompson that the provinces would have to set up their own commissions and that "the women of Canada would no longer tolerate the subservient role allocated to them by society. Thankfully, they are now on the march!"[50] That would turn out to be an interesting turn of phrase.

On November 8, 1966, the CEWC deputation that presented its brief to the government in Ottawa included Laura Sabia; Margaret MacLellan, then a vice president of NCWC; Margaret Hyndman from CFBPW; Julia Shulz from the Council of Jewish Women; and a representative from Fédération des femmes de Québec, an organization newly formed by Thérèse Casgrain.[51] There were also sixty observers in attendance. To their disappointment, the prime minister sent Justice Minister Lucien Cardin in his place, along with Labour Minister John Robert Nicolson, Secretary of State Judy LaMarsh, Senator Fergusson, and NB MP Margaret Isabel Rideout. They were cordially received but, as usual, left without any commitment from the government.

In January 1967, as the women waited to hear from the government, a historic headline appeared in the *Globe and Mail* suggesting that Laura Sabia was threatening to march two million women to Ottawa to demand a royal commission. Journalist Barry Craig, who wrote the provocative article, based his headline on a flippant remark Sabia had made during a telephone conversation in which they had discussed what she would do if Pearson refused to call the commission. After presenting a number of alternatives, she jokingly suggested she might lead a march. Or, at least, that's what she told her nervous supporters who were shocked to read the headline. But the paper had been careful to say that women "may" march and refused to print a retraction or Sabia's explanation.[52] The press went crazy with fear-mongering, creating ugly caricatures of women abandoning their kitchens and their babies to join militant feminist groups and march on the capital en masse. Sabia called it "an astonishing display of a prejudiced, untruthful and even vicious attitude toward women."[53]

The story took on a life of its own and became a kind of "creation myth" associated with the royal commission. Sabia later admitted that she doubted she could get two women to march, much less two million. To one nervous supporter she noted, "Thank heavens I am not the marching type—anyway it is too damn cold to march these days!! I dislike union tactics—however I'm not averse to 'arching men's backs.'"[54] According to Sabia, the threat terrified the government and they quickly called a commission. Judy LaMarsh pushed for the commission from within the Cabinet and credits Sabia's bold threat for making it a reality.[55] But as Cerise Morris notes in her history of the Royal Commission on the Status of Women, contemporaries also credit LaMarsh with playing a key role.[56] There were other pressures as well. In 1961, American President John F. Kennedy had called the President's Commission on the Status of Women to examine women's status in relation to education, the workplace, and the law. Segments within the media supported the cause and the Canadian government wanted to avoid embarrassment in the upcoming International Year of Human Rights. Setting up a royal commission would demonstrate the government's commitment to addressing women's issues. It was also an idea whose time had come.

On February 4, 1967, Prime Minister Pearson announced the Royal Commission on the Status of Women and on February 16 the privy council outlined its mandate: "to inquire into and report upon the status of women in Canada, and recommend what steps might be taken to ensure for women equal opportunities with men in all aspects of Canadian society."[57] It specifically mentioned political rights, labour, education, civil service, taxation, marriage and divorce, criminal law, and immigration and citizenship. Florence Bird, then known by her married name, Mrs. John Bird, was chosen as RCSW chair, becoming the first woman in Canadian history to head a royal commission. An American-born Bryn Mawr graduate, Bird was known professionally as Anne Francis when appearing on

CBC radio and television as a political analyst. Other members of the commission included aeronautical engineer Elsie MacGill, daughter of Helen Gregory MacGill; demographer Jacques Henripin; John Humphrey, who helped draft the Universal Declaration of Human Rights; Lola Lange, a farm woman and activist; Doris Ogilvie, a New Brunswick juvenile court judge; and Jeanne Lapointe, a Laval literature professor. The commission's secretary was none other than a young Monique Bégin, future politician and CFUW member who had campaigned with Thérèse Casgrain for women's rights in Québec.

The year 1967 was not just the year of the RCSW—it was also Canada's centennial. Like most organizations, the federation had a centennial project, the publication of the biographies of women who had made history in Canada. With some funding from the Canadian centennial commission, they produced *The Clear Spirit: Twenty Canadian Women and their Times*, edited by Mary Quayle Innis, a Toronto Club member, dean of women at University College, and widow of historian Harold Innis. At a time when Canadian women's history was in its infancy, the book told the stories of accomplished women from various regions and periods of Canadian history, beginning in New France and moving to British North America, then examining modern women's contributions to literature, the arts, and women's suffrage. Included in the biographies was one of Margaret McWilliams. Two biographies written about French women by Québec authors were published in French, making the book a uniquely bilingual publication. Still a valued resource today, it won the Margaret McWilliams Award from the Manitoba Historical Society in 1968.

A number of CFUW members also received centennial medals that were given to outstanding Canadians, including Dr. Hilda Neatby, astronomer Dr. Helen Hogg, geologist Madeline Fritz, Senator Muriel McQueen Fergusson, June Menzies, and former CFUW presidents Martha Law, Margaret MacLellan, Laura Sabia, and Marion Grant.[58] Some clubs had their own projects, the most popular being support to libraries in public schools or universities. In Victoria, BC, the club helped to develop Gorge Waterway and its adjacent park, restore historical buildings, and construct an Indian Village.

The president who followed MacLellan and Sabia, Margaret Fyfe Orange, could not have been more different from her two predecessors. Born in Cobalt, Ontario, she studied modern languages at St. Michael's College at the University of Toronto, trained as a teacher, and did postgraduate work in French at McGill. She taught secondary school in Sudbury before marrying Dr. Robert Orange, with whom she had six children. She was active in the Parent Teachers Association, as well as in Sudbury hospitals and the Ontario Council for University Affairs. She was a founding member of the board of regents at the University of Sudbury and its dean of women. Prior to her CFUW presidency, she had been president of the Sudbury Club, Ontario vice president, and travelled with the 1966 IFUW delegation to the UNCSW. In 1977, Orange was elected fourth vice president of IFUW. Her personal philosophy adhered to a maternalism reminiscent of an earlier era. She believed that "because I am a woman, I possess special qualities and capacity—qualities of love, compassion, patience, and endurance, and the capacity to know, to care, and to create."[59] She certainly made a curious choice as chair of the Status of Women Committee from 1958 to 1961 as she stated in the *Chronicle* that women already had adequate status, thus undermining the purpose of the committee. Indeed, she suggested merging it with the Education Committee.[60]

Margaret Orange's presidency signalled a dramatic shift away from advocacy. In her president's report published just after the RCSW was established, she completely ignored it in favour of a triennial theme that stressed community service. Orange represented the school of thought, reflected in CFUW goals, that its primary focus should be on education and community service as a means of fulfilling the social responsibility of the educated woman. She encouraged her fellow members to turn their attention to the world's hungry, homeless, and oppressed; to accept responsibility as well-informed leaders; and, show their worth through their accomplishments.[61] She downplayed the importance of lobbying, even to the extent of undermining previous CFUW efforts in relation to the Citizenship Act.[62]

Orange also gave voice to the misgivings of some married women who viewed the trend toward work outside the home as devaluing homemaking and volunteer work. She pointed out, for example, that the Kapuskasing Club objected to the reference to women whose "careers were interrupted" that had been used in the 1965 resolution on continuing education; as far as some women were concerned, they did not see their time spent at home being wives and mothers that way.[63] A respondent in the continuing education survey conveyed a similar sentiment when she asked, "Where does the volunteer in assorted community activities at the executive level fit into this picture? It can amount to the equivalent of a full time job! Although there is no financial remuneration, there is tangible contribution."[64] These currents remain within CFUW and illustrate the mixed reaction among women to the new women's liberation movement. The Vancouver Club, settling into its new home at Hycroft just as the upheavals of the 1960s began, viewed these tensions as something that "seemed new to many, but to others was a resurgence of the old cause which they had never abandoned."[65]

Orange moved CFUW further in its quest for bilingualism during her tenure—she encouraged the use of French and approached the secretary of state for funds to translate new CFUW membership cards and fellowship posters. Still, by decade's end, the need for professional translation was being highlighted as a concern by the vice president for Québec, as many francophone members were overtaxed in providing voluntary translations and CFUW was equally hard pressed to pay for professional services.[66] Orange also secured $8,500 in federal funding to allow Indigenous Canadians to attend the triennial meeting in 1970.

As this activity was going on within the federation, the newly appointed Royal Commission on the Status of Women was busy conducting extensive cross-country hearings throughout 1968. The commission's work was clearly touching a nerve and women's dramatic testimony was converting many members of the commission and the press to the seriousness of women's issues.[67] The royal commission received 468 briefs and more than one thousand letters and testimonies, some of which came from CFUW. The federation advised clubs to study the issues and prepare submissions and the federation's Status of Women Committee called on clubs to ask for provincial inquiries as well, as Sabia had tried to do in Ontario. The Regina Club's brief focused on the age of marriage. The Vancouver Education Committee submitted a brief based on their 1965 conference on the mature woman and continuing education that stressed women's right, regardless of age, marital status, or family circumstances to pursue educational goals on the basis of equality with men. It also recommended counselling services, financial assistance, daycare, and program flexibility for mature students, especially in teaching and social work.[68] Encouraged by Laura Sabia, the Edmonton continuing education study group made six recommendations to the RCSW.[69] The Winnipeg Club's Status of Women Committee prepared a brief for the Manitoba government, in cooperation with Thelma Forbes, a Manitoba cabinet minister. They hoped that it would parallel the work being accomplished at the national level.[70]

The federation's brief to the RCSW was not published in the *Chronicle*. Nor was it listed in the Commission's final report, as were those submitted by a dozen or so clubs. That may have meant it was late to arrive, or that it was not submitted. A CFUW brief found in the archives represented a less than ringing endorsement of the commission's goals. The preamble to the brief noted that "some great battles have been won and that much of what is still to be done is in the form of clean-up operations."[71] It also pointed out that the views expressed were those of the membership as reflected at the 1967 triennial meeting, and that the organization reserved the right to submit a supplemental brief following their 1968 meeting. Sadly, no record of any supplementary brief was found in the files. The 1967 meeting saw the transition from the Sabia to the Orange presidency and, given the organization's penchant for intense debate, one can imagine that the discussion was lively.

In a section on women and public life, the recommendations in the CFUW "brief" focused on maintaining a roster of qualified women for positions on boards and commissions. In a discussion of why there were so few women in politics, the document suggests that this was regrettable but unavoidable and that the reasons lay with individual women themselves. Nonetheless, other sections, such as the one on taxation, do capture much of the CFUW policy passed through resolutions. The brief asks for assurances that women's economic role in the home will be recognized, for amendments to estate and succession taxes, and for recognition of joint enterprises when a wife and husband have a business together. It addresses income tax disincentives to working wives and appeals for allowable deductions for housekeeping and childcare expenses and points out that income tax legislation that treats the wife's income as belonging to her husband contravened provincial married women's property acts that were put in place in the 1880s.[72] In the area of employment, the submission calls for the introduction of measures to enforce equal pay legislation and asks that sex be added to the prohibited grounds for discrimination in documents such as the Canada Fair Employment Practices Act. It asked that Canada sign and adhere to the international conventions and declarations on the economic rights of women and that all jobs and educational institutions be open to women. In addition, the brief notes that Canada was behind other countries with regard to employment in the civil service, and could do more to ensure equality.[73]

What is left out of a document is often as interesting as what is in it. The brief did not deal directly with the Carter Commission on taxation that was established in 1962 and reported in 1966. Elsewhere, CFUW called upon the finance minister to re-examine the position of "married women in the tax system before a family unit for taxation purposes becomes an integral part of Canada's taxation structure," just as the Carter Commission had recommended.[74] June Menzies forecast that recognizing women's unpaid labour would require a major overhaul of the tax system, noting,

> Even after 20 or 30 years of housekeeping, rearing children, participating in public life through voluntary organizations essential to the quality of public life in the community, a woman may have no property or money in her own name—no economic recognition or financial independence from it.[75]

The CFUW brief to the Royal Commission on the Status of Women did not articulate views on women's status within new social safety net programs such as the Canada Pension Plan, established in 1965.[76] Also absent from their brief were CFUW positions on birth control, and abortion, and, with respect to divorce, the only recommendation made was the need for "an independent domicile for married women" so that women could seek divorce where they lived, not where their former husbands lived.

The decade of the 1960s ended with CFUW's celebration of

its fiftieth anniversary and the publication of a new history of the organization. Some legislative changes at the end of the decade are noteworthy. The new federal Divorce Act of 1968 incorporated the concept of marriage breakdown as grounds for divorce and granted a married woman the right to her own separate domicile, although for divorce purposes only. Amendments to the *Criminal Code* gave women limited access to therapeutic abortions, and birth control was de-criminalized, while amendments to the estate tax laws provided some relief for widows.[77]

The following decade began with the December 1970 publication of the report of the Royal Commission on the Status of Women. Laura Sabia, through the newly formed National Action Committee on the Status of Women would press for implementation of its 167 recommendations, while CFUW struggled to redefine its place in a rapidly changing organizational landscape.

Footnotes for this chapter can be found online at:
http://secondstorypress.ca/resources

Chapter 8
THE 1970S: FOSTER THE ROSTER

The Peter Principle posits that a man is promoted to his level of incompetence. The Martha Principle posits that a woman is promoted to a level immediately below her potential so that her less than competent male superior may have someone to keep his incompetence from fouling up the machinery.[1]

—L. Gladys Harvey, *Chronicle*, 1978–1979

Ottawa Club member L. Gladys Harvey adapted *The Peter Principle*, a popular book published in the 1970s, to reflect women's unique position (or lack thereof) on the corporate ladder. Using Rudyard Kipling's declaration that the progeny of Martha keep the wheels turning, she added that while the Martha Principle was not universally true, it is true "often enough that we can all think of examples."[2] It certainly signalled women's frustrations with being unable to gain access to the higher echelons of power in government, business, academia, and other areas of Canadian life. Such sentiments led CFUW President Ruth Bell to launch a "Foster the Roster" campaign to coincide with the United Nations' International Women's Year (IWY) in 1975. Meant to place qualified women in leadership positions, the roster drew on the organization's strengths in fostering leadership. Recent trends in the 1970s were encouraging, with Senator Muriel McQueen Fergusson being appointed the first female speaker of the Senate and Pauline McGibbon, Ontario's first female lieutenant governor. By now, the organization had a good track record of producing leaders: Margaret McWilliams headed the committee on the postwar problems of women in the 1940s; Marion Royce was the founding director of the Women's Bureau in the Department of Labour in the 1950s; and Laura Sabia led the campaign for the Royal Commission on the Status of Women (RCSW) in the 1960s.

But Foster the Roster and IWY celebrations also represented a rebound for CFUW after a few difficult years in the late 1960s and early 1970s when the organization appeared shell-shocked by the new generation of activists. Change was certainly afoot. Consciousness-raising groups, rape crisis centres, abortion clinics, and women-only credit unions were springing up everywhere. As well, while student protests hit university campuses, divorce and birth control became much freer and sexuality more open. The landmark December 1970 report of the Royal Commission on the Status of Women made 167 recommendations for change and the Ad Hoc Committee on the Status of Women led by Laura Sabia came together to press the government for implementation. CFUW would soon find its niche within the new realities of the growing bureaucracy and shifting personnel of the women's movement.

In the 1970s, CFUW's membership remained at around 11,000. Some women preferred to join the newer women's organizations, and this no doubt slowed their previous growth. Vancouver and Toronto had memberships of one thousand or more, and the Ottawa Club's membership was close to five hundred, but many of the approximately 115 clubs were much smaller. Although the Vancouver Club still held more than half its events during the day, reflecting its membership of predominantly homemakers and volunteers,[3] the trend for women to go back to work or school meant that there were fewer members and fewer recruits for executive positions.

Growing financial problems led to a review of the executive function and the creation of an endowment fund to better manage the growing number and value of scholarships, and CFUW decided to incorporate. In 1970, the organization established a creative arts award to recognize a promising young music composer. In 1978, they established an Ontario Council to serve as an intermediary between clubs and the federation and play a role in provincial advocacy. As well, CFUW decided to only publish the expensive *Chronicle* every three years, although they introduced a new, smaller, journal.

The first major CFUW event of the decade was the triennial held in North York in the summer of 1970, where President Margaret Orange finished her three-year term. She had clearly decided that the Royal Commission on the Status of Women, whose report would be released in December, was best ignored, and when a reporter asked her about the women's liberation movement, she made a very post-feminist statement, commenting that "the things our forebears had to fight for, such as women's rights to higher education and equal pay for equal work, have been granted...now the emphasis is on the rights of all human beings, both men and women."[4] Clearly she was not alone. The dynamic group at the North York Club who organized the program decided to include study seminars on topics that had been identified in a club survey, including "'Indians' as Disadvantaged Canadians," "The Environment," and "Unrest in Education."[5] Not only was the royal commission nowhere to be found; curiously, the club invited RCSW Commissioner Florence Bird to be keynote speaker but asked her to speak on the conference themes rather than the RCSW. As Louise Slemin remembered it, "The whole idea of the triennial for us was to have a dual purpose: being educational and being in the Federation. I think Florence was happy to go along with our theme, which was 'New Ideas for a Changing Society.'"[6] It also fit well with Orange's view that CFUW should focus on community service.

The triennial program included twenty-six seminars, from which delegates could choose sessions that focused exclusively on one of the three topics or mix them. Experts—including one hundred people representing several Indigenous organizations—were invited to facilitate discussion and answer questions; President Orange had secured substantial funding from the governments of Canada and Ontario to pay their expenses. Although there is a sense of awkwardness among the delegates, the *Chronicle* reported that it was "a unique experience to sit among four or five 'Indian' people for two hours of close association, or to hear from an intelligent, long-haired student why he hated school."[7] Still, the club felt that they had opened doors of friendship, and there was some good-natured kidding. After showing a group of the guests to their residence, one club member jokingly asked if this qualified her as an

Gwendolyn Black, CFUW President 1970–1973.

"'Indian' guide." After attending some of the sessions, a chief from the group of visitors concluded that Indigenous people and white women shared the same problem—white men.[8]

The North York Club considered the meeting a triumph. Delegates numbered 450 and new conference features such as the daily bulletin "Delegatessence" and the "Buzz Sessions" were well received. Looking back to the event in 2015, Lou Slemin remembered the importance of that triennial in bringing the organizers closer together: "We did so much together that for a brief time, a group of us contemplated starting a business."[9] The meeting also provided a rare opportunity for the Indigenous groups to hold their own meetings. As always happened at CFUW meetings, there were vigorous discussions on resolutions, including disagreements on income tax reform relating to women and families; on the equity of partners in divorce; and the abortion issue. However, "there was almost total agreement on the resolutions meant to combat pollution."[10]

At the 1970 meeting, Margaret Orange passed the president's job on to Gwendolyn Black. Black was born in Alberta, but moved to Massachusetts with her widowed mother when she was six. She grew up in an academic setting, as her mother was dean of Lasell Seminary for Young Women. An accomplished pianist, Black earned a bachelor of music from Mount Allison University in 1933. She married and raised four children in Sackville, New Brunswick, where she was active in the Victorian Order of Nurses, the Sackville Art Association, the Imperial Order Daughters of the Empire (IODE), and the Canadian Association for the Mentally Retarded, now known as Canadian Association for Community Living. She was president of the Sackville Club, provincial director for New Brunswick, and vice president (East) before becoming CFUW president. Black later served on Mount Allison University's board of regents, senate, and library committee. She enjoyed travel, especially exchanging views with women around the world, and was active in the International Federation of University Women (IFUW).

As incoming president, Black stressed that members could be most effective when working in their own communities, which would in turn garner a better understanding of larger problems. She believed that CFUW opinions on national issues were "respected and welcomed" by the federal government due to their thoughtfulness and the excellence of their research.[11] During her tenure she worked on nominating capable women to federal positions, including boards and commissions, and the Senate.

Soon after Gwendolyn Black came to office in December, 1970, the long-awaited RCSW report was released that articulated four main principles. The first was that women should be free to choose to take employment outside their homes; the second, that the care of children is a shared responsibility; the third, that society has a special responsibility for women because of pregnancy and childbirth; and fourth, that, in certain areas, women would require special treatment for an interim period to overcome the adverse effects of discriminatory practice—that is, the report recommended affirmative action.[12]

The RCSW report's recommendations differed only slightly from CFUW policy as seen through its resolutions passed at triennial meetings since its founding in 1919. Indeed, they often mirror one another with differences primarily in emphasis. The resolutions that CFUW passed in 1973, for example, expressed opposition to discrimination on the basis of sex and marital status in fringe-benefit plans and support for affirmative action programs. CFUW asked the government to establish a human rights commission, including a division dealing specifically with the rights of women, for a period of at least seven to ten years—these related to RCSW recommendations 165 and 166.[13] It should be noted, however, that some club members expressed the view that human rights commissions should "look after the needs of all men, women and children,"[14] leading to the renaming of the federation's Status of Women Committee to the Status of Women and Human Rights Committee. The 1974 *Chronicle* noted that CFUW had supported only six of the 167 RCSW recommendations, including support for part-time workers; aspects of daycare funding, a federal-provincial national day care act; and, a national health and welfare advisory service on childcare. Nonetheless, many other CFUW resolutions fit within RCSW principles, including continuing education for mature women; support for "Indian" women denied status under the Indian Act due to marriage to non-"Indians"; care for and rehabilitation of women offenders; and the appointment of women to the Senate.[15] CFUW also supported the deduction of child care expenses from taxable income and the widespread availability of birth control information.

These similarities are hardly surprising. The RCSW report was a consolidation of previous research from a number of sources and had benefitted substantially from CFUW's own well-researched briefs. There were some differences, however. Both supported the removal of abortion from the *Criminal Code*, but CFUW did not explicitly support the liberal conditions spelled out in the RCSW.[16] Clearly not all CFUW members agreed with Margaret MacLellan, who remarked in 1971 that if section 247 of the *Criminal Code*—that decreed that any woman who ended a pregnancy was guilty of an indictable offence and liable for up to two-years of imprisonment—was enforced, the prison for women would have to put up tents![17] A cautious approach was also evident in a 1972 CFUW resolution calling for a comprehensive professional study of sound daycare services and philosophies to provide an adequate basis for the drafting of national daycare legislation.

In January, CFUW and the Manitoba Action Committee on the Status of Women under June Menzies wrote to Prime Minister Pierre Trudeau, asking for his careful consideration of the report, particularly Chapter 10, the "Plan of Action." This section called for implementation committees within government, human rights commissions to enforce existing laws, and an advisory council on the status of women to continue RCSW's work. Both letters noted that volunteers had carried the heavy load of working for equality for women in Canada and asked that the government "at long last" assume some leadership.[18] The government proceeded with caution. Prime Minister Trudeau created an interdepartmental committee on the status of women chaired by Freda L. Paltiel, a senior civil servant from the Department of Health with degrees from Queen's University, McGill University, and the Hebrew University Hadassah-Braun School of Public Health and Community Medicine. Paltiel produced a report on the commission's findings, but it was not made public. The government then appointed Paltiel as coordinator for the status of women, and her first report in that position was published in 1972. She left the job in 1973 and became an advocate for women in senior civil service positions. The government also named Robert K. Andras minister responsible for the status of women, a portfolio he held from 1971 to 1974.[19]

The National Ad Hoc Action Committee on the Status of Women also prepared a "report on the report" and submitted it to the government in February, 1972. Following that, the committee members organized a massive Strategies for Change Conference with $15,000 in federal funding, bringing together some five hundred women from across the country. Sabia's genius was in managing to bring together older women's organizations from the original committee along with some twenty feminist groups made up of younger women.[20] Sabia called it, "bringing the hobnail boots and the white-glove set together."[21] Representatives from organized labour, from all political perspectives, and from most classes, regions, and ethnic groups attended, and the result was the formation of the National Action Committee on the Status of Women (NAC). Laura Sabia served as the first president of this influential women's group, which had as its sole organizational mandate the implementation of the RCSW report. Gwen Black's reflection on her experience of attending this historic meeting shows CFUW's unease with the new movement:

> I found the radical group completely devoid of any concept of democracy, and all the while screaming about it; I found them arrogant and deaf and ignorant, but I am glad they were there—our traditional groups need to "change our heads" somewhat....[22]

At least some of this group represented a dramatically different culture from that of the formal CFUW, an organization that always had an official parliamentarian in attendance at every meeting, that was continually revising its constitution, protocols, and governance principles. To CFUW, these methods constituted the way that rule of law and democracy were supposed to work. CFUW members were horrified that NAC failed to use any rules of order at their meeting and were equally shocked at the lack of sober thought and research that went into their resolutions. Black and others commented on the eighty resolutions (!!) that were apparently later narrowed down to seventy-three, observing that any attempt to act on them all would lead to utter chaos. By contrast CFUW resolutions went through numerous revisions, negotiations, and debate often at the club, provincial, and federal levels before a resolution was passed and became policy. CFUW also had written protocols for how resolutions were to be dealt with at the political level.

Another sore point was the refusal of the young upstarts to credit earlier women's groups. When a representative from the Canadian Federation of Business and Professional Women (CFBPW) spoke in appreciation of Marguerite Ritchie, mentioning her professional prowess but ending with a note on her femininity and beauty, one young woman "leapt up and wanted to know what in hell she meant by calling attention to her femininity?"[23] Black did concede that she liked hearing Kay Livingstone and Jeannette Corbiere Lavell speak on African-Canadian and Indigenous women's issues respectively, although she acknowledged that they made her feel "like a worn-out fuddy-dud."[24]

Class conflict was always just below the surface. The meeting was for many their first encounter not just with the new generation of feminists, but also with groups from the left side of the political spectrum. At around the same time as the conference, Black received a request from one of the new groups, the Ontario Committee on the Status of Women, asking CFUW to give its support to striking workers at the Dare cookie factory. Black had to consult her contacts to find out who the group was and ultimately questioned the accuracy of their information because it differed from the company's viewpoint. She also expressed a dislike for strikes and boycotts.[25] Despite its negative publicity, the central issue of the strike was actually pay equity—the larger raise that the employer had offered to the minority of men on the payroll than they had offered to the women would further widen the gender pay gap.[26]

Despite their misgivings, CFUW joined NAC and worked toward implementation of the RCSW recommendations. But there were certainly conflicts. CFUW objected in particular to one of the resolutions passed at the 1972 conference that emphatically rejected the concept of a federally appointed status of women council. In a letter to activist (later politician) Rosemary Brown, Johanna Michalenko, chair of the Committee on the Status of Women remarked, "I cannot understand this great fear of use of federal funds for a council; that this means government control, etc. Whose money is it? It's ours."[27] Comfortable and experienced in dealing with government, CFUW found the creation of federal and provincial advisory councils on the status of women and human rights commissions an effective way to affect change and pushed for the inclusion of sex and marital status in human rights codes. Just before the big meeting, Michalenko had proposed ambitious plans to move quickly with a brief and a delegation to the government, but Black cautioned that this would "take some time to prepare if it is to reflect the consensus of CFUW."[28] Perhaps Black knew that a consensus on RCSW would be difficult to achieve. She still hoped that CFUW could assume an effective role in pressing for an advisory council, although she confided in MacLellan that she did not know how.[29]

Although there were some delays in obtaining enough copies, the federation encouraged clubs to read the RCSW report and promote its implementation. The National Council of Women of Canada (NCWC), in conjunction with the Fédération des femmes du Québec, was quick off the mark, writing and distributing a booklet in both languages called *What's in It?* Its synopsis was meant to make the report more accessible and to facilitate study and discussion by women's groups at the local level. Michalenko did begin to produce a similar document summarizing the clubs' responses, but it does not appear to have been completed. Certainly, it was not printed in the *Chronicle*.

Club response to the commission was mixed. The Saskatoon Club reported that the RCSW had served to re-invigorate its club, which had been questioning its purpose in the 1960s.[30] In Vancouver, seminars added to the exhilaration surrounding the commission report, one of them held at Hycroft on January 30, 1971, in conjunction with the University of British Columbia (UBC) Centre for Continuing Education, with Florence Bird as keynote speaker. After the meetings, the club established a group that met regularly to study the RCSW report. Their Status of Women and Laws Committee, which had co-sponsored a course on Law and Society with UBC, lobbied for provincial welfare services and submitted a brief on family law to the Family and Children's Law Commission of BC, family courts being one of the RCSW recommendations.[31]

In the meantime, the federal government established the Canadian Advisory Council on the Status of Women in February, 1973. The government overlooked Sabia as chair and appointed Dr. Katie Cooke, a public servant who contributed much to the women's movement over her long career. Cooke was also a founding member of the Canadian Research Institute for the Advancement of Women (CRIAW) and the Bridges for Women Society, an employment training service for abused women.[32] CFUW's June Menzies was named vice chair. In 1973, the provincial government created the Ontario Advisory Council and Laura Sabia was appointed to lead it. By 1976, four other provinces had created councils and there was a number of women's bureaus in provincial departments of labour.[33] On the federal level, the office of the coordinator for the status of women moved from the Privy Council Office to Status of Women Canada. CFUW breathed a collective sigh of relief, as it preferred to interact with government through formal structures where their solid research and quiet influence was appreciated. Privately, Black expressed concerns about working with NAC, which she believed had difficulty reaching a consensus. She was moving toward the view that CFUW might make more headway on its own.[34]

The first royal commission headed by a woman and composed primarily of women, the Royal Commission on the Status of Women, brought to light women's concerns and ensured that they were finally treated seriously. Before they heard women's dramatic testimonies in the 1968 RCSW's hearings, the media had savagely ridiculed the women's movement. But the sincerity of women's testimonies converted many to the cause and helped to re-invigorate the women's movement. As Cerise Morris writes,

> The RCSW...focused public attention on women's grievances, recommended changes in government policy aimed at eliminating inequality between the sexes, and mobilized a constituency to press for implementation of the commission's recommendation.[35]

Early legacies of the royal commission included the 1975 omnibus bill that removed discriminatory measures from the Immigration Act; from the Canada Elections Act; and from various pension provisions. It provided for maternity leave; permitted girls to join cadet organizations; and added marital status and age to the prohibited grounds of discrimination in the Public Service Employment Act. In 1978, the federal government passed human rights legislation that included sex and marital status and established a commission to monitor it.

CFUW members played a part in the early movement that led to the creation of the RCSW through its president, Laura Sabia. As well, CFUW joined NAC to help implement its 167 recommendations, many of which resembled existing CFUW policies. Some clubs worked on implementation at the provincial and municipal levels, addressing one of the royal commission's inherent weaknesses—although it was a federal document, it made broad recommendations that required implementation at all levels of government. Provincial governments were responsible for education, many social services, and some taxation and criminal justice issues. Local clubs had experience and contacts in these fields from their previous advocacy work and they put them to use. Another legacy of the commission was that it pushed CFUW to define itself on the moderate end of the feminist spectrum.

Ten years after the creation of the RCSW, a 1976 *Chronicle* article appeared written by Laura Sabia. A transitional figure, Sabia constructed bridges between the older organizations and the new players, but did not seem to fit into either. Many CFUW members found her too militant, while others within the new movement found her too moderate.[36] Disappointed that so little had changed in ten years, Sabia argued that divide-and-conquer strategies had been successfully used to pit women against women: the stay-at home-mom vs. the professional woman and "pro-life" vs. pro-choice. In Sabia's view, while all of this upheaval was happening CFUW was busying itself with amending its constitution, raising fees and, passing resolutions—"all grammatically correct, to be sure, and submitted to government with polite, 'by your leaves.'" She saw this as "fiddling while Rome burns" and bemoaned CFUW's failure of leadership; the organization, she felt, "should have led the way to equality. It has all the leadership qualifications. It chose to drag its feet in refined clay."[37] Sabia certainly knew how to hit raw nerves—"grammatically correct" resolutions did reflect CFUW's pride in thorough research. And it's hard to argue that CFUW had not walked away from leadership—Margaret Orange ignored the RCSW entirely, Gwen Black failed to find consensus on it within the organization, and Ruth Bell launched a non-controversial project for International Women's Year.

For its part, CFUW felt it was protecting its greatest asset—organizational stability—in dealing with problems in the 1970s such as inflation, postal strikes, and rising costs. And, in the end, by adhering to the organization's stated goals, CFUW did outlast NAC and other groups whose primary focus was women's issues. When it was founded in 1919, the federation goals mixed community service, friendship, and international work with advocacy. The 1970 version of CFUW goals covers a broad range of interests, in which status of women issues constituted only part of one out of its four goals; also included were support to education through scholarships, fostering interest in public affairs, encouraging women to use their education for community good and to promote the status of women, and participation in international efforts.

Feminist advocacy was not the only focus of CFUW. The organization continued to do the other things it had always done. Born of the first-wave feminist movement, CFUW had grown out of tea parties, prohibition, and the social gospel, and many of its leaders were still active in their own churches and took their social responsibilities seriously. Once a small minority of well-educated women, federation members were protective of their status and placed priority on gaining leadership positions, preferring quiet influence to noisy militancy. Having lived through long periods when few cared about status of women issues and were at times actively hostile,[38] members learned to be moderate in public through their dress, language, and comportment. Even labour organizer Madeleine Parent always dressed "in a conservative dark suit," especially when meeting with government ministers. Her colleagues on the Ontario Committee on the Status of Women believed that her ladylike attire "belied both her thinking and her tenacity and that in itself was a decided stealth asset."[39]

Working with the newer women's groups represented a clash of cultures for CFUW. It seemed as if, suddenly, out of nowhere, women's issues moved to centre stage, warranting a prestigious royal commission and government agencies, and new groups devoted primarily to feminist activism. For many federation members, the "unladylike" strategies and militant tone in the new movement was symbolized by the term Ms., which some women began to use. As a Vancouver Club history related,

> We used to sit around the kitchen at Hycroft and wonder what we should do about Ms. The solution, worked out by the President, 1974/76 and her First Vice-President, was increased use of first names among members.[40]

Most clubs were still using the husband's initials when referring to a married woman, although the practice of using women's given names was increasing. In a 1971 newsletter, the executive used the term "Ms." just to gauge members' reactions. When former president Marion Grant remarked on it, Gwen Black explained that "Ms." had once been an accepted form of address when a woman's marital status was unknown, but that lately women had adopted it because they wanted to be "recognized as individuals" rather than in association with their husbands. But as Black relates many CFUW members still used "the feudal relic," because they believed they could "maintain or even enhance their pride of person and their independence" within a marriage.[41] CFUW did change, but it took time. The North York Club observed, for example, that it took twenty-six years "for us to decide that we could be identified by our own names alone,"[42] and husband initials disappeared completely.

At the nineteenth CFUW triennial meeting held in Ottawa in August 1973, Gwen Black reflected on the events of her presidency. Much had changed in that period, and her remarks reveal a lot of anxious looking back at the 1970 triennial before the watershed RCSW report was released. She recalled uncertainty over the "defiant energies" of the 1970s, when women's status had been in a twilight zone "halfway between the report and the recommendations." Believing that changes in attitudes and laws could only be affected through the slow, steady pressure of stable organizations like CFUW, groups with a history, a constitution, and accumulated expertise, Black nonetheless feared that CFUW would be swamped by the "rising tide of the more arrogant but not always well balanced groups."[43] Still, Black conceded CFUW members could learn from the new voices and privately expressed sympathy with Sabia's frustrations, noting that most club members were "more study-oriented than action-oriented.... Eleven thousand women could set the world on fire, but we only want to dally with the 'important social issues of the Day' not deal with them."[44]

Some clubs seemed oblivious to the Royal Commission on the Status of Women. In line with the organization's goals, they provided members with friendship, learning opportunities, and the chance to perform community service, especially by raising money for scholarships. Social events remained an important attraction as women organized and participated in club programs and the regular meetings that blended light entertainment with intellectual stimulation and often made use of club members' talents. Many clubs wrote and performed plays, sometimes on women's rights. In the tradition of the earlier mock parliaments of the suffrage campaign days, non-threatening humour was used to deliver political messages. Betsy Boyce, CFUW recording secretary, wrote a clever play called *Oh Men! Oh Women! Oh Unisex!* that was performed at the Eastern Ontario regional conference in Belleville in October 1969. In May 1978, at the Hamilton regional conference, *Where Do We Go From Here?* presented women's position in society using music and verse.[45]

In 1974, the Montréal and Québec City Clubs celebrated their twenty-fifth anniversaries and the Winnipeg Club marked Manitoba's centennial in 1970 with an account of its historic Ralph Connor clubhouse. The Toronto Club celebrated its seventy-five years with a new history, *75 Years—In Retrospect*, and the Vancouver Club observed its sixtieth anniversary at Hycroft. In 1973, the club also began a city tradition called "Christmas at Hycroft" that was still ongoing in 2019. Part fundraiser and part community outreach when it began, this four-day showcase and open house allowed members with an artistic bent to arrange dried flowers, decorate the house, and make Christmas handicrafts and treats to sell. There was an admission fee and for a time the money raised allowed the club to keep its fees down.[46] The upper floor was given over to such groups as the Young Women's Christian Association (YWCA) and United Nations International Children's Emergency Fund (UNICEF), a space that was at other times used as a gallery for young artists to present their photography; realist and abstract art; prints, watercolours, oils, acrylics, mixed media; sculpture; ceramics; and weaving. Vancouver's membership numbers were at a healthy level in the 1970s but the fear remained that the clubhouse would sap the energies of members for social reform. The Vancouver Club president, Beatrice Sperling, commented that

...not all members come to the Club for intellectual stimulation. Some come for relaxation and there has been a tremendous upsurge in bridge playing and bridge lessons. Most of our social functions are over-subscribed. Most of our luncheons have waiting lists.[47]

Many of the clubs felt a responsibility to do community service, volunteering with specialized programs for special children, or French-language programs.[48] Some took their cues from the news or from triennial conference themes. Under the leadership of Dr. Jean Lauber, for example, the Edmonton Club's environmental concerns study and action group launched a paper recycling initiative. Working in the schools, women taught children the value of recycling and arranged to pick up old telephone books. They also made a presentation that contrasted images of natural scenery with garbage, then created an ecology caravan and hired a university student to tour with it. They prepared an anti-pollution resolution for the 1970 triennial in Toronto, which CFUW passed, and then, after taking the slide show to the 1971 IFUW conference in Philadelphia, it became IFUW policy.[49] The Montréal South Shore Club submitted a brief to the Commission of Inquiry on the Situation of the French Language and Linguistic Rights in Québec—the Gendron Commission—and the North York Club made a submission to the white paper on taxation, "Income security for Canadians" (1970). There were many others as well.

The cultural groups within the clubs supported community and school libraries and, especially in small or isolated towns and cities, filled a wider cultural role. The Sudbury Club sponsored a Canadian Opera Company performance, and the Regina Club pulled off a coup in 1974 when they brought in the Bolshoi Ballet. Dr. Morris Shumiatcher, prominent human rights lawyer and patron of the arts, said that, "Whatever else the ballet performances did, they clearly defined the chief ornament of our city...the members of the University Women's Club who were the enterprising impresarios that brought the Bolshoi here."[50] In this decade, however, newer, better-financed institutions were emerging to fill that need. Over time, particularly after the Saskatchewan Centre of the Arts opened in 1970, the club stopped sponsoring shows.

The North York Club conducted a successful seminar on second careers, teaching resumé writing and job interview skills, and providing job-market information, and the clubs in London, Georgetown, Oshawa, Truro, and Saint John all organized career counselling days. Montréal's South Shore Club worked with the YWCA to create a "Wheel of Fortune" vocational readiness game, which it took to local schools. The English club in Québec City had an active Consumer Affairs Committee that researched consumer products and services.

Federation committees also continued to work on a broad range of issues. As mentioned above, the Standing Committee on Libraries and Creative Arts administered the Creative Arts Award that was established in 1970 to recognize an original chamber work by a promising composer "under 30 years of age, on the threshold of a career in composition." The Canadian Music Centre arranged a professional premiere of the piece on a CBC national network broadcast. As well, the committee prepared study guides on literature, art and a musical guide on Canadian composers. The committee's writing project gave CFUW members an opportunity to submit manuscripts to be assessed, which motivated writers and helped readers develop techniques of literary criticism.

The federation's Education Committee conducted a follow-up to its earlier continuing education survey and investigated the availability of counselling and other services for mature women at universities. Monique Bégin, RCSW research director, encouraged the Edmonton Club to expand its 1968 RCSW brief in which they had created a composite character called "Mrs. Rusty Baccalaureate," who had worked in the home for ten years, raised three children, and was encountering barriers to returning to school. The club also lobbied the provincial government and the University of Alberta for improved financial aid for students and, after connecting with a support group for mature students, established a mature woman's bursary.[51]

Ruth Cooper Bell served as president of CFUW from 1973 to 1976. The daughter of a widow, she grew up in modest circumstances. After graduating from high school, she supported herself with office work, then married and became a faculty wife. After

Ruth Bell, CFUW President 1973–1976.

studying part-time for ten years, she earned a bachelor of arts degree in political economy. When her husband died, she moved to Ottawa, joined the university women's club there, and worked for the Progressive Conservative Party, where she collaborated with MP Ellen Fairclough to draft equal pay for equal work legislation. She later moved to Montréal, where she worked in the business sector and became a committed advocate for women after being told that only male employees could contribute to retirement pensions because women do not support families. She then began studying public finance, which led to a job as instructor and dean at Renison College at Waterloo University. In 1963, she married Dick Bell, a Progressive Conservative MP and cabinet minister, and turned her attention to full-time writing, teaching, and advocacy for legislative and social change for women.

One of Ruth Bell's major contributions to CFUW was to launch the previously discussed rebound project after the tumultuous RCSW years—the Foster the Roster campaign. It was launched in 1975, UN International Women's Year and was specifically aimed at promoting the appointment of women to government boards and commissions and executive positions in business. Bell liked to tell the inspirational story of attending an annual shareholders' meeting of the Royal Bank of Canada and asking why there were no women on the board. Bank president W. Earl McLaughlin replied that there were no women qualified and asked her, "Why don't you be a nice girl and let me exercise your ballot?"[52] From then on, she was committed to putting women into board positions.

At the 1973 CFUW meeting where Bell assumed the presidency, Muriel McQueen Fergusson, recently appointed speaker of the Senate, "received CFUW members in the beautiful speaker's chambers, making a splendid finale to the tour of the Parliament Buildings."[53] It was a richly symbolic gesture. In 1972, CFUW member Sylvia Ostry was appointed chief statistician at Statistics Canada and became the first woman of deputy minister rank to be responsible for an agency.[54] The federation took pride in such examples and set out to add more to the list.

While Bell inspired women to get behind the project, the roster idea had actually originated with the Ottawa Club in 1970 and was taken on nationally by Gwen Black who established contact with the Privy Council office. Black submitted names and biographies and called it the "roster of qualified women."[55] But Bell expanded and promoted the concept extensively and secured funding from the secretary of state to hire administrative staff. With plenty of contacts in government, Bell aggressively presented women's names to cabinet ministers, various government departments, and businesses. She claimed that the federation was performing a service that government departments could not duplicate at several times the cost. Reinforcing the point made by many women's groups, Bell argued that women's volunteer services should be recognized as credentials for public service jobs.[56] This was a tough sell—then as now. Still, whenever a male executive or politician claimed, as had Bell's bank president, that there were no qualified female candidates for any given position, the roster allowed CFUW to prove them wrong and send names to potential employers. By 1976, there were 550 names in the roster and more than sixty-six clubs watching for openings to which women could apply.[57]

At the federal level, the organization's successes were limited. Bell cited difficulty getting appointments with busy ministers and the "long-established, but unmentionable, tradition of political patronage."[58] But there were exceptions. June Menzies, former vice chair of the Canadian Advisory Council on the Status of Women, was appointed vice chair of the federal Anti-Inflation Board in 1976. CFUW also obtained a position on the Canadian Standards Council for Johanna Michalenko. The roster had much greater success provincially and locally, where many club members served on boards of education and in city government. The emphasis on women in public life spurred some club initiatives. The Vancouver Club organized a workshop in May 1975 on the theme "Why Are There So Few Women in Public Life?" and the club's parliamentarian held workshops to teach women the procedures of running a meeting and on the "Mechanics of Politics." They were designed to build women's competence in political campaigns.[59] The Montréal Club's Roster Committee created a talent bank and secured appointments on the Advisory Council on the Status of Women in Ottawa and the Superior Council on Education in Québec. The club also established a file on corporations such as Radio-Canada, Canadian National Railways, the chartered banks, and Bell Canada.

CFUW did not—at least not publicly—acknowledge that these successes sometimes came at the price of compromising women's effectiveness as reformers. Menzies, for example, had been a member of the Manitoba Action Committee on the Status of Women that opposed the very inflation controls the board imposed because the committee feared that the controls would make pay equity more difficult to achieve.[60] Laura Sabia left her position on the Ontario Status of Women Council because of bureaucratic resistance and her own fear of being co-opted, deciding instead to focus on journalism and some unsuccessful runs as a Progressive Conservative M P.[61]

Foster the Roster was the national component of the three-pronged International Women's Year campaign. At the provincial level, the campaign addressed family property law reform and locally, the federation asked clubs to campaign against sexism in education and to promote women and girls in non-conventional fields such as business and engineering. In the previous decade, women's organizations had addressed the issue of family law, focusing on the reform of estate and succession taxes predicated on a widow's right to a share in family property. Betty Sims, who chaired the Committee on Legislation, explained to members in a *Chronicle* article that under common law, in what was called "separate property," husbands held all marital property except that placed explicitly in the wife's name, or for which she had provided all or part of the purchase price.[62]

In a landmark case, the Supreme Court of Canada ruled in 1973 that Irene Murdoch of Alberta had only done what any "ordinary rancher's wife does" and thus had no right to a share in the ranch's value when she and her husband divorced. Women's groups were outraged to learn she was only entitled to a lump sum of secured maintenance under the federal Divorce Act, and that she had no right to a share of the ranch under provincial law governing the division of property on marital breakdown. It was made all the more infuriating when women learned that Murdoch had broken his long-suffering wife's jaw.[63] The case so angered one Edmonton Club member, Marjorie Buckley, that she wrote a two-part play called *Twin Pack* for the fiftieth anniversary of the Persons Case in 1979. While the first part dealt with the Famous Five, the second "brought women's struggles for basic justice up to the time of the Murdoch case," focusing on it in a moving and visual way. The play gave expression to women's feelings of powerlessness in the face of a system that refused to recognize the value of women's work in the family.[64]

This was clearly an issue that united all women. In 1975, CFUW passed a resolution calling for a searching review of legislation relating to matrimonial property and support. CFUW's Status of Women and Human Rights (SWHR) Committee held a workshop at the Victoria Council meeting in June 1975 at which a panel of CFUW members and experts from seven provinces provided an overview of the current legislation and some proposed changes. Clubs actively pushed for change. In 1974–1975, the Regina Club studied the working papers of the Saskatchewan Law Reform Commission, prepared a brief, and later suggested a retraining program for judges. They also asked for the appointment of more women judges because they did not trust the impartiality of male judges. The Ontario Law Reform Commission produced a report that led to the passage of the *Family Law Reform Acts* of 1975 and 1978.[65]

At the local level, International Women's Year was marked with an educational focus that dovetailed with the Foster the Roster campaign. Bell asked clubs to push educational authorities to improve school career counselling in order to encourage girls and women to consider a broader range of choices, including science, engineering, and other non-traditional fields. As part of this initiative, the federation also asked clubs to address sex stereotyping in textbooks. To give this a research foundation, the SWHR Committee did a survey that asked members, "What is it about our educational process, at home and at school, that sometimes locks girls into thinking of themselves as second class citizens?" Of the four hundred women who replied, half thought that having one or both parents encourage them made all the difference. About one-quarter cited receiving a scholarship or award as critical, or being selected from among peers to attend a conference, winning a competition, or achieving highest marks in a course or exam. Some also mentioned the importance of role models.[66]

The responses showed that many CFUW members had earned their degrees late after taking care of family duties, or a period working at a boring job. Because a number of respondents had taken the advice of guidance counsellors, there were also a lot of frustrated medical doctors and lawyers among the group, women who had drifted—or were advised into—fields thought to be "good choices for a woman." Some admitted to having ambitions thwarted by admission quotas, lack of money, well-intentioned advice, or peer pressure. To counter these trends, the federation's Education Committee prepared kits and resource materials for clubs, having first tested them at a Saskatoon high school. The Edmonton Club put out a booklet called *They Jumped So High They Reached the Sky: Famous Canadian Women*. Geared to girls in Grades 5 and 6, the book included stories about the Edmonton Grads, a phenomenal women's basketball team of the interwar years, and other exceptional women.[67] The Kitchener-Waterloo Club created a guidance book called *100 Alternatives* that featured women in various occupations.

CFUW also addressed the paucity of women in educational administration. The Edmonton Club came to the aid of faculty members at the University of Alberta who were trying to find statistical data on the hiring and promotion of women at the university and then helped them launch a petition that resulted in the university establishing a task force.[68] This, in turn, led to a CFUW submission to the Association of Universities and Colleges of Canada (AUCC) pointing out that women faculty earned $4,000 per year less than men and held only 15 per cent of full-time teaching positions. To address this issue, the AUCC conducted their own investigation.[69] There were several other studies on women faculty and an Edmonton study group on education submitted a brief to the city's school board titled "Program of affirmative action regarding the employment and promotion of female professional staff by boards of education."[70]

At the end of International Women's Year, Bell announced that "we are no longer 'ladies in white gloves,' we are working women who have donned our hard hats. If IWY's theme in 1975 was 'Why Not?' 1976's will be 'Let's.'"[71] There was a bit of bravado in this statement, as elsewhere she complained that only 47 per cent of clubs had taken part in IWY projects, interpreting this to mean that "53 per cent of Clubs think the status of women is not a nice subject for university ladies." Although the low participation rate was concerning, she herself was reluctant to call herself a feminist, preferring instead to say that she was "a person working to improve the status of women by bringing about equality," adding that her approach was "to persuade and to educate."[72]

Bell had accurately assessed the pulse of the organization. A 1979 survey revealed that more than half the clubs did not have a convenor or study group on women's status. When these issues were discussed, the most popular topics were family law, International Year of the Child, violence against women, sexual stereotyping, poverty, appointments to boards and commissions, and money management. Most of the clubs believed their purpose was to return some of the benefits of their education through projects that benefited the community rather than their own status; to take an active part in public affairs; and to encourage higher education.[73]

In 1976, the twentieth CFUW triennial was held in Saskatoon on the theme "Growing up Canadian," and Jean Battersby Steer was elected president. She had an Honours BA in French and English, and a BEd with distinction, from the University of Saskatchewan, where she had been active in the student Christian movement. While she was teaching, she married Paul Steer and had two children. In 1976, she had been teaching Latin and French for twenty years at Luther College in Regina, was active in church and women's issues, and was on the women's auxiliary of the Regina Symphony.[74] As regional director and vice president (West) before becoming CFUW president, she promoted and developed provincial councils, including the formation of the Ontario Council in 1978. Her term coincided with a period of organizational difficulties that Laura Sabia had referred to, that were the result of escalating inflation and rising costs.[75]

Steer also addressed issues of Canadian regionalism, especially Québec nationalism. While Canada had survived the FLQ crisis in 1970, tensions remained and when the Parti Québécois was elected in Québec in 1976 the new government announced its intention to separate from Canada. Steer obtained a three-year bilingual development grant from the secretary of state for translation and the 1977 *Chronicle* appeared in a fully bilingual format for the first time. Privately, some members wondered if the expense was justified, given that there were only five French-speaking clubs with a total of 187 members, but Steer saw it as a political imperative. Another grant was used to assist clubs and regions to hold mini-conferences, which coincided with the federal government's Task Force on Canadian Unity chaired by Jean-Luc Pépin, former federal cabinet minister, and John Robarts, former Ontario premier. CFUW and the clubs in St. John's, North York, Vancouver, and the Québec Council all presented briefs stressing cooperation and the need for constitutional reform to remove inequalities—and, of course, the role of education in fostering understanding.[76]

Steer also led a CFUW delegation to the Destiny Canada Conference at York University in 1977 and travelled extensively, speaking on the subject of Canadian unity at sixty clubs, eight regional conferences, and a number of workshops. She arranged for Québec members Yseult Taschereau, president of the Montréal French Club; Thérèse Casgrain; Norah Bengough, CFUW vice president (Québec); and Anne Marie Trahan, provincial director (Québec) to visit CFUW clubs so they could communicate the feelings of members in Québec to those in the rest of Canada. CFUW's newly created Program Resources Unit also produced a "National Unity Kit" for each club.

Like many of her predecessors, Steer would have liked to establish a head office with more paid staff. Although Mount Allison University had provided Gwen Black's office free of charge, Ruth Bell's office in the AUCC in Ottawa was more costly. Inflation added to their difficulties and the organization ran deficits through most of the decade. Steer helped put the organization on a more solid financial footing through a review of the executive "to make it less costly and more effective."[77] In 1977, Steer established the Charitable Trust, which could issue charitable receipts. The organization hoped that it would eventually fund all of CFUW's fellowships and awards, and keep them separate from their operating budgets.[78] CFUW became incorporated, a requirement for the Charitable Trust, which also protected the organization's name, granted personal immunity from lawsuits, and allowed the organization to testify in a court of law.[79]

When 1979 was declared the International Year of the Child by the United Nations, the Edmonton Club formed a special interest group that addressed the issue of speech therapy, and the Peterborough Club launched a local chapter of International Parents Anonymous, paying its operating costs for two years. Parents Anonymous, a self-help peer group for parents who were having difficulty dealing with their anger and hostility toward their children, provided a hotline service for times of crisis and weekly meetings to give support and advice. There were also resolutions to promote pre- and post-natal care and to protest female genital mutilation in Africa. Many clubs also promoted parenting and human relations classes which they felt should be mandatory in elementary, intermediate, and secondary schools.[80]

The twenty-first CFUW triennial was held in Québec in 1979 with 462 registrants and the theme "New Attitudes for a Changing Society." It was CFUW's diamond jubilee, and to mark it, the federation published a new history in the form of a calendar. Incoming President Eileen Clark recalled the Québec City meeting where French and English women realized how much they had in common.[81]

The decade to follow would bring critical scrutiny of women's place under the Canadian constitution. As discussed in greater detail in Chapter 14, tensions were mounting between IFUW and CFUW, in part due to a proposed increase in fees, as both organizations were dealing with inflation and rising administrative costs. A proposal jointly arrived at between CFUW and AAUW was prepared for the international meeting to be held in Vancouver in 1980. How would their proposal on fees be received?

Footnotes for this chapter can be found online at:
http://secondstorypress.ca/resources

Chapter 9
THE 1980S: PORN WARS
AND THE CONSTITUTION

All of us can be activists, without having to make speeches or march. Be involved with issues and concerns (Influence in other words).[1]

—Margaret Strongitharm

In 1985, CFUW President Margaret Strongitharm summed up the organization's goal of being a moderate and informed voice in public affairs. By the end of the decade, CFUW put that belief into action by sending delegations to Parliament Hill to meet with Barbara McDougall, minister for the status of women. The 1980s began with the organization hosting a very successful International Federation of University Women (IFUW) conference in Vancouver, only the second time that the gathering had been held in Canada. Having negotiated a ceasefire in their war over fee increases, more members became active on the international front. CFUW also joined many Canadian women in ensuring that their rights were protected in the constitution "patriated" in 1982—and launched an unambivalent attack on pornography.

Some new clubs were established in the 1980s, many of them in the West and in smaller towns and cities,[2] and others in new suburban areas such as Markham-Unionville (near Toronto) and Calgary North. CFUW membership was at around 12,500 despite the graduation of 60,000 women each year, prompting President Linda Souter to challenge members to double their numbers. She was not the first, nor the last, president to do this. A special Ad Hoc Committee was created to survey CFUW to determine what members considered the organization's most important goals. To address membership issues at the policy level, CFUW decided that clubs could accept any woman who supported the goals of CFUW, whether she was a graduate from a post-secondary institution or not. It was hoped this would counter the perception that the organization was elitist. The federation, looking for consistency, also asked clubs to change their names from, for example, the University Women's Club of Toronto to Canadian Federation of University Women/Toronto, or CFUW Toronto.[3] Neither directive was universally followed among the largely autonomous clubs.

At the club and national leadership levels, there was a growing shift away from professional or academic women toward volunteers, as executives were predominantly recruited from that dwindling demographic of women who could afford not to be in the paid labour force. The professional and executive roster was discontinued, although CFUW still sought appointments for women. The federation finally established a permanent head office in Ottawa, various organizational reforms allowed the executive to act more quickly between meetings, and ushered in the era of annual general meetings (AGMs). Councils were established in British Columbia, Saskatchewan, and Alberta. After the *Chronicle*, which had provided a detailed record of business decisions, was discontinued, the federation launched a shorter, newsier journal and the president's newsletter to improve communications with clubs.

Eileen Crawford Clark became president in 1979. Born in Scotland, she was a teenage math prodigy who received a government scholarship to take an accelerated degree in mathematics and physics at St. Andrews University; she earned her bachelor of science degree at age nineteen and joined the Women's Auxiliary Air Force to become a radar technical officer when World War II broke out. In 1945, she came to Toronto as a war bride and her new sisters-in-law introduced her to CFUW. She and her husband later settled in Montréal, where Clark served as CFUW provincial director, Québec (English) from 1970 to 1973 and vice president for Québec from 1973 to 1976. She also chaired the Committee on International Relations from 1968 to 1979, a position soon to become an automatic

appointment for past presidents. Clark was also elected fourth VP of IFUW.

Left to right: unidentified person, Eileen Clark, and Laura Sabia.

Clark rented office space at the Université de Montréal and got to work on resolving the simmering fee dispute with IFUW and planning the 1980 IFUW triennial in Vancouver. It was, by all accounts, a tremendous success with 825 delegates attending from forty-four countries. Clark reported at the meeting that the contentious IFUW fee dispute had been resolved in a spirit of goodwill and that CFUW would remain a member in good standing. The friction between the two organizations is explored more fully in Chapter 14, but suffice it to say that the IFUW reduced Canada's fee based on membership, and streamlined its administration. This paved the way for renewed support for IFUW in Canada, with some Canadian leaders taking on an active role.

In keeping with its longstanding defense of women's rights, CFUW joined other women's groups in a campaign to ensure that women were represented in Canadian constitutional discussions.[4] International developments in human rights were having an impact in Canada, first with the Universal Declaration of Human Rights in

1948 and then with John Diefenbaker's Canadian Bill of Rights in 1960. The UN Convention on the Elimination of all Discrimination Against Women (CEDAW) was adopted by the General Assembly on December 18, 1979, and signed by Canada July 17, 1980. Women's groups were becoming increasingly aware that they could not rely on the wording of the 1960 Bill of Rights that had proven ineffective in protecting women—the Supreme Court of Canada ruled that it only applied to how a law was administered, not to the content of the law. This meant that reform was possible only through the laborious process of amending legislation piece by piece. When federal-provincial talks in the late 1970s discussed transferring divorce jurisdiction to the provinces, which would have made tracking down support payments even more difficult than it already was, women's groups protested. The government dropped the idea, but the incident prompted women to study constitutional issues more seriously.

When Pierre Trudeau returned to government in 1980—just after the first Québec referendum on separation—and introduced a plan to "patriate" the constitution and enshrine a Charter of Rights and Freedoms within it, women were ready.[5] The first version of the charter tabled by the prime minister relied heavily on the wording of the 1960 Bill of Rights for its equality guarantee. Because the charter entailed a new formal judicial review of laws in terms of basic principles, which had not previously existed, it was critical that it have the strongest possible equality guarantee, one that gave Canadian women confidence that it would further women's equality agenda. Anglophone women lobbied extensively for improvements to the equality provision and, in January 1981, Minister of Justice Jean Chrétien announced that section 15 of the proposed charter would read, "Every individual is equal before and under the law and has the right to equal protection of the law and equal benefit of the law."[6] This was a good start but it was missing one key ingredient— women wanted a place at the negotiating table.

In January 1981, the Canadian Advisory Council on the Status of Women (CACSW) was planning a women's constitutional conference to be held in February, but it ended up being postponed for a second time, and CACSW president and former *Chatelaine* editor Doris Anderson accused Lloyd Axworthy, minister responsible for the status of women, of orchestrating the delay. She resigned in protest, taking some of her staff with her.[7] It was a newsworthy, dramatic move that mobilized women. They established the Ad Hoc Committee of Canadian Women on the Constitution and organized their own Ottawa conference with no government funding. Ottawa MPs Flora MacDonald, Judy Erola, and Margaret Mitchell booked the Confederation Room in the West Block for the conference and were instrumental in subsequent lobbying of their fellow Members of Parliament. Progressive Conservative (PC) Leader of the Opposition Joe Clark and his wife Maureen McTeer held a reception at Stornoway, their official residence, and CFUW members were among the 1,300 women present at this wildly successful three-day meeting.

After intense debate, the women delegates decided that they would support the entrenchment of women's right in the charter only if there were significant improvements and they were given input into the wording. The Ad Hoc Committee proceeded to lobby cabinet ministers, Members of Parliament, and female senators. The women demanded that the government accept the resolutions adopted at their conference, send them to the House of Commons for debate, and either amend the charter or abandon it. The new CFUW-FCFDU *Journal* reminded its readers that if the proposed charter did not grant women equality, then neither would the courts.[8] The Ad Hoc Committee members sent letters and telegrams, launched a national phone campaign to update women, and held T-shirt demonstrations in the House of Commons. The media covered it all, of course. It was pure drama. Finally, the government announced in the House on April 23, 1981, that the equality provisions of Section 15 would be bolstered by Section 28, which states "Notwithstanding anything in this charter, the rights and freedoms referred to in it are guaranteed equally to male and female persons."[9]

As is true with any major lobbying effort, the women needed to maintain vigilance. In November of that same year, during federal-provincial negotiations, a majority of provincial premiers agreed to the inclusion in the charter of an override clause that would allow provinces to pass special time-limited legislation *notwithstanding* the guarantees of the charter—in effect enabling them to negate various fundamental rights, including women's rights.

Another intense period of lobbying followed as women fought to protect their hard-won guarantees in the charter. CFUW President Eileen Clark sent telegrams to the prime minister, the minister of justice, and all provincial premiers during the federal-provincial constitutional conference. CFUW clubs, vice presidents, and provincial directors all demanded that women's equality be protected. In the end, Trudeau and the premiers had to partially back down—they exempted Section 28, which guarantees that the charter must be applied equally to both sexes, but not Section 15, which guarantees all equality rights, from the controversial Section 33 override power that allowed Parliament or provincial legislatures to override certain portions of the charter. Although Québec did not sign on to the patriation package, the constitution and charter apply everywhere in Canada; Québec women, in addition to the protections of the federal charter, are also protected under the 1975 Québec Charter of Rights. The patriation process did little to bring women inside and outside Québec together, and these tensions would only increase during the debates over the 1987 Meech Lake Constitutional Accord discussed below. The feminist movement in Québec was closely allied with Québec nationalism and remained somewhat separate from the anglophone movement, a reality that is reflected in CFUW's low numbers in Québec.

In summing up the campaign, Eileen Clark noted that, "It seems almost incredible that governments would have been quite happy to ensure rights to male persons, but not for the remaining 52.4 per cent of Canada's population, had we not protested." She advised members, "to pay close attention to the Charter, and oppose any possible attempts to enact legislation with notwithstanding clauses that would have discriminatory applications."[10] CFUW's Legislation Committee report at the 1982 triennial noted that the constitution, with the inclusion of the *Charter of Rights and Freedoms* was now law. Women all across Canada had succeeded in retaining Section 28 on women's rights after a strong last-minute campaign.[11] CFUW passed two resolutions in 1982 to support the charter. The first called on the organization to be continuously vigilant "concerning any overriding provincial or federal legislation which may seem to contravene the spirit of the *Charter* as expressed in Section 1, *Guarantee of Rights and Freedoms*." The second resolution asked the

"Government of Canada and provincial and territorial governments to delete Section 33 (1–5) of the 1982 Constitution Act, which may override the fundamental freedoms, legal rights, and equality rights of the *Charter*."[12]

The constitutional battle, fought and won—not once but twice—has come to rival the Persons Case as a landmark in the struggle for women's equality in Canada. Through it, women again made a considerable contribution to constitutional reform in Canada, one that history will one day acknowledge.[13] CFUW played a role in these constitutional reforms that forced legislatures to change laws to conform to Section 15. These in turn influenced future legal decisions. After 1982, feminist lawyers and constitutional experts, many of the same women who led the constitution campaign, established the Legal Education and Action Fund (LEAF) to support cases important for women's equality.

In 1987, the Mulroney government launched new efforts to bring Québec into the constitutional fold with the Meech Lake Constitutional Accord that contained a highly contentious "distinct society" clause. While CFUW "applauded the inclusion of the province of Québec in Confederation and the specific recognition given to Aboriginal people and the multi-cultural heritage of Canadians," it expressed concerns that "the First Ministers had failed to respect the guarantees of equality contained in Section 15 of the *Canadian Charter of Rights and Freedoms*."[14] In their brief to the government, CFUW also cautioned against provincial rights undermining the universality of health and welfare programs, and renewed their request for the appointment of more women to the senate, the supreme court, and other federal institutions.[15]

Another shift that took the whole world by storm in this decade was the personal computer that revolutionized the way Canadians worked, played, and lived. CFUW kept its members up to date on these technological changes in various ways, big and small. The federation worked with others on "The Future Is Now," a women and micro-technology conference held in Ottawa in June 1982. As the organizers commented, "We are in the middle of a revolution, which will probably have more impact than the industrial revolution, and that initially, the greatest impact may well be on women."[16] CFUW conference partners in this endeavour included the Canadian

Congress for Learning Opportunities for Women (CCLOW), the Canadian Research Institute for the Advancement of Women (CRIAW), and the National Action Committee on the Status of Women (NAC).[17] Conference delegates were encouraged to lobby MPs and government officials for courses to help women integrate into the burgeoning micro-technology industry and encourage girls to study math and science in order to take leadership roles in these fields.[18] There were also proposals for a charter of rights related to micro-technology; for safeguards against de-skilling[19] and reductions in the workforce; for lobbying efforts in favour of freedom of information; and for protective legislation against theft or sale of personal information.

CFUW also chose as its 1982 triennial theme "Our Technological Society." The meeting's keynote speaker was Dr. John Madden, president of Pacific Microtel Research Limited in Burnaby, BC. The Program Committee had been asked to choose a speaker for the banquet who was a non-political woman. They chose Dr. Naomi Griffiths, dean of arts and professor of history at Carleton University, who spoke about the "Ethical and Social Implications of the New Systems of Communications" and mused about the non-technical aspects of the computer revolution. The overall program was worthy of the largely liberal arts graduates in attendance.

Some of the clubs also joined the timely discussion. A mini-conference held at Hycroft included a workshop on "The Computer in Education" and the Winnipeg Club ran a series entitled "Computers and the Human Brain." CFUW's Education Committee focused on computers in the school. Technology reappeared as a theme at the Calgary triennial meeting in 1985, where "Women's Work—The Reality of Tomorrow" was explored. One of the meeting highlights was a panel discussion moderated by Sylvia Teare of the Calgary Club on the "Social Impact of Women's Changing Work." Invited speakers included a psychologist who talked about "Superwomen, the Stress, Guilt Cycles" and Pat Cooper from CACSW who addressed "Social Change, Women's Work, Family, and Society." Clearly change was in the air!

CFUW meetings retained an element of past formalities, despite changing times. The 1982 triennial at the University of Winnipeg began, as usual, with the singing of "O Canada," followed by a moment of silence for deceased members, welcome remarks from the Winnipeg Club president and the chancellor of the university. Then came the granting of charters to three new clubs, and greetings from the presidents of IFUW, the British Federation of University Women (BFUW), and the American Association of University Women (AAUW). Past presidents Marion Grant, Doris Saunders, and Vivian Morton were also introduced before the resolutions, speakers, and workshops followed with vigorous debate. At the end of it all, the gavel was passed from outgoing president Eileen Clark to new president Margaret Strongitharm.

A University of British Columbia (UBC) nursing graduate in 1940, Strongitharm worked as a public health nurse, married a lawyer, raised four children, and was committed to voluntary work and advocacy. She followed the usual trajectory from club to regional to national level of leadership. CFUW's *History and Heroines* stresses that Strongitharm "maintained her important status as a wife and mother while being recognized as a 'lady,'" which meant showing genuine interest in the lives of others "while being fastidiously groomed and appropriately dressed for every occasion."[20] Such a description would have undoubtedly angered younger members of the women's movement but it reflects CFUW values. Strongitharm epitomized the undervalued female volunteer whose roles as executive, administrator, and politician were persistently minimized because they were performed not only by women but by volunteers.[21] Aware of tensions within the federation and the movement, her presidential address in 1983 emphasized unity:

> We must head off the confrontation between home-based and job-based women for economic recognition. We must bridge the gap between moms and career girls, unionists and managers; we must educate ourselves about the strategies of affirmative action and equal pay and TOGETHER build a platform that will lead, however slowly, to greater economic justice

for women and a more humane work/home world for women, children, and their men.[22]

Through the special Ad Hoc Committee, Strongitharm launched a study of CFUW aims, objectives, policy, procedures, and resolutions. The study surveyed members about their opinions on the importance of the various goals of the organization and found that they were split three ways—maintaining high standards of education; stimulating interest and participation in public affairs; and encouraging women graduates to put their education at the service of the community.[23] Some 70 per cent of the members also gave priority to friendship as a goal. The review also looked at demographics, finding that the membership was aging and a substantial number of them were long-time members, and that a whopping 65 per cent of members had already served on the executive.[24]

As CFUW's relations with their international colleagues warmed in this decade, Strongitharm helped chair the International Women's Peace Conference in Halifax and a very successful Asia-Canada Women in Management Conference held in Victoria.[25] CFUW also worked on "Women, Leadership and Sustainable Development," a conference in Ghana in 1989, and established its own Committee on Peace and Security following a failed IFUW resolution.[26] The committee sponsored an essay contest on the topic of peace for schoolchildren and some of the winners' essays were read at an AGM; a Truro Club study group produced a kit for teaching about peace in schools. At the end of the decade, CFUW asked the Canadian government to refuse US President Reagan's invitation to participate in the US strategic defence initiative infamously known as Star Wars.[27]

As always, clubs remained the backbone of the organization, with meetings, social events, and study groups filling the need for friendship and fun mixed with fundraising and learning. The Hamilton UWC established a gourmet cooking group in 1975 that followed the format of accepting ten women plus spares:

> The hostess decides on the menu and provides the food. Then each member takes one task and begins to prepare one part of the meal. Somehow it all comes together, and by 10 p.m. they are all sitting down to enjoy a gourmet homecooked meal. With wine, of course.[28]

Through study groups and committees, CFUW members kept up to date on issues such as pensions, educational reform, part-time work, and child care. The Kingston Club had an armchair travellers' group; the Perth Club researched its town's history; and in Oshawa, members set up a school for gifted children. Several clubs had successful children's film series. The St. John's program ran from 1962 to 1982 and won a *Chatelaine* award for "combining fund-raising with imaginative public service, the showing of children's classic movies at a University theatre."[29] There were new investor groups and CFUW North Bay helped establish a Hands-On Museum for children aged four to twelve, a project that had originated with the International Year of the Child in 1979. Interestingly, the museum featured the role of Canada's voyageurs, "Native" people, and French Canadians in history, but apparently no women.[30]

The Toronto clubhouse underwent major structural alterations and redecoration in the latter part of the decade and the Vancouver Club won a Heritage Award in 1982 for Hycroft. In 1989, the Christmas at Hycroft event featured an immense Christmas tree decorated with puppets hand-made by club members. In the previous year, the Peace and Security Committee decorated the tree with doves to symbolize peace.[31]

CFUW placed great importance on role models to inspire the young and were always looking for ways to draw attention to women's potential through the recognition of outstanding women. The organization was happy to report, for example, that two CFUW members won the 1981 Persons Award that had been established in 1979 on the fiftieth anniversary of the Persons Case: Governor General Edward Schreyer presented the awards to Florence Martel of Montréal and Agnes Davidson of Regina.[32]

Although the CFUW executive decided in September 1980 to cease promoting its roster at the federal level, it continued to collect the information.[33] In 1982, the federation passed a resolution urging the government to give women equal access to appointments on government agencies, boards, committees, commissions, councils, and crown corporations. CFUW also continued to be active in mentoring young girls. The twenty-third triennial held at the University of Calgary featured astronaut Roberta Bondar, who was also a zoologist, neuroscientist, and medical doctor as a keynote speaker.

Dr. Roberta Bondar (left) presenting a picture to Margaret Strongitharm with Dolly Kennedy.

The organization made her an honorary member, which required a change in CFUW bylaws but most members felt that she made a fine role model. When she took a CFUW banner and T-shirt into space with her in 1992, President Peggy Matheson was thrilled. She was invited to watch Bondar take off at the launch of the Space Shuttle Discovery STS-42 at Kennedy Space Center and remembers it as a highlight of her tenure:

> The tension and excitement was almost tangible as the count-down progressed, was halted, and then re-commenced.... Lift-off was heralded by the familiar spurt of flame and cloud of smoke, and after a significant pause, by the tremendous bang, "Discovery" broke the sound barrier, metaphorically severing her connection with earth...a thrilling experience and one in which all Canadians, especially Canadian women can take pride. Dr. Bondar, an honorary member of CFUW is a remarkable person who has dedicated her life to scientific discovery.... As a mentor and role model, no one could serve the young people of Canada better than Roberta Bondar.[34]

A 1987 *Journal* article quoted Bondar as saying that the sky was the limit, advising girls to keep their options open and take math and science.[35]

More provincial and regional councils, some of which mirrored the national CFUW structure with committees on education, library, status of women and human rights, etc. were established in this period. As Lyn Hardman, VP Ontario noted, the councils provided a valuable training ground for future CFUW presidents.[36] The Ontario Council's Education Committee, for example, monitored the 1984 Bovey Commission on the Future Development of the Universities. Its Status of Women Committee worked on resolutions to ensure pensions and benefits for part-time workers. While part-time work had been proposed specifically for married women with children in the 1950s, employers soon discovered that by denying part-time workers pensions and other benefits, they had created a cheap source of labour.

Councils and clubs did not always agree with the federation's policy directions, particularly in relation to daycare. At the Ontario Council meeting in 1985, a seminar on "Social Change and Mental Health" given by Edwin Clarke, executive director of Family Services in Windsor, Ontario, led group members to conclude that "there should be money provided to keep mothers who need to work to support their family at home," as is done in Finland.[37] Similarly, CFUW Etobicoke's Daycare Committee rejected a proposal for universal publicly funded daycare largely because of cost and because they felt it would exert "even more pressure on a woman to work outside the home and place her child in an organized setting where individual needs may not be fulfilled." The group did concede that subsidized and partially subsidized places were needed for those whose family income was below the poverty line. CFUW's official policy as expressed in a 1978 resolution was to ask federal and provincial governments to increase financial support for "quality daycare, including daycare for infants, private home daycare, lunch and after-school programs, as well as licensed daycare centres."[38]

Provincial Council meetings provided a forum for discussion, learning, and fun. In British Columbia three mini-conferences dealt with multiculturalism, genetics, and society, and the computer revolution. In Kelowna BC, a daylong workshop taught participants how to research resolutions and lobby for them. There was also a skit called "Have you the Minutes? Please say you have the Minutes." The Québec Provincial Council conference at Sherbrooke in May 1984 held a "Hands Across the Border" conference with AAUW, where they discussed mutual concerns such as acid rain; the Sherbrooke Club invited Dr. Mariafranca Marcelli of the University of Vermont and a member of the Burlington Club to speak on this topic as well.[39]

At both provincial and especially federal levels, resolutions dealt with postwar social welfare programs, which CFUW monitored to ensure that women were dealt with fairly. The "feminization of poverty" that put elderly and single women at the highest risk of living in poverty was a growing concern. Lester B. Pearson's government had introduced the Canada Pension Plan (CPP) in 1965 and it was amended in 1978 to allow for the equal splitting of pension credits between spouses after divorce or marriage annulment. However, less than 1 per cent of those eligible were taking advantage of it. Former CFUW member and senior civil servant June Menzies conducted research leading to a CFUW proposal that CPP and the Québec Pension Plan (QPP) make the splitting of Canada pension plan credits acquired during marriage mandatory, automatic and unrenounceable following divorce or annulment. CFUW worked on this with Monique Bégin, federal minister of health and welfare, whose department sponsored eighteen conferences across Canada on "Pensions—Focus on Women." The high attendance at these conferences reflected women's interest in planning for old age, especially in the event of divorce or widowhood. Such experiences reinforced the importance of having sympathetic women in government.

CFUW also played an active role in one of the most heated controversies of the women's movement in this period—pornography. There was a heightened realization within the women's movement of the 1980s that rape, incest, wife battering, and violent pornography needed to be addressed along with the long-standing economic issues, and events relating to violence against women began to appear on club programs.[40] Some women linked violence to the widespread dissemination of pornography, and it became a subject of fierce debate in the 1980s. CFUW joined a coalition formed in 1983 called the Canadian Coalition Against Media Pornography, led by Maude Barlow, then an advisor to Prime Minister Trudeau on women's issues.[41] The organization sought to raise awareness and lobby politicians, protesting to the Canadian Radio-Television and Telecommunications Commission (CRTC) in January 1983 against "First Choice" pay-television channels that were planning to broadcast "soft porn" movies. It also wrote letters to Ronald Reagan urging him to take action against the US pornography industry.

Several government reports dealt with the issue. The Badgely report, released in August 1984, shocked many Canadians by detailing the prevalence of child sexual abuse,[42] and stressing the importance of protecting children.[43] In June 1983, Canada's Liberal justice minister, Mark MacGuigan, established the Special Committee on Pornography and Prostitution chaired by BC lawyer Paul D. K. Fraser. CFUW's members put forward their position to the Fraser committee, and Legislation Committee chair Theodora Carroll Foster called the response by clubs "superb." She remarked that the issue had "grabbed women emotionally" and showed what can be done when women are galvanized."[44] At least twelve clubs submitted briefs and others took local action. One of these briefs, submitted by the Vancouver Club asked the government to

> ...stop the manufacture, importation, and distribution of pornographic material. We expect the government of Canada to guarantee the right of all Canadians, including women and children, to live with dignity in a society free from pornographic exploitation.[45]

At its 1985 triennial, CFUW showed the controversial documentary *Not a Love Story*, a landmark production from Studio D of the National Film Board, that examined the pornography industry and made a powerful statement on pornography's inherent violence against women. One woman sitting in that audience was particularly moved by this evocative production—Tammy Irwin, who later became a CFUW president. She had joined the Edmonton Club in search of friends, then got involved in their recycling and environmental initiatives. Seeing *Not a Love Story* convinced her to study the issue; she heard Maude Barlow speak and even took the subject to her church social committee, arranging to show the film there.[46]

CFUW's first anti-pornography resolution had originated with the Montréal South Shore Club in the late 1970s and had requested that the Canadian government define pornography to facilitate regulation, set up a committee to study it, raise public awareness, and enforce anti-pornography laws. They were especially concerned with protecting minors against the contempt, hatred, and violence transmitted by pornography.[47] In 1985, CFUW passed three more resolutions on the issue, which primarily focused on protecting children from exploitation in both the making of pornography and exposure to it. One resolution, that came from the North York Club, called for more research into long- and short-term alternatives to censorship. Other resolutions asked that municipal bylaws be enacted to protect minors from the display of pornographic materials and that the government implement the recommendations of the Badgely report. Finally, in 1986, CFUW took a resolution to the IFUW meeting in New Zealand to draw the problem of child pornography, its widespread circulation, and its transportation across borders to the attention of all national affiliates. It passed unanimously.

The Fraser committee was called largely to satisfy women's groups and took a legal and human rights perspective.[48] There were well-qualified women on the committee, such as constitutional expert Mary Eberts, Montréal lawyer Andrée Ruffo, human rights champion Joan Wallace, and sociologist Susan Clark, who was dean of human and professional development and director of the Institute for the Study of Women at Mount St. Vincent University. In the end, the report avoided concluding that pornography was a manifestation of male violence against women and ignored feminist recommendations for increased funding for women's organizations that provided assistance to victims of male violence and did public education on sexuality.[49] The pornography issue proved one of the most divisive issues within the women's movement. While most feminists saw pornography's degrading and sometimes violent portrayal of women as sexist, not everyone agreed that there was a direct causal relationship between it and sexual violence, and many women were uncomfortable with any form of censorship. Radical feminists did not trust the *Criminal Code* and the police to enforce anti-pornography laws equitably, fearing that gay and lesbian materials, rather than commercial pornography, would be targeted. It was for this reason that the media dubbed these debates as the "porn wars."

CFUW was careful to distinguish between pornography and erotica. Following the 1984 election, Progressive Conservative Minister of Justice John Crosbie became a CFUW ally when he proposed changes to legislation to stem the flood of pornography coming into Canada through the United States. Those opposing the legislation on the grounds of censorship included the Canadian Periodical Distributors and the Canadian Association of University Teachers. In 1987, when R.E.A.L. (Realistic, Equal, Active, for Life) Women of Canada appeared on the scene, CFUW felt the need to distinguish themselves on this issue. R.E.A.L. Women gained a significant amount of media coverage by claiming that feminists did not represent all women and demanded the same access to government funding as other women's groups. That summer, CFUW President Linda Souter noted that while both groups opposed pornography, R.E.A.L. women did not recognize the difference between erotica and pornography, and was opposed to both sex education and abortion. CFUW opposed government funding for R.E.A.L. Women because the organization could not demonstrate their support for the *Charter of Rights and Freedoms* and the UN Convention on the Elimination of All Forms of Discrimination Against Women. She also pointed to their lack of accountability and undemocratic procedures. While the PC government did formally recognize R.E.A.L. Women after 1984, it is not clear how much, if any, funding they received.[50]

Linda Palmer Souter assumed the president's chair in 1985 and was the last to preside over a triennial meeting. A McGill graduate, who had done extensive volunteering and worked her way up from club president in Sudbury to the national office, her profile was similar to her two predecessors, underlining the fact that the demands of the president's job nearly precluded candidates who had full-time employment.[51] Adept at fostering decisions through consensus and at organizing people, Souter went on to a second career with IFUW, becoming the second Canadian president.[52]

Linda Souter was the first president to benefit from the new CFUW office established on Parkdale Avenue in Ottawa, and she moved to the city with her husband to take up the position. Elizabeth Cureton, a qualified pilot and a niece of the artist Emily Carr, served as its first executive secretary—later director—from 1985 to 1994.[53] With operating funds always tight, the office had to also rely on a

Linda Souter, CFUW President 1985–1988.

number of part-time paid staff as well as volunteers from the Ottawa Club to take on everything from scholarships to advocacy, but the stability of an office allowed the organization to accomplish more.

Souter continued the reforms begun by Margaret Strongitharm's Ad Hoc Committee, such as the creation of an Executive Committee to deal with the new emergency resolutions that could be brought to the AGM on twenty-four hours' notice. Urgent resolutions could be voted upon by mail, provided that two-thirds of the Resolutions Committee and the majority of the board agreed that the matter could not wait until the next AGM.[54] Other improvements included the creation of a policy handbook that included all CFUW resolutions, a new logo that incorporated the Fédération canadienne des femmes diplomées des universités (FCFDU), and membership kits were sent to clubs with ideas on how to recruit and retain members.[55]

One of Souter's lasting achievements was to open more sustained access to government. This strategy took advantage of the increased number of women holding political office and reaped some early rewards from the successes of the women's movement. One friend and CFUW member was the Honourable Flora

MacDonald. Having earlier helped on the constitutional issue, she spoke at the 1984 CFUW council meeting[56] in Saint John, New Brunswick on "Human Values—Women's Responsibility" the day after the federal leaders' debate on women's issues. Organized by NAC, this was the only such debate in Canada before or since. In preparation for the election,

The CFUW delegation that met with representatives of the federal government, circa, 1985–1988. Left to right: Suzanne Coallier (Finance), Betty Tugman, (VP Ontario), Tammy Irwin (VP Prairies/President elect), Linda Souter (President), Eleanor Chilacombe (Oakville Club), Theodora Caroll Foster (Legislation).

NAC published extensive information on the candidates and their platforms.[57] The organizing committee had asked MacDonald not to speak on the debate, so instead she spoke about the concept of a women's debate. She argued that all issues were women's issues and while she conceded that a women's issues debate was necessary today, she hoped that someday women would reach a level of participation when it was no longer needed. In September 1984, when the Progressive Conservatives won the federal election, twenty-seven women—a record number—were elected. MacDonald was one of the six women appointed to Cabinet.

Linda Souter persuaded Barbara McDougall, then minister for the status of women, to hold an annual briefing with CFUW, ushering in a new era in advocacy. Apparently, it all began when CFUW representatives cornered her while she was eating lunch at her desk. This led to McDougall inviting CFUW to appear before House of Commons standing committees on issues such as generic drugs and the Meech Lake Accord. Near the end of her term, Souter took advantage of CFUW's links within government and challenged its proposed amendment to the Patent Drug Act, which would extend the period of protection for drug companies and delay the production of cheaper, generic drugs. Unfortunately, the government went ahead with their amendment despite CFUW efforts, which led to an escalation in the already rising cost of drugs.[58]

In 1987, McDougall invited sixteen women's organizations to a public policy forum designed to improve consultations between government and the women's groups. Advisors from fourteen federal departments attended the meeting and gave advice on how to approach government by focusing on major issues and learning when and where to key those issues into the system. In 1988, CFUW was granted their first "bilateral consultations" with the federal government. McDougall distributed sections of CFUW policy briefs, derived from resolutions from the previous council meeting, to the appropriate cabinet ministers, briefs relating to peace, daycare, equal pay for work of equal value, part-time work, pensions, the Meech Lake Accord, and protests against funding cuts to women's programs. Each minister responded to CFUW on the appropriate item, then the CFUW team gathered to study the responses and plan their strategy for the ministers' meetings that McDougall arranged.

CFUW delegations usually consisted of the president, president-elect, and executive director, but, depending on the issues to be discussed, they might be joined by committee chairs and, sometimes, provincial council representatives. In 1988, CFUW delegations met with McDougall and Jake Epp, minister of national health and welfare, to discuss child care and abortion, and with Benoît Bouchard, minister of employment and immigration, to discuss a job strategies program. They also had discussions with Shirley Potter, special assistant to David Crombie, secretary of state, and with the undersecretary of state regarding post-secondary funding and adult literacy. Ministers often sent their experts; Joe Clark, for example, sent in his place a representative of the External Affairs'

Arms Control and Disarmament Division to a planned meeting on the establishment of a nuclear weapons-free zone.[59] The women described the experience as a "hectic, exciting and rewarding day on Parliament Hill." They believed that they had established themselves as a group that could make a valuable contribution to policy discussions.[60] It is impossible to know for certain whether this was a polite comment or a sincere belief, but CFUW did get invited back.

The following summer the CFUW executive was busy planning for the next year's meeting on the Hill, where they again found themselves dashing from one minister's office to the next. Connections always helped and one delegation proudly reported that the half-hour they had scheduled with Perrin Beatty, minister of health, was extended to more than an hour—his wife was a CFUW member. There was an aura of excitement around these encounters and the women found "individual presentations to be effective in establishing a rapport" with the minister and his or her staff. They discussed the 1988 resolutions and other areas of concern. On the Meech Lake Accord and funding for R.E.A.L. Women of Canada, they "agreed to disagree" but overall the members of the delegation felt that their positions were given a fair hearing.[61] Thanks to the efforts initiated by Souter and carried on by subsequent presidents, CFUW began its regular and fruitful consultations with the federal government. This was a period before power became more concentrated in the prime minister's office and federal ministers became less open to discussion and input from the public.[62]

Toward the end of the 1980s, women began to reap the rewards of an increasingly effective *Charter of Rights and Freedoms*. When Angelique Lavallee was acquitted of murdering her abusive common-law husband in 1987, the battered wife syndrome was used successfully as a defense for the first time, and it renewed women's faith in the courts.[63] CACSW estimated that one million Canadian women—one in eight—had been abused by a spouse. In 1984, Flora MacDonald, PC minister of employment and immigration, had named Judge Rosalie Abella to lead the Royal Commission on Equality in Employment. Her report, released the following year, included visible minorities, Aboriginal women, and women with disabilities, and it sought definitions for what came to be called employment equity. While some thought that the federal legislation

The CFUW delegation in Minister Barbara McDougall's office, Ottawa, April 1989. Left to right: Elizabeth Cureton, Susan Mohamdee (Russell), Tammy Irwin, Barbara McDougall, Linda Souter, and Rose Beatty.

passed in 1986, the Employment Equity Act, was weak, it was a beginning.[64] In Ontario in 1988, pay equity came into effect, phased in over several years and including the private sector. Nova Scotia began applying employment equity with the civil service in 1990, and other provinces followed.[65] This not only lessened the gender gap in pay but encouraged people to think differently about how work was defined and valued.

In 1986, Sylvia Gold, president of CACSW, spoke to the Vancouver Club about the legacy of the Royal Commission on the Status of Women, still in the process of implementation. She pointed out that forty-three of the 122 recommendations within federal jurisdiction had been fully implemented and fifty-three more had been partially implemented. There was still work to be done on issues such as the enforcement of court orders in custody settlements, benefits for part-time workers, and improvements to pension benefits for women, but all in all, things were looking up. She even expressed hope that the masculinized version of "O Canada" that they had just sung would one day be replaced with words that included daughters as well as sons.[66] Gold did signal one note of caution—CACSW funding had not kept up with inflation. CFUW's resolutions on family law reform, recognition of midwives, violence against women and children, pension reforms, and daycare made a significant contribution to these measures of progress.[67]

Change was coming in many areas, even within CFUW. Theodora Foster, Ottawa Club member and chair of the Status of Women and Human Rights Committee, initiated language reform. In considering a 1987 CFUW resolution to urge governments "to draft all future federal and provincial laws in non-sexist language," she pointed out that this contradicted CFUW's own practices. Foster had earlier chastised this federation of university-educated women for not taking the lead in challenging language that masculinized women or made them invisible.[68] This discussion led to reform of language conventions and the persistent term "chairman" was finally dropped from federation records.

Tammy Elder Irwin came to the CFUW presidency in part through her interest in the anti-pornography campaign in Edmonton. She was a graduate of UBC in English and psychology, was born in Tillsonburg, Ontario and grew up in Sarnia and Winnipeg. She joined the university women's club in Winnipeg, sponsored by two of her mother's friends, while she was employed as a welfare worker for the Manitoba government. She moved back to Vancouver in 1962 at the time of the Hycroft acquisition and in 1968 relocated again, this time to Edmonton.[69] Irwin and her husband had a long involvement with social justice issues in the United Church and with truth and reconciliation issues.[70]

President-elect Irwin had advocated for the change to a biennial structure to attract more candidates for the job, but did not know until the vote was taken at the 1988 meeting in Ottawa whether her term would be two years or three.[71] The two-year presidential term and the establishment of CFUW's new head office in Ottawa made leadership transitions go much more smoothly. Before these changes came into effect, the new president and secretary had had to devote months to finding inexpensive space, moving files, then hiring and training staff. With the biennial format, executive members also only had to commit to two years instead of three. As part of this transition, CFUW began having annual general meetings, which meant that policy could be established every year at the AGM instead of every three years. Irwin chose as her biennial priorities increased efficiency, increased membership, and a strong study and action program.[72]

The 1980s reflected an optimism born of women's accomplishments. Satisfied with their growing contribution to advocacy and community service, CFUW chose as its theme for the 1988–1990 biennial "Our Health, Our Planet, Our Future." At the AGM in Edmonton delegates attended workshops on recycling, garbage, and the environment interspersed with relaxed trips to Fort Edmonton and the West Edmonton Mall.

In December 1989, tragedy struck when an angry, young, anti-feminist man shot and killed fourteen female engineering students at Polytechnique Montréal. Leaving behind a hit list of Québec's feminist leaders, he sent anger, sadness, and shock through the community and across the country. The CFUW president acknowledged the sad event by portraying Lépine as a "disturbed" young man; it was the commonly held, moderate viewpoint. Some feminists characterized his actions as a madness that reflected Western society's resentment of the progress women were making; some of them even characterized it as a hate crime. Today CFUW remembers the lives of those fourteen women with fellowships offered through the CFUW Fellowships Committee.

In the 1990s, CFUW would continue to find the federal government open to its representations and conducted a major survey of the place of women on university campuses. But there were challenges ahead, including cuts to the funding of women's programs.

Footnotes for this chapter can be found online at:
http://secondstorypress.ca/resources

Chapter 10

THE 1990S: GOVERNMENT
DELEGATIONS AND AUSTERITY

One Member Plus One Member Equals Two Members; One Club Plus One Club Equals Two Clubs; Action plus visibility equals membership.
>   —Margaret Cugnet, Membership Committee[1]

Over the years, CFUW devised many slogans to increase membership as the organization sought to attract a larger percentage of university graduates. But by the 1990s, it was becoming a worry—one with financial implications—and the federation worked diligently to address it. In 1990, there were 129 clubs and membership had dropped to 11,000, or a decline of about 300 members a year across the country. This represented a serious loss of revenue in a self-supporting organization with a growing number of officers, which resulted in reduced influence and profile in the community and, as some of the smaller clubs closed, a decline in the breadth of geographic representation. The organization made efforts to increase visibility, conducted more studies, and even hired a press officer for a time.

As was increasingly common practice, President Peggy Matheson, who served from 1990 to 1994, was recruited to stand for the presidency and was flattered to be asked. It was difficult to recruit people because of the considerable demands on a president's time, even with the help of a paid executive secretary/director. The decision to move from a triennial to a biennial system, with two- instead of

Margaret 'Peggy' Matheson, CFUW President 1990–1994.

three-year terms for the president and executive helped, but as one regional director commented, it was "almost impossible to put together an executive, because so many women had a multitude of family and community commitments."[2]

• • • • • • • • •

As it became clear in the middle of the decade that increased membership was not going to solve CFUW's growing budget problems, a task force led by Robin Robinson of Edmonton resulted in a major constitutional change that reduced the number of executive on the board to fourteen.[3] Previously it had included four vice presidents and seventeen regional directors as well as chairs of standing and special committees. Regional director positions were removed from the executive and some positions were consolidated. By 1998, there were four regionally based vice presidents and directors of communications; international relations; development; educational affairs, libraries, and creative arts; and legislation, resolutions, and the status of women and human rights. The only standing committee left was the Fellowships Committee. With the exception of Ontario, vice presidents served as their own regional directors and most vice presidents (VPs) served as chairs of their provincial councils, which met twice a year between annual general meetings (AGMs).[4]

Despite the worry about membership and a federal government that was increasingly preoccupied with fighting deficits and controlling social spending, CFUW kept active in advocacy and conducted a major study on universities in Canada. It submitted briefs to the 1989 Royal Commission on New Reproductive Technologies and responded to the December 1989 Montréal massacre by joining coalitions to combat violence against women through gun control legislation and helped achieve, in 1989, the successful ratification of the international convention to prohibit the use of landmines.

Peggy Matheson chose to serve two terms (four years) because she felt that two years was not long enough to consolidate the biennial-related constitutional changes that she had worked on in her earlier committee roles. She also thought that it was important to maintain strong ties with the clubs and visited almost every one during her term. A psychology major from the University of British Columbia (UBC), Matheson and her husband settled in Victoria, where she worked successively as a social worker and a stay-at-home mother, then worked for the Canadian Mental Health Association and the Greater Victoria Art Gallery.[5]

Matheson linked CFUW visibility with membership and funding and promoted Elizabeth Cureton from executive secretary to executive director. In that new role, Cureton often represented CFUW at local meetings and events, thus increasing the organization's visibility and effectiveness. A fax machine was installed in the president's home to allow easy communication with head office. By 1992, CFUW was officially incorporated and had created a database, with information on club members' academic backgrounds, interests, occupations, and potential for appointment to provincial or national boards. The financial books were also moved to head office, relieving some of the work of the Finance Committee.

Matheson's first biennial theme was "Time to Care," which focused on healthcare, threats to the environment, violence against women, and the status of women on campus. Her second biennial theme, "Visions for the Future," centred on membership, leadership, and mentoring. The chair of the Education Committee cited an American Association of University Women (AAUW) study of three thousand children in Grades 4 to 10 in twelve different communities that found that eight- and nine-year-old girls were confident and assertive but in the succeeding eight years they became much less so. Pointing to a strong relationship between mathematics and science education and adolescent self-esteem, they recommended, among other things, that girls be encouraged to tackle these subjects.[6]

CFUW did not take the membership issue lightly and the federation tackled the problem from several angles. Phyllis Scott

chaired the Forward Planning II Committee that developed a Public
Relations Standing Committee "with a budget to promote CFUW
nationally and regionally"[7]; produced recruitment slogans, bro-
chures, kits and posters; updated federation logos; and gave awards
to clubs that produced noticeable gains in membership. The committee also set a goal of increasing membership by increments of 250
a year and targeting underrepresented groups such as francophones,
women of colour, and recent graduates. There were mini-workshops
on membership for six clubs at the Saskatchewan Council meeting
as the survival of several clubs was in jeopardy without an influx
of new members. The organization also made efforts to reach out
to universities to raise CFUW's profile and interest new graduates
in joining. The results, however, were disheartening and CFUW
membership continued to decline, although not as dramatically
as that of its southern neighbour. The American Association of
University Women (AAUW) numbers dropped from 186,800 to
115,897 from 1980 to 1991, while CFUW's decline in the same period
was somewhat slower, falling from 12,109 to 11,552. Other women's
organizations were also experiencing similar declines.

Francophone membership remained at about five hundred in
1992. In addition to overburdening a few members with translation
duties, there were continuing class and philosophical divergences
between the Québec and anglophone women's movements. CFUW
largely appealed to affluent white, English-speaking women with
university education, many of whom stayed home with their children for a time and/or did volunteer work, often at an executive
level. This lifestyle was becoming increasingly unaffordable.

Using data from their newly established members' database,
CFUW found in 1994 that 40 per cent of its members were age sixty-
four or older, with decreasing numbers in younger age groups.[8] A
survey by the Montréal Lakeshore Club provides a glimpse into
members' professional affiliations. Among its 190 members, there
were seventy teachers, thirteen medical and health professionals,
eight secretarial workers, and forty-nine housewives or volunteers.[9]

Another federation survey looked into women's reasons for
joining the organization and found, once again, that friendship
was the biggest attraction. Other reasons included a desire to influence social problems, to participate in interest groups, and to find

intellectual stimulation. Asked why they left CFUW, most respondents replied that it was because of a husband's transfer to another city, insufficient time and conflicting commitments, or competition from women's groups with lower membership fees.[10] Many clubs tried to make their programming more interesting; some clubs discovered that being involved in local issues such as environmental recycling or advocacy attracted new members, and others reached out to smaller cities or towns in their region.

A year later, the organization hired a public relations coordinator on a contractual basis,[11] and on October 1992, held its first national press conference to announce its support for the latest attempt to amend the constitution, the Charlottetown Accord. It was well attended, especially by the francophone media as Québec had not formally signed on to patriation of the constitution.[12] In 1987, Brian Mulroney had negotiated the Meech Lake Accord with its "distinct society" clause, but CFUW, like most women's groups, opposed it out of concerns the controversial clause would override the hard-won *Charter of Rights and Freedoms*. Mulroney appointed the Honourable Joe Clark as minister of constitutional affairs and assigned him the task of bringing Québec into the constitutional fold. CFUW took part in the wide-ranging consultations with Canadians that were followed by government negotiations with the provinces and Indigenous groups. The result was the Charlottetown Accord, unveiled in August 1992. The National Action Committee on the Status of Women (NAC) opposed it, fearing that concessions to Québec, the provinces, and Indigenous Peoples would erode women's rights, including the rights of Indigenous women.[13] Most national women's groups, including CFUW, supported it, however, in the interest of Canadian unity. But it was all for naught; the accord was rejected in a national referendum.

CFUW held another Ottawa press conference on December 9, 1992. It was not as well attended as the previous one, being overshadowed by other news stories that day. Or, perhaps, the subject matter was just not as interesting to the media. The press conference launched CFUW's latest survey, "The Women in Universities Project: A survey of the status of female faculty and students at Canadian universities." The study had an interesting genesis. In 1990, Tammy Irwin, in the wake of the Montréal tragedy, urged clubs to contact the universities in their communities to assess what measures were being taken to tackle sexual discrimination, campus violence, alcohol abuse, and other issues affecting female students.[14] The Education Committee then proposed a resolution that urged universities to attract and keep more female professors. When it passed in 1992, the CFUW resolution called on universities to implement employment equity, affirmative action, flexible part-time employment, a safe environment, and to support programs for women. The Oakville Club, frustrated with the glacial pace of change in Canadian universities, began a survey that soon morphed into a national study. It investigated ten areas of academic activities that affected women, asking questions that were meant to elicit descriptive and qualitative information rather than statistics. Club volunteers personally undertook the distribution and pick-up of the questionnaires and most clubs participated, with the French-speaking clubs providing translations. The highlighted issues in the survey included equity, hiring and tenure, course content, prevention of harassment, and ensuring both a safe working environment and adequate support services for female staff and students.[15]

This was a timely initiative as many universities were beginning to address these issues of their own accord. The legacy of the survey was a profile of a woman-friendly university environment that was widely circulated to both high schools and universities and included a checklist of things to consider in making a campus welcoming to women. Both the Association of Universities and Colleges of Canada (AUCC) and the Canadian Association of University Teachers (CAUT) endorsed the profile and Marilyn Taylor of CAUT noted that it "will generate important discussion about priorities and specific objectives."[16] The survey was later published in the collection *The Illusion of Inclusion: Women in Post-Secondary Education*, edited by Jacqueline Stalker and Susan Prentice, and was featured in a March 1993 article in *Policy Options*, published by the Institute for Research on Public Policy.[17] By 1994, two of the survey's designers were preparing a national conference on equal opportunities for women in post-secondary education.[18] The survey also gave clubs a welcome opportunity to reach out to university presidents, staff, and students. In the earlier years of the organization, CFUW had had much closer access to universities—campuses were smaller, there were regular social events with students, and many of the federation members were academic instructors and/or deans of women. CFUW had lost that connection.

Another royal commission of importance to CFUW, was the Royal Commission on New Reproductive Technologies, the Baird Commission, appointed by the Mulroney government in 1989. Past President Margaret Strongitharm had watched with interest the social implications of reproductive technologies, and that year CFUW passed a resolution calling for appropriate legislation to regulate them. Headed by UBC professor Patricia Baird, the commission studied the legal, ethical, and social implications of technologies such as in vitro fertilization, surrogacy, and artificial insemination. CFUW had requested that the commission focus on "new" reproductive technologies to ensure that the controversial issue of abortion be excluded.

Like computers, these technologies were opening up possibilities that were both exciting and frightening. Many Canadians resisted any effort to play with nature in the sacred area of motherhood and worried about the potential for "designer babies." Feminists were particularly concerned about sex selection and the exploitation of low-income women as baby factories for the wealthy. Still, as long as the technologies existed, the need to regulate them was pressing.[19] CFUW submitted a brief to the commission that was so well received that commissioner Maureen McTeer asked the organization to pass resolutions on the regulation of specific issues such as in vitro fertilization and the donation of gametes and embryos. She thought that such resolutions would further passage of legislation and that CFUW was the best organization to undertake such research. With the help of molecular geneticist Dr. Mary Saunders, Oakville Club member, CFUW responded to this request.[20]

In November 1993, the commission issued its final report entitled, *Proceed with Care*, reflecting the topic's intrinsic controversy. The report's recommendations were aimed at providing oversight on the development and practices of the new reproductive technologies and protecting Canadians from unsafe applications and misinformation. After the commission's report was released, the government shared proposed federal legislation with CFUW, and the organization passed resolutions asking the government to enact and enforce laws based on respect for individual rights and prevention of the exploitation of individuals through commercialization. CFUW also specified prohibitions on certain procedures such as the use of nuclear transfer technology for the cloning of complete human beings; purchase or sale of human eggs, sperm, and embryos for profit; the culling of sperm or eggs from cadavers except in the case of informed prior consent; and the arranging or advertising of surrogacy services for profit. These resolutions blended the need for ethical restrictions with giving hope to infertile couples and offered some protection to the public from misuse and/or excessive commercialization. The legislation was long in coming, but a bill, after consultation with CFUW and other women's groups, was finally passed in 2004.[21]

Phyllis Scott served as CFUW president from 1994 to 1996,[22] coming into office just as the effects of the 1990s economic recession were beginning to hit. Economic restructuring and government cutbacks were becoming common buzzwords and politicians and other commentators worked up the perceived need to reduce the deficit to a level of near hysteria. Both the Progressive Conservative (PC) government—in power until 1993—and the Liberals—who governed from 1993 to 1997—made major cuts to government services that affected CFUW, the larger women's movement, and many social safety-net programs. Adapting to economic realities, Scott conducted executive meetings by teleconference, taking advantage of the generosity of the nearby regional federal Status of Women office, which made its phones available. A great believer in exercise, she was known to interrupt meetings that had dragged on too long and lead her fellow delegates in an exercise break. She did this while dressed up as Carol Burnett's cleaning lady character, complete with mop and pail.

Government budget cuts—especially provincial education cuts—had an effect on a variety of programs. The Library Committee reported a sharp spike in applications for its reading stimulation grant in Alberta, where severe budget cuts had forced some libraries to charge a fee for membership. Women's programs that supported services such as women's shelters and rape crisis centres also felt the effects of cutbacks because of budget cuts to the advisory councils on the status of women. Women's organizations that relied on government funding were forced into major restructuring or faltered altogether. CFUW, on the other hand, became aware that one of its strengths was its lack of reliance on government funds.

CFUW joined other women's organizations in protesting many cuts such as the 1992 cancellation of the court challenges program. Originally introduced in 1978 to protect minority language rights, it had been extended in 1985 to include any equality rights challenges to federal laws. In its resolution, CFUW called it a unique program that assisted disadvantaged individuals and groups—including women, the disabled, the poor, Indigenous Canadians, minority groups, immigrants, prisoners, lesbians, gays, and refugees—to exercise their equality and language rights under the Canadian charter and resolved to work with other equality-seeking groups to restore and improve the program. An article in CFUW-FCFDU *Journal* highlighted the work one of these groups, the Women's Legal Education, and Action Fund (LEAF) which was assisting a female civil engineering professor who had been denied a tenure-track position. In this case, LEAF was trying to establish the important principle of systemic discrimination in the courts. LEAF, established by many of the same women who had fought the earlier constitutional battles, had already taken on seventy-five cases and won decisions of benefit to Canadian women.[23]

Although it happened in late 1989, the shooting of fourteen female engineering students at Polytechnique Montréal cast a shadow over women's groups in the 1990s and beyond. Initially, there was mourning and CFUW created a new memorial scholarship to honour the women. Then, when women were able to move on from grieving, they turned to anger and to action, making demands for changes that might ensure that such a thing could never happen again. Following two years of advocacy by women's groups, the Canadian Parliament named December 6 as the National Day of Remembrance & Action on Violence Against Women. AFDU Montréal asked the federation to distribute a petition in favour of gun control and CFUW joined other women's organizations in this demand.

With these calls for change coming from women's groups as well as some male allies, the PC government of Brian Mulroney established the Canadian Panel on Violence Against Women in 1991.

While it brought visibility to the issue, the panel also duplicated the work of a House of Commons subcommittee on the status of women, which recommended "adequate funding for shelters and rape crisis centres, an affordable housing policy, mandatory gender equality training for judges and Members of Parliament," and violence-prevention/gender-equality education in schools across the country.[24]

Mary Collins, minister of the status of women, spoke at the 1991 CFUW AGM and later announced an initiative to counter family violence, promising $136 million over four years to combat wife battering, child abuse, and elder abuse. CFUW congratulated her on this initiative, but many were skeptical of the government's announcement in light of recent budget cuts that had reduced support for child care, women's shelters, and affordable housing—the very things that would help women escape domestic violence.[25]

In the end, the panel's report, "Changing the Landscape: Ending Violence—Achieving Equality," was published just before an election campaign and was thus largely ignored. Its failure was helped along by NAC and the National Organization of Immigrant and Visible Minority Women of Canada (NOIVMWC), both of which vehemently condemned the report because it lacked representation from women of colour and gave short shrift to their issues. By now growing internal divisions within the women's movement, based on diverse socioeconomic status, ethnicity, and sexual orientation, foreshadowed the later collapse of NAC. In the meantime, CFUW continued to stake its claim on the movement's moderate wing—feminism had become too big for one organization.

CFUW took tremendous pride in its advocacy role, which was gaining in strength and confidence. A photo (see next page), used on the front cover of the 1991 CFUW-FCFDU *Journal*, shows Peggy Matheson and other CFUW executives seated at a table with Mary Collins.[26] The federation's advocacy was built on the foundation of its own grassroots—clubs and committees put forward resolutions that were discussed, amended, debated, and voted on at the AGM. It was a lengthy and vigorous process. Once resolutions were passed, they were sent to the relevant level of government. At the federal level, the federation continued its advocacy through a week of consultations during which CFUW's representatives made presentations

March 1991 meeting with Hon. Mary Collins, minister responsible for the status of women. Left to right: Peggy Matheson, Susan Mohamdee (Russell), Elizabeth Cureton, unknown, unknown, unknown, Mary Collins; standing is Kay Stanley (Coordinator, Status of Women Canada).

to government on relevant resolutions. The meetings with government officials were initially arranged through the minister for the status of women, but after 1993, they were scheduled by the federation's executive director. In 1990, CFUW began to include IFUW resolutions in their briefs to the government.

Over time, CFUW's advocacy with the federal government grew from an annual meeting to year-round consultations with various cabinet ministers as well as with the Liberal and New Democratic Party (NDP) Members of Parliament, often with their critics for women's affairs. Growing contacts also meant more invitations to consult. In 1994, for example, the federal government invited CFUW and twenty-six other national women's organizations to participate in a teleconference following the speech from the throne that opened the first session of the thirty-fifth Parliament. Secretary of state for the status of women outlined the government's position on women's issues and gave each organization the opportunity to ask a question.[27]

CFUW did not confine itself to so-called women's issues. The new Global Peace and Security Subcommittee on Legislation protested the Gulf War in 1990–1991 and called for the abolition of nuclear weapons. It is unlikely that the government listened very carefully to either of these delegations, but there were other issues on which the federation had more success. CFUW clubs had a strong interest in the environment and this was reflected in resolutions, passed at the AGM, that were aimed at stopping ozone depletion (1993); dealing with the disposal of household hazardous waste (1990); promoting alternative energy resources; and conducting a review of the Canadian nuclear industry (1997).

Clubs were encouraged to follow up on federation initiatives, although coordination on issues that crossed jurisdiction was sometimes a challenge. Matheson created a summary of the federation's meetings with government and urged clubs to direct their efforts to persuading local MPs and provincial governments of their policy decisions. While clubs were encouraged to support federal advocacy, they also passed local resolutions addressing issues at the municipal government level.

Regional and provincial councils conducted their own process of provincial advocacy, especially in education.[28] In 1992, Nova

Scotia regional director, Jean Wagener, presented CFUW policies to the Nova Scotia government, to members of the official opposition, and to Mary Clancy, the federal Liberal status of women critic from Halifax.[29] The Ontario council met with the provincial minister responsible for women's issues at Queen's Park.[30]

CFUW attracted leaders interested in advocacy. In 1996, new president Betty Bayless, made advocacy a priority choosing the theme "Democracy Is Not a Spectator Sport." She had earlier made her presence felt as chair of the Legislation Committee by conducting workshops at the 1993 AGM that taught women how to hold all-candidates meetings, and presenting CFUW policy to newly elected MPs. Bayless, working with Susan Russell—who was at that time chair of the Status of Women and Human Rights Committee and soon to become CFUW's executive director—and Marilyn Letts produced a handbook called *Nuts and Bolts* in 1995. The project was funded through a grant of $20,000 from Status of Women Canada and over the years the useful book underwent many revisions. Russell later recalled that CFUW had originally asked for a grant of $5,000—ever the fiscally responsible organization—and she thought the meeting was over when a bureaucrat announced, "We don't give out grants for $5,000." She was about to leave when the government official told her that, "We do give out grants of $20,000!"[31] CFUW had to learn some important lessons in this changing environment; in accordance with the Lobbyists Registration Act that came into effect in 1989 to govern the registration of paid lobbyists, their delegates were instructed not to use the word lobby.[32] CFUW could advocate, but it could NOT lobby.

American-born Betty Bayless studied mathematics and computer science in St. Paul, Minnesota, and began her career working for Sperry Univac, where she helped develop software for missile guidance and automated computer design. Although she was a whiz at computers, her true love was advocacy and she became executive director of Common Cause Minnesota, a state branch of the American National Lobbying Association. During her varied career, she worked for the League for Women Voters and the AAUW in St. Paul. But she found herself putting her husband's career ahead of her own and followed him to Montréal in 1984, where she joined two university women's clubs. When her husband's employment took them to Saint John, New Brunswick, Bayless became a member of the Kennebecasis Valley (KV) Club from 1987 to 1990 and worked on sports for the disabled, including the Special Olympics. Returning to Montréal, she became president of UWC of Montréal Inc. and the public relations director of UWC of Montréal Lakeshore. When she began her term as CFUW president, it was her husband's turn to follow her to Ottawa, where she helped to advance reform on gun control and landmines through strategic coalitions.

Bayless expanded on CFUW's consultations on Parliament Hill by instituting the tradition of "a day on the hill"—when board members went to CFUW meetings in Ottawa, they would attend Question Period, visit their own member of Parliament, or take a tour of the House of Commons. In one of the CFUW major initiatives mentioned above, Bayless partnered with Mines Action Canada in a campaign to ban anti-personnel landmines. These weapons, activated by pressure, tripwire, or remote detonation, were intended to kill or disable soldiers but, as with all war weaponry, they also victimized—and continue to victimize—civilians. The late Princess Diana was among the more famous spokespersons for an international coalition that came together in 1992 to campaign against them. CFUW passed a resolution in 1996 calling for a ban on the production, sale, import, export, stockpiling, and operational use of antipersonnel landmines. The federation also opened political doors for the larger group, Mines Action Canada, using their political connections to give the coalition access to government officials, particularly Foreign Affairs Minister Lloyd Axworthy. CFUW believes that their approach to winning him over helped ensure the campaign's success.[33] The organization convinced the federal government that it could become a world leader by establishing a Department of Defence Demining Action Centre, sponsor an international conference to develop strategies for a worldwide ban, and define mine-free zones in regions and hemispheres. Out of the conference, formally called the Convention on the Prohibition of the Use, Stockpiling, Production and Transfer of Anti-Personnel Mines and on Their Destruction, came the Ottawa Treaty. This legal document obligated each signatory state—Canada signed along with 121 other states—to eliminate landmines from its arsenal within a set time frame. Susan Russell was present at the signing in Ottawa in

December 1997 and considers this one of CFUW's biggest advocacy successes.[34] It was considered a major achievement for the governments who signed on to the treaty as well as for the vast network of international non-governmental organizations (NGOs) that played a key role in generating support for it.[35]

In response to the tragedy at the Polytechnique Montréal, CFUW's other major successful coalition, also mentioned above, dealt with gun control. Even before the Canadian Panel on Violence Against Women had concluded its report, CFUW had passed a resolution in 1990 calling for a ban on automatic and semi-automatic rifles and restrictions on firearm permits. In the summer of 1992, the organization considered four resolutions on gun control and, true to form, carefully researched the issue before articulating its policy two years later. An interim resolution, which originated with the Nepean Club, called rather vaguely for appropriate steps to prevent violence against women. When they were ready, the 1994 resolutions asked the federal and provincial governments to establish a cost-effective national registry of all firearms and to monitor gun permits; to seize firearms from any person under a restraining order; to institute a total ban on assault weapons; to enforce the ban on importing prohibited weapons; and to sponsor gun amnesty days for disposal of unwanted weapons.

The other resolution dealt with the sale of ammunition. Under Bayless' guidance, CFUW endorsed the position of the Coalition for Gun Control. After several aborted efforts, Justice Minister Allan Rock ushered in Bill C-68, the Firearms Act (1995) that created the Canadian firearms registry to be managed by the RCMP. CFUW, which had handled some of the back-and-forth negotiations with Rock, joined other groups in celebrating the victory. In the process of helping to bring it about, Mavis Moore, who became CFUW president in 1998, became something of an expert on the bill.[36] Again, there was a need for vigilance, as there had been with the constitution. Later governments would cancel portions of the registry due to alleged "cost overruns," although political considerations always lurked in the background. Perhaps CFUW regretted its earlier resolution calling for a "cost effective" registry.

Ministers, deputy ministers, and staff sometimes sought out CFUW opinions. In 1998, Bayless reported that government asked for their input into the closure of the Health Canada research lab, as well as on issues such as birth control, Canada Pension Plan reform, the 2001 Canada census on unpaid and volunteer work, and child custody. Many of these concerns were of special interest to the CFUW demographic. As well, in 1998, Bayless testified at the pre-budget hearings of the House of Commons standing committee on finance and met with Minister of Finance Paul Martin about the need to maintain funding for women's programs.[37]

When Mavis Moore followed Bayless as president, she continued and expanded the "day on the Hill" tradition, speaking with great affection of these opportunities to influence legislators. Susan Russell remembers being invited to go with her to visit her friend NDP MP Svend Robinson on one of these expeditions.[38] Born in Saskatchewan on a prairie farm, Mavis Moore was a member of the CCF/NDP, served on the Saskatoon Citizens Advisory on Transit, the Saskatchewan Legal Aid Commission, and the University of Saskatchewan senate.[39] She was the exception among presidents of this decade in two respects: one, she declined the chair of the Committee on International Relations after her term, and two, she continued to work throughout her presidency as ward clerk of the intensive care unit in the Saskatoon Hospital.

When CFUW needed a new executive director, Moore hired Susan (Mohamdee) Russell, who served from 1999 to 2010. Chosen for her experience in advocacy, she had chaired CFUW's Status of Women and Human Rights Committee in the mid-1990s and before that was vice president of Ontario and Ontario East regional director. A committed internationalist, Russell was CFUW representative to UNESCO from the mid-1980s to mid-1990s.[40]

How effective were CFUW's lobbying efforts? Advocacy is a delicate art.[41] Timing is important—the right amount of pressure must be exerted at the right time; confrontation that embarrasses the government can be effective but it can also backfire. Conciliation, the area in which CFUW excelled, especially when done behind the scenes, can also be effective. CFUW had success with the landmines treaty and the gun registry, where it had formed part of a much larger coalition. Susan Russell felt that while CFUW was small, we "knew people who knew people who knew people." Her own maxim was that once inside the door of the minister's office, "be nice to the woman at the front desk."[42] CFUW had connections, but not numbers, and was reluctant to be confrontational. Teaming up with groups who were willing to be confrontational could be effective; this had worked in gaining a Royal Commission on the Status of Women in 1967.

Advocacy can also be frustrating. In 1999, President Moore noted that members expressed a keen interest in our dealings with government. "We are making a difference but sometimes it doesn't happen as quickly as we would like."[43] As a 1998 report of the Status of Women Committee complained,

> Senior's Benefit and Phase II of the CPP have still not been introduced, nor has the long-awaited Bill on New Reproductive Technologies. The Child Custody and Access Hearings have revealed such a high level of emotionalism that it is sincerely hoped the primary focus—the best interests of the child—will not be lost. Pay Equity still has not been achieved.[44]

Sometimes it took repeated tries, and saying the same thing over and over again, like water "dripping on a stone."[45] But then, suddenly, the message got through.

President Phyllis Scott thought that CFUW passed too many resolutions and proposed that, "we could become highly visible if we focused on one or two resolutions, which we pursue diligently in all sorts of ways until our goals are met."[46] While she certainly had a point, these resolutions originated with clubs, and clubs were the foundation of the organization. Too many resolutions were perhaps the price to be paid for democracy.

Records seldom indicate how often CFUW resolutions translated into legislative outcomes, and CFUW officials noted that tracking the status of established policies was difficult. But it does appear that CFUW spoke with some authority on behalf of their constituency— women. In 1992, the Alberta regional director reported that the legalization of midwifery was imminent and credited CFUW's 1991 pro-midwifery resolution.[47] Governments found CFUW a congenial women's group to consult, especially considering their modest fiscal and political demands and their good connections with elites in government, business, and the civil service. Reading CFUW's oft-repeated adages about governments respecting their reasoned views, does, however, bring to mind Laura Sabia's observation that women's groups were politely listened to, complimented on their stylish appearance, and then ignored. Now they were being complimented on their thorough research. Perhaps that is progress.

In the next decade, CFUW would face new and ongoing challenges—the long-gun registry, the Kyoto Protocol, violence against women, and women's poverty. In response to setbacks (compounded by federal spending cuts) and backlash in regard to the achievements of the women's movement, CFUW became leaders in new coalitions created to address them.

As a self-funded women's organization, CFUW was not silenced as effectively as others were during the tenure of the Conservative government of Stephen Harper, when advocacy was seriously curtailed, and only the opposition parties were listening.

Footnotes for this chapter can be found online at:
http://secondstorypress.ca/resources

Chapter 11
THE MILLENNIAL DECADE

Never retract, never explain, never apologize—get the thing done and let them howl!

— Nellie McClung

This famous quote from a member of the Famous Five still resonates with Canadian women today. To usher in the new millennium, a group led by Frances Wright of the Famous Five Foundation, obtained permission to put up statues of these heroines of the Persons Case. The memorials, sculpted by Alberta artist Barbara Paterson, depict the Famous Five hearing the news that the Judicial Committee of the Privy Council (JCPC) had ruled in their favour, making women "persons" under the Canadian constitution. The first statue went up in Olympic Plaza in Calgary in 1999, and another went up on Parliament Hill near the Senate in Ottawa in 2000. A millennial project worthy of all Canadian women, the placement of the statues in such prominent locations represents a major victory.[1] In 2008, CFUW joined the Famous Five Committee in an event on the Hill to celebrate all those who worked on this project to recognize women in the commemorative landscape.

On Persons Day, October 18, 2000, clubs in Winnipeg, Portage la Prairie, and Brandon launched their publication *Extraordinary Ordinary Women: Manitoba Women and Their Stories.* Proceeds went to scholarships, and, by telling the stories of forty-two remarkable Manitoba women during the past 250 years, the book contributed to the social history of Manitoba.[2] Other successful publications and historic markers appeared in this millennial decade, including the launch of an updated history of the Vancouver Club, *Women Lead the Way*.[3] UWC Montréal marked their eightieth anniversary by holding an event with members dressing up as flappers, in accordance with the era of their founding.

But the millennial decade was not a happy one for women as government funding cuts and attacks on former gains continued. The previous decade's successes with the landmines treaty and with establishing the gun registry encouraged CFUW to seek coalitions with other groups. The federation hoped that these alliances would help give it greater visibility and relevance and increase its membership, which was now fluctuating between nine and ten thousand. In another attempt to increase its numbers, CFUW instituted two new membership types—associate and student. The organization gave certificates of recognition to clubs with significant membership increases over the previous year and CFUW began to publish a slick new annual report directed toward outside stakeholders. As

We Are Persons! Famous Five Monument (Ottawa) commemorating the Persons Case.

small clubs were at the greatest risk of closure, a new small club grants program helped them send representatives to the national annual meeting. AGM registration went online, and the Ontario Council became incorporated.

At the national office, CFUW maintained as many as four full-time staff members through most of these years. Executive director Susan Russell guided CFUW through this challenging decade. With the office now on Bank Street, she was aided by long-time staffer, Betty Dunlop, who took over from Dorothy Holland working on fellowships, a time- and paper-devouring enterprise before it too, went online. As well, there was a receptionist and various part- or full-time staff to deal with bookkeeping, advocacy, and member services. Volunteers from the Ottawa Club continued to help out as well.[4] Later in the decade, during Patricia DuVal's tenure as president, CFUW incorporated more changes that allowed the executive to respond quickly to events and government requests for information in those situations where CFUW did not have a policy. CFUW also created an Ad Hoc Committee to examine the policy book, looking for possible gaps and omissions that might be remedied. But the major challenges of the millennial decade would be political.

Roberta Brooks, a self-professed professional volunteer, was the first CFUW president of the millennial decade, serving from 2000 to 2002.[5] In 2001, she instituted a town hall format for the AGM plenary session.[6] During her presidency, Canada hosted the successful 2001 IFUW triennial conference in Ottawa in honour of Linda Souter, who was elected IFUW vice president, and then president in 1998. CFUW presented three resolutions, four Canadians ran for office, nine hundred delegates attended, and, to top it all off, CFUW clubs raised $85,000. Some of the highlights of the meeting included a Canadian workshop on "Globalization and Peace: Conflicting Agendas,"[7] poster presentations, and events at the Canadian Museum of Civilization in Hull, Québec (now the Canadian Museum of History in Gatineau, Québec). There were intense debates on resolutions related to such issues as child soldiers, while old friendships were renewed and new ones forged.

Many Canadian members who participated in the popular Links of Friendship program, that twinned clubs from different countries, hoped to meet their email pen pals in person.[8] One of the first clubs

CFUW delegates to meetings with government, March 2000.
Left to right: Sheila Laidlaw (Status of Women), Barbara
Himmel (Legislation), Mavis Moore (CFUW President).

to take part in this program was AFDU Québec, which twinned with Montpellier, France. By 2001, forty-eight Canadian clubs were linked with IFUW affiliates. Expanding on connections made at the 2001 meeting, CFUW Sherbrooke and District sponsored a 2005 exchange between the Netherlands Federation of University Women (VVAO) and ten clubs in the Québec and Ottawa areas. CFUW members hosted Dutch members for several days while they visited Ottawa, Sherbrooke, Québec, and Montréal, taking in meetings, conferences, potluck dinners, and sightseeing excursions.[9] The highlight of the clubs' year, the exchange garnered national, provincial, and local media coverage for CFUW. It might even have contributed to an increase in membership. The Canadians were soon making plans to visit their counterparts in the Netherlands in anticipation of the 2009 IFUW conference in Manchester, England.[10]

In the early years of the decade, federal advocacy delegations still spent three or four days on Parliament Hill meeting with ministers to discuss resolutions and other issues.[11] The resolutions of 2001 covered conservation of the Canadian water supply with a categorical rejection of water exports, and research and education into the non-essential or cosmetic uses of pesticides, particularly in parklands and gardens. CFUW delegates also presented a brief to a senate committee on the Endangered Species Act.[12]

In the field of health, CFUW asked for a federal inquiry into health care and the inclusion of home-care services in the Canada Health Act. The organization also requested the development of ethical guidelines regarding stem cell research as recommended by the Canadian Institutes of Health Research and advocated for organ and tissue donation.[13] In 2001, Prime Minister Jean Chrétien appointed the Commission on the Future of Health Care in Canada under Roy Romanow to find ways to ensure the sustainability of the public health-care system. In preparation of the CFUW brief to this commission, Margaret McGovern, the Ontario Council's status of women chair, conducted a nation-wide health-care questionnaire.[14] Romanow's 2002 report recommended additional budget transfers from the federal government to provincial and territorial governments.[15] Although some health critics were disappointed that the report did not suggest innovations in health-care delivery that would reduce costs, CFUW still credited this as an advocacy win.

CFUW Welland members sort books for their 1973 book sale, held annually to raise money for scholarships.

Provincial and/or regional councils and clubs responded to severe educational budget cuts that were eroding the quality of public education and leading to an upswing in private education with a resolution to affirm the value of public education.[16] Other resolutions called for a cap on primary grade sizes and the provision of tax relief for teachers who used their own resources to support their classrooms.[17] After some clubs had done charitable work with inner-city dwellers, including people with disabilities and those suffering from addiction, the British Columbia provincial council passed a resolution on addiction services for their province. Working with the federation, the director of legislation also launched a letter-writing campaign to provincial ministries.[18]

With CFUW policy in hand, clubs reinforced the various messages at the community level by speaking to town councils and, occasionally, local members of Parliament. CFUW Prince George worked with Capsule College and the Start Where You're At Society, a transition house for recovering addicts. In Vaughan, Ontario, the club partnered with the York school board to host "Spotlight on Women in Science and Technology," inviting speakers to Seneca

College to encourage young girls to study math and science. More than three hundred Grade 7 and 8 girls participated.[19] Clubs could also author their own resolutions, although some chafed at the amount of work this entailed. A well-researched resolution could take a year to prepare and clubs would then be asked to state their resolution in no more than four pages, including background notes.

Club members, becoming more activist, perhaps, than in previous decades, began to join women in a growing number of marches and vigils, particularly to remember the victims of the Montréal massacre and to raise awareness about violence against women. In 2007, the South Shore Montréal Club organized a Polytechnique Montréal candlelight memorial in conjunction with the Montréal city mission and the Sherbrooke Club held a vigil at Bishop's University.[20] CFUW members also attended events commemorating International Women's Day on March 8. While this day had been marked in Europe much earlier than in North America, it was recognized in Québec in 1973, the United Nations in 1977, and in English Canada (Toronto) in 1978. Organizers of the Toronto event, the International Women's Day Coalition, had to negotiate internal conflicts between white women and women of colour, between socialist and radical feminists, and between lesbians and straight women. By the mid-1980s, however, the coalition and the women's movement generally, had become more inclusive, paving the way for moderate groups such as CFUW to join their marches.[21] As will be further explored in Chapter 14, CFUW members also participated in international women's events such as the World March of Women.[22]

The bread and butter of most clubs continued to be the social and fundraising events such as garden tours, fashion shows, book sales, public lectures on a wide range of topics, and travelogues.[23] In Vancouver, Hycroft was the social focus, although the building demanded a great deal of maintenance and had to be rented out to make it financially sustainable. Nonetheless, the heritage building continues to be a source of pride for the Vancouver Club and a place for club activities, entertaining, and social events.[24]

Jacqueline Jacques, who served as president from 2002 to 2004, was motivated to join CFUW by the Montréal massacre that occurred not far from her home. Shocked and angry, she was moved by a television interview given by the mother of one of the fourteen victims. As the woman was herself a member, she suggested that people who wanted to help could contact FCFDU. Jacques did just that and soon found herself working on a draft resolution for a firearms registry, a major political initiative of the 1990s. Jacqueline Jacques had graduated from the Université de Montréal in 1969 with a BA in the humanities. She was really interested in computer science, but it was not then offered at the university. So she went to the head of the science department and told him that they should create such a program. When the university did so, Jacques transitioned into it and graduated with a BSc in computer science in 1973, one of only seven women in a class of eighty-eight. The program equipped her well for a career that gave her the autonomy and financial security she believed all women needed. Multi-talented, she was equally at home as a producer, comedian, and actor.[25] She was pleased to become the first francophone president of CFUW in 2002 and embarked on making its website bilingual. She also put the CFUW policy book online, complete with a search function that made all the resolutions easily accessible to members, clubs, and councils. Jacques visited almost all the clubs during her term, a task that many presidents described as the most enjoyable part of their terms, albeit time-consuming.[26]

Jacques attributed CFUW successes in advocacy to being well known to government, articulating policies that were accurate and reflected consensus.[27] She extended a thank you to her predecessors for writing *Nuts and Bolts* and encouraged clubs to follow its useful guidelines. The gun registry resolution that Jacques had first worked on when she joined the Montréal Club was eventually presented to the AGM and passed. Many women's (and men's) organizations were calling for such a measure in the aftermath of the tragedy. Jacques witnessed the finalization of the registration of firearms under the new gun control legislation during her time as president, but there would be many setbacks on this issue and many more years of advocacy ahead for the federation.[28] Another highlight of these years was seeing Canada sign the Kyoto Protocol in 1997 and ratified in Parliament in 2002. This international environmental accord set Canada's target at a 6 per cent reduction in carbon emissions by 2012, but Jacques was disappointed to learn that there were no plans for implementation. She had reason to be concerned.

There were occasions when the government needed a friendly reminder. In June 2002, for example, the Refugee Appeals Division (RAD) had been scheduled to come into effect, under the provisions of the *Immigration and Refugee Protection Act* (*IRPA*). When this had still not happened by 2004, CFUW, always sensitive to human rights, decided to jog the federal government's memory. The federation also passed a resolution asking the government to update Sections 318 and 319 of the *Criminal Code* on hate crimes to include sexual orientation in the definition of "identifiable group," which at the time included colour, race, religion, and ethnic origin. National origin, age, sex, and mental or physical disability were added in 2014, and gender identity and expression in 2017.[29]

There were still times when the federal government requested CFUW input. Senator Landon Pearson, on behalf of the prime minister, asked for help in preparing Canada's National Plan of Action for Children (NPA) as a follow-up to the 2002 special session on children at the UN General Assembly. Two Guelph members, Pat Fisk and Liz McGraw, who had helped craft the CFUW child-care policy, worked on it, stressing the need for accessible, affordable, quality care for preschoolers. They also emphasized the need to support families and expressed concerns about children living in poverty. In another initiative, Deborah Cook, vice president of CFUW Kitchener-Waterloo advised on the Prime Minister's Task Force on Women Entrepreneurs. She outlined some of the challenges that women faced such as access to financing, child care, education and training for girls, and second-language training for immigrant women.[30]

Rose Beatty[31] began her two-year term as president in 2004 and at the 2005 AGM in Oakville articulated the new five-year strategic goal of becoming nationally recognized as a women's equality-seeking organization by parliamentarians, other organizations, the media, and the general public. It proved to be a timely decision—the 2006 election of Conservative PM Stephen Harper saw dramatic slashes to funding of women's programs and restrictions on advocacy work by non-profit organizations. By the end of Beatty's term, the National Action Committee on the Status of Women (NAC) had effectively ceased to function, and many other women's organizations were struggling. This CFUW gesture represented a shift in emphasis more than a substantive change. CFUW had always played a role in advocacy to varying degrees, from suffrage to the Royal Commission on the Status of Women (RCSW). Now, in the wake of government funding cuts and threats to non-profit advocacy, CFUW re-focused its efforts toward the advancement of women's equality.

In 2005, CFUW was still able to arrange meetings with federal government officials, although trouble was brewing. The status of women portfolio, for example, was added to the Department of Canadian Heritage and the overloaded minister found little time to meet with women's groups. In a meeting with Bruce Carson (assistant to Stephen Harper), and Lynne Yelich (status of women critic), representatives of the Conservative Party (who were then in opposition), the latter chose to focus on the education section of CFUW's brief. When the women tried to raise the gun registry issue, Yelich indicated that the Conservative Party supported gun control, just not the gun registry. CFUW persisted despite indications that some parliamentarians (from all parties) were considering voting against it—ostensibly out of concern for the cost of the registry. With clearly eroding support on the Hill, CFUW re-established contact with the Gun Control Coalition and participated in its postcard campaign to support the registry. CFUW encouraged members to write to their MPs as well as to Canadian chiefs of police, furnishing them with statistics on the positive effect gun registration had on preventing violence against women.[32] CFUW clubs and provincial councils wrote to their local representatives in record numbers on this issue and to encourage and assist them, the federation established a new tool, the *Women in Action e-journal*. The gun-control issue demonstrates how slow change can be, how necessary vigilance is, and how easily victories can turn into defeat.

CFUW also returned to an older issue in this decade. Following a complaint that women were being mistreated in federal prisons, the federation participated in a coalition of non-governmental organizations initiated by the Canadian Association of Elizabeth Fry Societies in 2002.[33] The group met with Correctional Services Canada (CSC) and the solicitor general's office to complain that little progress had been made in response to a 1996 Commission of Inquiry into Events at the Prison for Women in Kingston. Chaired by Madam Justice Louise Arbour, the commission report recommended the elimination of male guards and a holistic, woman-centred approach to corrections. CFUW passed a resolution urging the government to establish an independent, external, oversight mechanism for federal prisons for women and held consultations with CSC in 2004. They reported that although the government was not abiding by the Arbour report or had plans to make any changes, the meeting still left them feeling optimistic but "not hopeful."[34]

CFUW members continued to be devoted stewards of the environment. In 2007, the Ontario Council chose CFUW member Elizabeth May to be guest speaker at their AGM. May had recently left her job as executive director of the Sierra Club of Canada to run for leadership of the Green party and she spoke on bulk water exports, water sustainability, and the threat to Canada's sovereignty over its water resources.[35] This issue was one that the Ontario Council was familiar with. It had served on the provincial government's advisory panel on the Great Lakes Charter Annex Agreement in 2006 and commented on the proposed Clean Water Act of 2005.[36] CFUW also passed a resolution concerning the pollution of fish and their habitat in Canada's coastal waters, stressing the need to enforce the Fisheries Act.[37]

In 2005, the Ontario Council also led a major advocacy initiative related to family law. It joined a vocal coalition of groups opposed to the use of private and/or faith-based arbitration to resolve family law disputes in the Muslim community. The controversy began when the privately owned Ontario-based Islamic Institute of Civil Justice announced that, under Ontario's *Arbitration Act*, Muslims could use faith-based arbitration to resolve family disputes. With fears of terrorism running high so soon after the 2001 attack on the World Trade Centre in New York City, there was a public outcry against what was perceived to be an imposition of sharia, or Islamic law on Ontario. Most Canadian feminists asserted that the law infringed the rights of Muslim women under the Canadian *Charter of Rights and Freedoms* and the Ontario government was forced to order a full review of the legislation chaired by Marion Boyd, former NDP attorney-general. Boyd issued a report in 2004 that defended faith-based arbitration so long as it did not violate Canadian law and noted its use by Jews and Catholics in Ontario to avoid costly court battles.[38]

In meetings between Marion Boyd and the Canadian Council of Muslim Women (CCMW), the National Association of Visible and Minority Women of Canada (NIOVIMC), and other women's organizations, it became clear that support for the charter by minority women's groups was tempered by their marginal status as immigrants, their relative poverty, and their limited access to quality legal representation. While the Muslim women's groups opposed the particular form of arbitration in this case and acknowledged the difficulties of putting such a process into practice across widely different Muslim communities, they were not categorically opposed to a good system of family arbitration.[39] Boyd herself cautioned that the Ontario situation could set a precedent, leading to universal rejection of any system of private arbitration.[40] The eventual outcome was the *Family Statute Law Amendment Act* of 2006, which eliminated private arbitration in family disputes. The Ontario Council's vice president called it "an important force in preventing the equality-destroying religious arbitration in Ontario,"[41] and counted the win as an advocacy success. CFUW was proud to have been cited in Hansard, the official transcript of debates in the legislature.

Near the end of Rose Beatty's term, the advocacy terrain shifted noticeably. Having grown tired of funding women's organizations only to be criticized by them, governments had already begun to tie funding more closely to specific projects rather than to operational costs.[42] But the funding issue would take on new dimensions with the election of Stephen Harper, who had united the Reform and Progressive Conservative parties to form the new Conservative Party of Canada. Despite being in a minority government, Harper launched a series of funding cuts that devastated women's groups. The budget for Status of Women Canada was slashed by 40 per cent, twelve of its sixteen regional offices were closed, and any reference to equality and research were removed from its mandate. The new federal government also took measures to muzzle its critics and placed controversial restrictions on advocacy by non-profit organizations. At the same time, the government stated its intention of promoting direct services at the community level and "for-profit" organizations were granted access to women's program funding. In response, CFUW joined reform coalitions, in some cases providing leadership to a demoralized feminist community.

But not everything was bleak. Beatty addressed declining membership by working on getting younger women into active roles in the organization and faced rising board expenses and the high cost of maintaining the national office—no longer called head office—by using teleconferencing and emails instead of face-to-face meetings. And, she ended her term by bestowing an honorary CFUW membership on Flora MacDonald at the 2005 AGM and receiving a $50 bill featuring the Famous Five monument signed by sculptor Barbara Paterson.

When Ardith Toogood became CFUW president in 2006, this internationalist, mother, and volunteer,[43] chose the theme "Visible Voice—*Voix Visible.*" As the federation's director of development from 2004 to 2006, she had led the organization's initiative in declaring itself an equality-seeking organization. Her term coincided with the massive federal cuts to women's and social programs, later compounded by the financial crisis of 2008, and she reported in 2007 "the relentless advocacy because of cuts and changes at Status of Women Canada and the cancellation of many programs and services directly related to CFUW policy." A sense of being under siege is evident in her remark about writing several times to "our IFUW sisters, keeping them informed on equality issues in Canada, and receiving pledges of solidarity from them."[44] Language like "sisters" and "solidarity" was new for CFUW and began an era in which the federation and the government agreed on very little.

The cancellation of the federal-provincial-territorial Multilateral Framework on Early Learning and Child Care cut almost $1.2 billion in future federal child-care transfers to provinces and territories. Some funds were reinstated after advocates mobilized across the country, but the centrepiece of the government's child-care plan was a universal taxable family allowance of $100 a month for each child under six.[45] In an earlier period some CFUW members might have applauded this measure to return child care to families, but CFUW had recently updated its policy calling for a "quality, universally accessible, and comprehensive early learning and child care program, which emphasized the development of the whole child."[46] CFUW participation in various symposia reflects its support of child care as a social benefit, and that access to early learning and child care was important for women's equality.

CFUW reached out to other non-governmental organizations such as the Ad Hoc Coalition for Women's Equality and Human Rights created in 2006. The new coalition was made up of about one hundred women's organizations and its focus was restoring concessions that had been won in an earlier period and preparing for the next election. CFUW's executive director, Susan Russell, served as the coalition's treasurer and on the board of the National Association for Women and the Law, and provided them with a desk at national office.[47] Russell was busy in these years, attending meetings of many organizations including FAFIA, LEAF, CRIAW, and the Canadian Peace Initiative, among others. In an event organized by the Ad Hoc Coalition, CFUW members marched on Parliament Hill in front of the Persons Case monument on December 10, 2007, Human Rights Day. Federation members also took part in demonstrations against the closure of regional Status of Women Canada offices.[48]

With an unsympathetic government in power, President Toogood held meetings with various MPs, including a special session with opposition status of women critics. By the end of her term, she remarked on CFUW's ability to get its message out to politicians of all parties in all provinces due to the federation's reputation for fiscal responsibility and recognition by media and politicians. During Toogood's term, CFUW made explicit its non-partisan position, publishing articles such as "Advocacy 101" and "CFUW's non-partisan stance."[49] One article explained CFUW's approach to seeking out opposition members when governments officials would not see them. It highlighted some of the perks of this strategy—opposition voices were more vocal in the House of Commons than those of government members. Susan Russell notes she would sometimes go to the Hill, drop in on a member of Parliament, and suggest a good topic for question period in the House.[50]

Experience at the provincial level reinforced the federation's approach. In Alberta, CFUW members set up a meeting with Heather Forsythe, minister of child services, regarding child-care issues and, in preparation, Shirley Reid, CFUW regional director, visited a daycare centre and met with an employee of a rural supervision agency. Another representative from CFUW contacted a faculty member from a community college child-care program. The result was a long and productive meeting in which the minister expressed the view that CFUW input was valued because it came from outside of the child-care community; the organization's lack of political affiliations or "axes to grind" was an asset.[51]

In 2009, CFUW's director of legislation reported another atypical year, with another minority Conservative government. The opposition parties called for a stimulus package to mitigate the worst effects of the 2008 financial crisis and even formed a coalition. But the government managed to prorogue Parliament, the Liberals elected Michael Ignatieff as their new leader, and the coalition fell apart. When the Conservatives introduced a stimulus budget, it outmaneuvered the opposition with an omnibus bill (C-10) that combined fifty-one unrelated pieces of legislation. Among them was legislation meant to render pay equity nearly impossible to achieve. Ignoring the 2004 Pay Equity Task Force that had recommended a proactive system with a pay equity commission and tribunal, the government passed the Public Sector Equitable Compensation Act that required women in the public sector to be assessed not only according to the usual criteria of skill, effort, responsibility, and conditions of work, but also according to "market forces" and "the employer's recruitment and retention needs."[52] It also restricted the definition of a "female predominant" job group (from one in which women constitute 55 per cent of the workforce to one that required them to be 70 per cent of the workforce) and took away workers' right to challenge gender-based wage gaps under human rights legislation. No longer a right, "equitable compensation" was something that had to be bargained for collectively. To make matters worse, the legislation prohibited unions on pain of a $50,000 fine from assisting individual members with pay equity complaints. The Public Service Alliance of Canada (PSAC) of course protested, but little could be done.[53] CFUW wrote an open letter to all the leaders and appeared before a House standing committee, where it also represented NAWL, to discuss pay equity and other issues. Toogood was interviewed on CBC and widely quoted on pay equity as well as on the cancellation of the court challenges program.

Drastic reductions in federal funding and anti-feminist legislation did have one silver lining—they produced a dramatic escalation in advocacy by CFUW clubs. In 2007, 37 per cent of clubs had active advocacy and issues groups, were participating in International Women's Day events, conducting letter-writing campaigns, and visiting members of Parliament.[54] CFUW thus created a Visible Voice Wall of Fame, consisting of well over one hundred descriptions of club activities and posted it on the website and at AGMs and other meetings. Toogood also coordinated the feature *History and Heroines* to document the organization's history through its presidents.

The final president of this decade, Patricia DuVal, who served from 2008 to 2010, chose as her biennial theme "The Right to Speak, the Responsibility to Act." An American-born computer scientist, DuVal had once campaigned for Shirley Chisholm, the first Black congresswomen, the first woman to run for the Democratic presidential nomination, and the first Black major party candidate for president. Described as very business-like, but also a "bundle of focused energy" and a tomboy, DuVal liked to do things thought unsuitable for a woman. One of her innovations was to make conference calls four times a year to groups of clubs to help them feel better connected. After her presidency, DuVal served two terms as vice president of membership and remains active into the modern period.

The next chapter covers the period from the 2010s to the present day, followed by chapters on scholarships and the international work that CFUW did in conjunction with IFUW/GWI. Finally, the conclusion summarizes the many contributions that CFUW, its clubs, and its provincial councils have made in the areas of advocacy, friendship, cultural and educational services, reform, and internationalism.

Footnotes for this chapter can be found online at:
http://secondstorypress.ca/resources

Chapter 12
NEW BEGINNINGS AND
NATIONAL INITIATIVES

CFUW understands the importance of adherence to "the rule of law." Indeed, it underpins the organization's belief in equity and confidence in the democratic system. It is fundamental to its belief in human rights and continuing pursuit of positive ways to practise fair and just decision making.

—Doris Mae Oulton

In the early part of this decade, the federation continued to work through coalition groups and the opposition parties. In 2010, it joined protests against the Harper government's maternal health initiative that was announced in conjunction with Canada hosting the 2011 Group of Eight (G8) conference of industrialized nations. In an effort to reverse membership losses and to keep up with modern business trends, CFUW entered into a phase of re-branding with annual reports and mission statements. A New Beginnings Survey recognized the roles of club-level advocacy and the federation launched national initiatives on violence, child care, and Indigenous peoples. The update of a 1992 survey of women at Canadian universities highlighted the issue of sexual assault in post-secondary institutions in Canada.

At the national office, Robin Jackson took over as executive director from retiring Susan Russell in 2011. Jackson, a former CFUW member with an honours BA in French literature from Carleton University and a bachelor's degree in library and information science

(BLS) from the University of Ottawa, had been executive director of the Canadian Independent Film and Video Fund and worked with both the Canadian Radio-Television and Telecommunications Commission and Department of Canadian Heritage. At CFUW, Jackson reviewed office procedures, guidelines, and practices, and ran the office with the aid of Betty Dunlop on fellowships, and, at the time of writing, Rachel Deneault, member services, and Yasmin Strautins, advocacy. Neither finances nor membership numbers had improved and, as will be discussed in Chapter 14, the transformation of the International Federation of University Women (IFUW) into Graduate Women International (GWI) caused division within the membership. Still, the 2015 election of a Liberal government under Justin Trudeau, and his announcement of a gender-balanced cabinet, brought renewed optimism.

• • • • • • • • • •

The last major revision to the CFUW constitution occurred in 2014 and took three AGMs to be adopted. CFUW is an organization that takes governance seriously and pays strict attention to its constitution, which is a standing agenda item at every annual general meeting (AGM). Amendments to the constitution are circulated to affiliated clubs before voting takes place at an AGM, where they are vigorously debated. Changes require a two-thirds majority on the floor. CFUW governance manuals carefully outline the organizational structure, including the committees, terms of reference, and reporting relationships. AGM business meetings are governed by standing rules, which are adopted (and can be amended) at each AGM where there is always a parliamentarian present and Robert's Rules of Order are carefully observed. Club representatives are accredited at AGM registration and receive voting cards (now electronic devices) based on the number of members in their club—every club receives a minimum of one vote. Past presidents and regional directors also receive one vote, as do current board members.[1] CFUW policy, based on resolutions that are submitted and confirmed according to established governance protocols, ensures CFUW's accountability to and direction by the affiliated clubs.

Resolutions must be submitted for consideration according

to strict timelines, are then circulated to clubs, and refinements are negotiated. The proposing club has the final say about what changes they will accept to the resolution that is presented on the floor of the AGM. It is generally a collegial progression. When a club does not accept a change, there can be (and often are) amendments made to the resolution from the floor. Resolutions are first discussed at the club membership level, where members instruct their delegates how to vote at the AGM; the next step is a review process[2]; resolutions are then presented at a workshop before they go to the floor at an AGM; and finally they are put forward on the floor itself where each resolution is debated. Again, there is a strict process for presenting and debating resolutions and a two-thirds majority vote is required for a resolution to pass. Resolutions are sometimes sent back to a club for further work before they can be reconsidered at the next AGM. When a resolution is adopted, it becomes CFUW policy and the following year it becomes the primary focus of the federation's advocacy activities. After the AGM, the national office circulates an advocacy plan—that includes components such as template letters to governments and suggestions for additional actions—to help clubs with their local advocacy efforts. Even the advocacy tasks are governed by protocols—correspondence with the federal government is done by the national organization; overtures to provincial governments are carried out by the regional bodies (sometimes in conjunction with the national organization); and clubs are responsible for approaches to local political officials. This is not a hard and fast delineation since many clubs have access to federal and provincial politicians. In these cases, the advocacy is done cooperatively so that everyone is kept in the loop. There are protocols, however, including those governing interactions with international bodies. Resolutions going to GWI, for example, must first be passed at a CFUW AGM and then adapted as necessary for application to other National Federation Affiliates (NFA).[3]

• • • • • • • • •

Brenda Margaret Wallace, the first president of this decade, served from 2010 to 2012 and was one the few CFUW presidents who actually campaigned for election—there were two capable candidates running that term. Wallace continued with the same theme as the previous biennial, "The Right to Speak, The Responsibility to Act," because it addressed her own concerns. Born in Regina, she was raised in a family that valued education, sports, and music, and where her accomplished mother provided a strong role model. She taught for three years in Germany with the Department of National Defence and after she returned to Canada, she joined CFUW Regina because she valued the organization's contributions to education.[4] As noted, committees on communications and governance guided CFUW during her term to a new structure that brought the constitution and bylaws up to date in compliance with federal changes to the legislation governing non-profits. The organization also introduced the category of associate membership, which eliminated the previous two-tiered membership and recognized graduates and non-graduates as equal members.[5] An increase in fees/dues[6] and a reduction in the number of board members helped the organization cope with rising costs, and CFUW examined alternate methods of governance for clubs that were experiencing leadership problems.

In 2010, Doris Mae Oulton, then director of the Status of Women Committee, noted that it had been a difficult year. The Canadian women's ski jumping team, unlike the men's team, had been excluded from competition at the Winter Olympics in Vancouver, despite an appeal by women's groups on the basis of gender discrimination to the Supreme Court of Canada. The court ruled that it did not have the jurisdiction to enforce the *Canadian Charter of Rights and Freedoms* on the International Olympic Committee.[7] CFUW also protested the closure of an advisory council on the status of women in New Brunswick, with press conferences, rallies, online petitions, Facebook pages, and blogs. The opposition brought in a motion to have it reinstated and CFUW members were interviewed on TV and radio, but nothing would change the government's mind.[8]

For the most part, government doors still remained closed. Teri Shaw, vice president of advocacy from 2010 to 2016,[9] never even went to a government briefing—she lived in the Toronto area and the government kept cancelling meetings in Ottawa at the last minute. Instead, she relied on Tara Fischer, the staff advocacy person at that time. Shaw had a master of library science degree from McGill and had run the department of library and cultural services in a small city near Montréal. She had experience with advocacy at the Ontario Council, dating back to 2000, and at the national level.[10] Shaw recalls two approaches to the changed political climate during the time of the Harper government. First, CFUW ramped up previous efforts to seek coalitions and affiliations with other women's groups; this was made possible by a motion to remove previous restrictions on CFUW affiliation. It joined the Voices Coalition for Human Rights and Democracy, another organization that was founded in response to unprecedented federal funding cuts targeting progressive organizations.[11] The Ad Hoc Coalition on Women's Equality and Human Rights, despite some help from the Canadian Labour Congress, folded in 2011 in favour of putting resources into preparing for the next election. As such, CFUW joined a large group of organizations, including the Alliance for Women's Rights and Oxfam Canada, in organizing the initiative Up for Debate.[12] The group mounted a campaign that called on all political parties to commit to a federal leaders' debate on women's issues. Had it been agreed to, it would have been the first such debate in thirty years. Political parties were also asked to commit to ending violence against women and gender-based economic inequality, and to support women in leadership roles. As of 2019, CFUW was actively participating in meetings for the next Up for Debate campaign.

The federation also developed briefing papers on key issues in preparation for the 2015 election and individual clubs helped get out the vote. Despite the gravity of the political climate, CFUW was always able to turn a serious matter into fun. CFUW Southport members, for example, dressed up as suffragettes—their term—wearing banners and encouraging people to vote in the election. CFUW White Rock/Surrey also invoked the memory of the suffragists in their federal all-candidates panel with the theme "From Then to Now."[13]

Getting their views across to government in this new political environment often took public protests. In October 2012, CFUW joined the Ontario Association of Interval and Transition Houses in a rally to call for a National Action Plan to End Violence Against Women and Girls. CFUW also joined in the condemnations of the federal government's controversial maternal health initiative announced in conjunction with the G8/G20 meetings being hosted by Canada in Toronto and Huntsville, Ontario in June 2010. It was meant to be Canada's flagship proposal on overseas development assistance and was initially met with shock, as the Harper government was known to be stingy with foreign aid of any kind and had shown even less interest in women's health either at home or abroad. As it was, the plan ignored access to safe birth control and abortion which, as women and humanitarian groups were in near universal agreement on, was essential to maternal health. CFUW found "particularly disturbing" the government's "elimination of foreign aid for contraception and safe, legal abortion as part of maternal healthcare."[14] CFUW's coordinator of international relations even urged clubs to participate in peaceful demonstrations prior to the summit, although reports do not indicate how many did so. With widespread anger related to the economic recession, globalization, and government secrecy many of those demonstrations turned out to be anything but peaceful.

Despite the many areas of contention, Ottawa staff members did occasionally get meetings with government members but only on topics of mutual concern. For example, CFUW met Guy Lauzon, national caucus chair of the Conservative Party to discuss ways to counter the "hypersexualization" of children; and with MP Joy Smith concerning opposition to human trafficking.[15]

In its advocacy initiatives, CFUW usually acted as part of a coalition. CFUW drafted material on gun control for use by the Ad Hoc Coalition and Canadian Labour Congress, but while they tabled a brief, they were not called to present it. In October 2012, CFUW again worked with the Canadian Labour Congress, the Young Women's Christian Association (YWCA) Canada, and the Public Service Alliance of Canada on a Roundtable on the Future of the Women's Movement in Canada. Along with several other roundtables, in 2012 and 2013 CFUW attended the Women's Forum des Femmes hosted by Niki Ashton, official opposition critic on the status of women. The forum included a diverse group of young feminist speakers. For International Women's Day, some thirty CFUW Clubs organized public screenings of the 2012 documentary film, *Status Quo: the Unfinished Business of Feminism in Canada*, in partnership with the National Film Board (NFB). Among its other partnerships with women's organizations, CFUW made a joint submission with YWCA Canada to the House of Commons standing committee on finance to address the growing problem of homelessness and joined a call for a national housing strategy. The federation also passed a resolution in 2013 for a basic income program to ensure that all adult residents of Canada, as defined for tax purposes, receive an income adequate for the necessities of life as a means of moving people out of poverty. The organization also supported private members bills on gun control, climate change, and pay equity. Karen Dunnett, VP Atlantic, was interviewed on the latter issue on TV and radio and the federation participated in a press conference with Liberal leader Michael Ignatieff.

There was one case in which the federation took the lead in advocacy. During the term of President Susan Dyer Murphy from 2012 to 2014, CFUW sponsored a 2011 resolution on non-state-actor torture. Their involvement began when two nurses, Jeanne Sarson and Linda MacDonald, came to CFUW asking for their help in creating a new category in the *Criminal Code* to cover extended torture and extended campaigns of physical and emotional abuse—often associated with human trafficking and domestic abuse—perpetuated by individuals or groups other than the state. The women wanted non-state torture identified as a crime—to validate women's experiences and create a database to track it—so police and physicians could be trained to recognize its signs and sufferers would be more willing to come forward. Despite CFUW's 2011 resolution to the UN anti-torture committee recommending that Canada change its *Criminal Code* to recognize non-state torture, the measure has not yet led to any legislative change.[16]

President Susan Murphy earned a Certified Management Accounting degree and took executive training through the civil service Career Assignment Program. She then held various senior positions in the Manitoba government, became active in the Business and Professional Women's Association, and, after discovering that UWC Winnipeg was NOT a group of women professors, joined the club. In 1999, she relocated to Nanaimo, BC and first became that club's vice president, then president, before she moved to the national executive.[17] Murphy brought a sense of adventure and physical fitness to the job—she and a friend raised $4,200 by walking the Camino de Santiago in Spain and donated it to the Nanaimo Scholarship Fund. They later raised another $18,000 walking the Santiago de Compostela trail.

As noted earlier, CFUW entered into a new phase or re-branding of the organization with external annual reports, in part to reverse its losses in membership and in part to keep up with modern trends. It also published a separate stand-alone report on the Charitable Trust's scholarship program and undertook market research on membership that identified a potential market of 4.5 million women in Canada with post-secondary education between the ages of forty-five and seventy-five who shared the organization's values. Comparing itself to seven other women's organizations, CFUW concluded that it was unique in offering social, educational, and advocacy activities.[18] As a result, the federation created annual report headings that aligned with its four perceived strengths: education, life-long learning and leadership; advocacy; being present in the community; and helping women to pursue their education. In 2011, CFUW further identified three target audiences for its membership drives: newly retired women and empty-nesters, young mothers at home, and recent graduates. The next step was to develop plans to approach each of these target audiences.[19]

The 2013–2014 annual report also articulated the organizations' strategic aims.[20] The CFUW mission statement stressed its role as "a national, bilingual, independent organization striving to promote equality, social justice, fellowship and life-long learning," and mentioned its consultative status with the UN Economic and Social Council, and with the Education Committee of the Canadian Sub-Committee of the UN Educational, Scientific, and Cultural Organization. As well, the federation created a new masthead, with a new colour scheme and the tag line "The Power of Women Working Together," a Facebook page, and a Twitter account.

President Doris Mae Oulton, who served from 2014 to 2016, had overseen many of the web and branding changes in her role as regional director and vice president of communications and governance. To strengthen relations between clubs and the federation, she and CFUW staff created an interactive website feature and set up their own press agency to provide news on CFUW events and relevant articles to club newsletters. In 2014, the first CFUW election occurred under the new Industry Canada rules that required all nominations to be posted on the CFUW website. In 2018, under President Grace Hollett, CFUW held its first virtual AGM.

Doris Mae Oulton showed an early interest in leadership through Canadian Girls in Training (CGIT), and as yearbook editor and choir director. After several community development jobs in remote areas, Oulton moved to Ottawa to coordinate Algonquin College's program. She moved again, in 1983, to Winnipeg, where her mother-in-law gave her a CFUW membership and she served as president of UWC Winnipeg from 1990 to 1992 before moving to the national level.[21] She also held senior positions with the Manitoba government and volunteered with YM/YWCA.[22] During Oulton's tenure, CFUW began making plans for their 100th anniversary in 2019 by focusing on their history, through biographies of past presidents and commissioning a centennial history.

CFUW must have been delighted with the 2015 federal election results—as a large number of women were elected, including at least four CFUW members. In addition to Green Party leader Elizabeth May, there were three Liberals: Brenda Shanahan (Châteauguay-Lacolle), Karina Gould (Burlington), and Karen McCrimmon (Kanata). Prime Minister Justin Trudeau's appointment of a Cabinet made up of 50 per cent women prompted President Oulton to write an opinion piece for the *Winnipeg Free Press* entitled "Gender parity was the bold change we needed." While clearly relieved to see the end of the former Conservative government attacks on women, Oulton nonetheless noted that since 1994, before the cuts and the backlash, "Canada held the highest ranking on the United Nations' Human Development Index (HDI)," but by 2015 the country had fallen to twenty-third place. She reminded readers that women employed in full-time jobs only earned seventy-one cents to every dollar earned by men. Still, it was important to see women in political roles and she was encouraged by the trend.

As if energized by the growing number of women in political office, CFUW established a National Mentorship Pilot Program in 2015 that connected mentors with women who had a similar field of interest. The program focused on three areas: CFUW members who had leadership portfolios; women interested in entering politics; and women in the science, technology, engineering, and maths

National President Grace Hollett with other CFUW leaders attending the 100th Anniversary AGM at The Fort Garry Hotel, Winnipeg.

(STEM) fields. The federation partnered with the University of Waterloo's Women in Engineering Committee, the Ontario Network for Women in Engineering (ONWIE), and the Laurier Centre for Women in Science (WinS) to "promote women's leadership and economic empowerment."[23] As well, they created a mentorship award to be given to a CFUW/FCFDU member (or to members), group, or club in recognition of their work mentoring women and girls in the STEM fields and politics.[24] Clubs worked to inspire young women. In 2017, the Montréal Club launched the first North American *Les Olympes de la Parole* competition that gives high-school girls an opportunity to join the global conversation on gender equality and education. Ten Montréal high schools submitted written essays and three-minute videos explaining their findings. Villa Maria College won for their project "Using Raspberry Pi Technology to Disseminate Mental Health Information Amongst Nunavummiut Girls and Women." Developed in the UK by the Raspberry Pi Foundation, these credit card-sized computers promote the teaching of basic computer science in isolated schools and developing countries.[25]

Following the 2015 election, access to government opened up again. CFUW met with the minister of the status of women on violence against women and presented briefs on legislation regulating violence and harassment for employees in federally regulated workplaces, on medical aid in dying, and on increased funding for gender equality programs and Pharmacare.

CFUW clubs continued to mark International Women's Day. In 2017, the Ottawa Club worked with Inter Pares, Amnesty International, Oxfam Canada, and other women's groups to organize an annual event at Library and Archives Canada with an activist fair featuring local and international organizations. More than three hundred people attended.

Clubs worked on local projects while providing friendship, lifelong learning, and advocacy work to women. In 2014, CFUW had more than two hundred book clubs across the country and one hundred lecture series. An increase in daytime programming reflected the growing number of retired members—CFUW Calgary North, for example, established four new daytime interest groups. Clubs held film screenings, often along with panel discussions following such relevant productions as the National Film Board (NFB) documentary *Buying Sex*; *Wadjda*, the first film ever shot in Saudi Arabia by a woman; and CFUW Edmonton sponsored three free movie nights, with films featuring strong women who overcome challenges to make a difference in their communities, such as *Maudie*, which explored the life of Nova Scotia folk artist Maud Lewis, who struggled with arthritis, an unsupportive family, and the loss of a child.

Events such as CFUW Brampton's fashion show, Christmas parties, and annual dinners often functioned as both fundraisers and social events. Popular fundraisers included books sales, raffles, lectures, and house tours.[26] CFUW Etobicoke held weekly English-language conversation circles for newcomers and the Nanaimo Club had a unique Seashore Program, in which members collected intertidal marine specimens every spring. They then showed them to local school children and gave lectures on animals that live between the tides, emphasizing the need for preservation of the marine environment.

There was a growing focus on advocacy at the club level. As Teri Shaw explained, a survey called New Beginnings showed how widespread local advocacy was becoming and expressed CFUW's recognition of the clubs' community action.[27] Three national initiatives gave further structure to club efforts. The National Initiative on Violence Against Women and Girls emerged from clubs that identified ways to support women and girls who are victimized by violence. In announcing it, CFUW highlighted the need to raise awareness, improve aid and prevention, and put pressure on all levels of government to support women and children who experience violence.[28] The survey found that this was one of the most popular club advocacy issues and more than half the responding clubs worked in coalitions with community organizations such as women's shelters. Kanata, for example, organized Shoe Box Projects to provide women moving out of Chrysalis House with cleaning supplies. Clubs in Orillia, North Bay, Kelowna, and Sudbury marched in Canada's National Walk for Homelessness on February 24, 2018.

The other two national initiatives came later—in 2016 the Early Learning and Child Care Advocacy project, "Telling Our Stories," and, in 2017, the National Initiative on Indigenous Peoples. CFUW's approach to child care was broadly conceived. At CFUW Victoria, the club held a public forum on Raising Children Out of Poverty, and CFUW Aurora/Newmarket gave a $1,000 grant to a ward of the Children's Aid Society who was transitioning out of care and into postsecondary education.[29] The BC Council's work led to a provincial poverty reduction strategy through projects in twenty-three communities and included an initiative to gather stories from communities regarding their child care experiences. Some clubs worked with women's advisory groups or councils, libraries, and the Grandmothers to Grandmothers campaign that supported women, orphans, and grandmothers living with HIV/AIDS in Africa. The latter project particularly appealed to the growing number of retired members.

The National Initiative on Indigenous Peoples was introduced in 2017 with a webinar and a resolution on access to safe drinking water and sanitation in Indigenous communities. CFUW had long been interested in Indigenous women's rights, expressing its opposition to discriminatory sections of the *Indian Act* that Canada only started to address when the equality rights section of the *Canadian Charter of Rights and Freedoms* took effect in 1985. The Ontario Council, where the Aboriginal issues group became a national group, focused on pressuring the federal government to improve education in Indigenous communities.[30] In 2013, CFUW passed a resolution calling for the government to collaborate with Indigenous leaders and provide indexed funding for "Early Childhood Education, school infrastructure, equipment, books, information technology, skills development and a core approved curriculum which is culturally sensitive."[31] Clubs took up the issue and the BC and Québec Councils sent submissions to their provincial governments.

This new initiative combined with the other national initiatives—especially violence against women, which had been dramatically symbolized in the tragic murders of fourteen engineering students on December 6, 1989. But the case of Tina Fontaine, a young Indigenous woman murdered in August 2014, drew attention to violence against women compounded by racism. Fontaine was certainly not an isolated example. As Marie-Claude Landry, chief commissioner of the Canadian Human Rights Commission asserted, "The murder or disappearance of some 600 Aboriginal women and girls over the past 30 years is a national tragedy.... We must get to the root causes of these disturbing facts."[32] CFUW added its voice to the call for a national inquiry, writing letters to more than one hundred politicians and distributing a sheet of suggested actions to clubs. The federation also passed a resolution urging the government of Canada to adopt and implement the recommendations of Amnesty International's 2004 report "Stolen Sisters: Discrimination and Violence Against Indigenous Women in Canada."

Clubs participated in protests by joining events for 16 Days of Activism. CFUW Peterborough, for example, joined the YWCA Freeze Mob at Lansdowne Mall in 2013, where fifty women held up roses and signs such as "We remember" and "600 + missing and murdered Aboriginal Women—Speak for them" to draw attention to women's issues. The national office developed materials for the more than 40 per cent of clubs that participated in similar events.

Grace Hollett, from Flat Island and Mt. Pearl, Newfoundland and Labrador came to the presidency after Karen Dunnett resigned as a result of the conflict over IFUW/GWI (See Chapter 14). Although she expressed regret at Dunnett's resignation, Hollett agreed to be nominated as CFUW president in January 2017. Hollett had been serving on the board as VP Atlantic and the position now known as acting president. In consultation with the CFUW parliamentarian, the organization fulfilled the procedures for nomination during a biennial period and her position was ratified by the membership at the 2017 AGM. She ran again at the June 2018 electronic AGM and won election as president for the 2018–2020 term.[33]

A product of a small rural school at Flat Island and Bishop Spencer College, a girls' school in St. John's, Hollett received a BA in history and mathematics, a BEd, and an MEd at Memorial University. She taught in the Newfoundland school system, lectured in mathematics education, and worked with teacher-interns in Memorial University's faculty of education. She was on the elected executive of the Newfoundland and Labrador Teachers' Association (NLTA) for eight years and on the staff of NLTA for two years as the field service executive assistant.[34] She also served on the Newfoundland and Labrador Labour Relations Board and the OXFAM board, and attended the AGMs and conferences of the Canadian Teachers' Federation and Canadian Research Institute for Advancement of Women. In 2000, she joined CFUW, moving from publicity chair to VP to president of CFUW St. John's, then to regional director for Newfoundland, and on to the national board as VP Atlantic for two terms. While she was chair of the regional group, Hollett led a committee to develop, administer, and report on the New Beginnings Survey of clubs that helped direct the work of the organization.[35] She also chaired an editorial committee in St. John's, led by Faith Balish, to edit and prepare the biographies of the thirty-eight past presidents for publication on the CFUW website. In addition to her other CFUW work involving all the committees except nominations, Hollett takes great pleasure in travelling to CFUW councils and clubs, in her family, and in the fellowship of CFUW members united in worthwhile causes. With VP finance, Dominique Racanelli; VP education, Kathryn Wilkinson; and executive director, Robin Jackson, Hollett was a member of the CFUW/GWI negotiating team chaired by VP international Joy Hurst that recently signed a Memorandum of Understanding between the two organizations.[36]

In 2018, CFUW conducted an Advocacy Survey to canvas clubs on their priorities. Its findings were not surprising. It defined advocacy broadly enough to include raising awareness of an issue with members and the public and dealt with "Turning Support into Action," which included member training and resource development; as well as advocacy for specific goals as members met with, or wrote to, elected officials and formed partnerships with other groups. The report found that 77 per cent of clubs had an advocacy committee or interest group but that when clubs undertook independent advocacy initiatives, they were usually based on local needs. Indeed, some 80 per cent viewed local issues and education/ awareness as their predominant concern. But the national initiatives were pertinent—84 per cent of clubs surveyed had taken action on one or more of the three national initiatives.[37] In terms of club priorities, the survey found that violence against women and girls was considered to be of paramount importance, but so too was the awarding of scholarships. Other topics of importance were poverty, the environment, human rights, and gender parity.[38]

During Hollett's presidency, CFUW published a follow-up to the 1992 study called "Women in Universities: 25 Years Later" that led to efforts to address violence against women on university campuses. The new study was conducted through the national Advocacy Committee's subcommittee chaired by Margaret Therrien of CFUW Halifax, who had been involved in the original study. The project used the same categories as in the previous one and the report found improvements in the number of female faculty members in tenure-track positions, more gender studies programs, and incentives to enrol women in male-dominated fields.[39] Areas in which progress was lagging included gender-balance in course content, pay equity for female faculty, and access to child care with flexible hours, both on and off campus. The final report also highlighted the need for universities to do more to promote equality, especially for women who are racialized, Indigenous, LGBTQIS+ students and staff, and those with disabilities. One area in which there was an especially great need for progress was in protocols and reporting procedures for women experiencing violence or harassment; many Canadian post-secondary institutions still did not have them.

Women in the Vancouver Club had already acted locally on this issue. Having heard reports of the harassment of women students at UBC, they pressured the university to establish the UBC President's Advisory Committee on Women's Safety.[40] Elsewhere, media reports were drawing attention to the issue. In their editorial "Studying in Safety" on November 21, 2014, *Toronto Star* reporters Emily Mathieu and Jayme Poisson reported that only nine out of seventy-eight Canadian universities had a specific policy on sexual assault.[41] Thelma McGillivray of the Burlington Club requested that CFUW consider contacting universities concerning their sexual assault policies. This resulted in a national study, the Sexual Assault in Post-Secondary Institutes in Canada Research Project, led Dr. Sharon Crabb and the Status of Women Subcommittee of CFUW's Standing Committee on Advocacy. CFUW shared its findings at a meeting with Status of Women and Statistics Canada for the New Survey on Sexual Victimization in Post-Secondary Institutions commissioned by the Ontario government. Representatives of the federation also met with Dr. Dubravka Simonovic, UN Special Rapporteur on Violence Against Women, to present specific recommendations related to sexual violence in schools.[42]

Another resolution that CFUW passed during this period called for non-discriminatory management of refugees and asylum seekers. In light of the reaction to the influx of immigrants into Canada through the "back door," CFUW provided a moderate and humane voice, asking the federal government "to protect the world's most vulnerable by continuing to increase the number of vetted refugees and asylum seekers accepted, settled, and integrated into the country." It also asked the government to suspend the Canada-US Safe Third Country agreement, in response to the US forcing asylum seekers to make their refugee claims in the first "safe" arrival country, and in response to ongoing violation of human rights in the US.

Having brought the history of CFUW up to the present, the following two chapters will deal specifically with the scholarship program and the international situation, respectively.

Footnotes for this chapter can be found online at:
http://secondstorypress.ca/resources

Chapter 13
HIGH ACHIEVERS AND FINE MINDS

*The men, of course, have their Rhodes Scholarships, but there is
nothing for the women.*

— Dorothea Sharp, 1924 scholarship winner[1]

The Travelling Scholarship was one of the first initiatives undertaken
by the new federation and local clubs soon followed suit with undergraduate awards. Over the years more awards were added, creating
one of the most costly, and the most highly prized, of all CFUW programs. In the absence of women-only scholarships and in recognition
of the barriers—both formal and informal—against women being
able to access mainstream academic funding, the CFUW scholarships,
later called fellowships, for advanced study gave women a foothold
of sorts into the realm of higher education. In spite of this, women
continued to face many obstacles and, in the federation's view, too
few of them gained the academic positions they sought. Despite their
struggles, most of these women made stellar research and teaching
contributions in numerous fields; some of them became loyal and
hardworking members of CFUW clubs and a few volunteered at the
federal level. While the careers of some of these women, scientists
in particular, have received some scholarly attention, most of the
recipients remain largely unknown.[2] The following exploration of
their lives—as much as the sources allow—provides a glimpse into
the achievements of some exceptional young women. Proud of their
accomplishments, the federation tried to keep track of their successes,

at least until the early post-World War II era. One of the first tasks the new federation archivist completed in the early 1920s was to conduct a survey of the educational pioneers who had fought for the right to attend university, many of whom became CFUW members. After that, the federation began publishing regular updates on scholarship winners in the *Chronicle* in order to keep their members—the very people who supported the program through their membership dues—informed. While a collective biography of the scholarship winners, which remains a good idea, was contemplated several times, this has not yet come to fruition.

The Travelling Scholarship supported overseas study because Canadian universities, some still relatively new, lacked the same prestige that those in Britain and Europe enjoyed. As well, the federation, as a new member of the International Federation of University Women (IFUW), joined their compatriots in seeking international exchanges to further understanding among the nations of the world and to promote peace. Thus, early scholarship winners almost invariably travelled to Europe or to England to study, although during World War II many of them attended universities in the United States. The federation's stringent selection criteria were based on a candidate's ability, promise of research, and character. The Scholarship Committee sought candidates with at least an MA and often a partially completed PhD, and had several times rejected suggestions that financial need be considered. Thus, rather than disqualifying a candidate for winning another award, the federation was proud that many of its recipients had won prizes in other competitions. The committee felt that this reinforced their choices. The range of study areas among applicants was broad. While many scholars were working in the more traditional fields for women such as literature, languages, classics, and history, and even natural sciences such as biology and botany, where women had developed a solid track record as gifted amateurs, the organization showed a slight preference for women working in science and in non-traditional subjects. By 1938, for example, of the eighteen women who had won CFUW Travelling Scholarships, ten were in the humanities and eight were in science, four of them studying biology. Later, the social sciences such as psychology, sociology, and political science would figure prominently.

Scholarship committees, tasked with the selection of scholarship winners, were continually delighted with the number of well-qualified applicants that came forward. Despite the economic downturn in the 1930s, for instance, University of Alberta classics professor Geneva Misener, reported that Canadian universities were producing "more and more women with the gift and love of learning."[3] The number of applicants rose from eleven in 1928 to twenty-two in 1931. Committee members frequently expressed regret at the number of applicants who had to be turned away and, when finances permitted, they added new scholarships. A Junior Scholarship to assist students who were exceptional but not as far advanced in their studies as the Travelling Scholarship applicants became a reality in 1940.

Interestingly, the initial Junior Scholarship that went to Dorothy Lefevre of Saskatchewan marked the first time that household science (nutrition) was recognized as worthy of support. The 1942 winner, Helen Stewart, assessed the scholarship's value to her by saying, "the most difficult step financially in postgraduate work is the first year of graduate study. After that, assistantships and fellowships are more easily available." Thus, she concluded "Your Junior Scholarship is of particular value, and I am very grateful to have been one of its recipients."[4]

Applicants were invariably exemplary in their academic achievements. In 1921, the first Travelling Scholarship winner, Isobel Jones, was a 1917 University of Toronto graduate with first-class honours in Greek, Latin, English, and history, who then obtained an MA in English. While teaching at the University of Saskatchewan, however, she discovered that history was her true passion. Typical of most candidates that the committee chose, she had good social and leadership skills and had shown great initiative in learning to type to put herself through school. She used her scholarship to go to France to study the early French period of Canadian history. In her case, as in others in this period, the issue of marriage arose when she married Spanish historian Raymonde Foulché-Delrose before her scholarship was completed and changed her thesis topic from French to Spanish history. In 1928, the committee had decided upon Ellen Hemmeon as the winner, but she soon announced her upcoming marriage. The committee was uncertain how to proceed and the executive eventually decided they could not rescind the award. With apparent relief, they noted that Hemmeon herself had concluded that she could not accept, and the scholarship went instead to E. Beatrice Abbott, a teacher at the Ottawa Ladies' College. After its 1928–1929 report, the Scholarship Committee raised the question of "whether we should not require that candidates give us some assurance that they will continue their studies until they obtained the desired degree for which they sought the assistance of the scholarship."[5] This was incorporated into the terms of the scholarship program. The committee noted that the only alternative would be to "support the continuance of married women in their posts," but that most educational institutions would not permit this.

The trend soon shifted to combining marriage and study. Phyllis Gregory, the 1927 winner, attained a bachelor's degree in economics and political science from the University of British Columbia (UBC) and an MA from Bryn Mawr College before using her scholarship to study at the London School of Economics. While she was in England she married Leonard Turner but continued her studies and became one of CFUW's many success stories. After she was widowed, she returned to Canada—now as Phyllis Gregory Turner—where she became chief research economist of the Canadian tariff board during the Depression, served on the Dominion Trade and Industry Commission, and was an economic advisor to the Wartime Prices and Trade Board. Credited as "an outstanding administrator and a major force in the direction of Canada's wartime economy,"[6] Gregory nonetheless received only two-thirds of a man's salary. After moving to British Columbia, she became the first female chancellor of UBC. Her son, John Turner, became Canada's seventeenth prime minister.

Active in the Ottawa Club, Turner showed great loyalty to the federation. Isobel Jones, even though she had left to marry, came back to volunteer with her club after her husband's death. In 1936, she lived in Québec and conducted research into French Canada's history.[7] Doris Saunders, the 1925 winner, became CFUW president in the 1950s, and Dr. Margaret Cameron, the 1923 winner, was a lifelong CFUW member. Having studied at the Sorbonne, she lectured in the French department at Smith College and earned a docteur de l'université de Paris in nineteenth-century comparative literature. She then left briefly for the United States, but ultimately found a home at the University of Saskatchewan, where she taught for many years.

The Scholarship Committee expressed concern over losing scholars to the United States—where the large number of women's colleges afforded more job opportunities for women—and tried to find places for returning scholars in Canadian universities. The 1922 scholarship winner, Dixie Pelluet, an amateur naturalist who had gotten her start collecting specimens in the Rocky Mountains with her father, went to University College, London and in 1927, earned a PhD at Bryn Mawr College.[8] She then lectured at Rockford College, Illinois and headed the biology department at Teachers College, Kentucky. A leading scholar in fish embryology, Pelluet was also assertive with regard to her position as a female academic. Before accepting a position at Dalhousie University in 1931, which was offered to her for $2,200, she asked for and received $2,600. When she was set to marry fellow zoologist Ronald Hayes, Pelluet extracted a promise from Dalhousie president Carleton Stanley, that she could keep her job after the wedding.[9] Stanley agreed but her salary was frozen. The couple earned honorary doctorates of law from Dalhousie, which created the Ron Hayes and Dixie Pelluet Bursary in biochemistry and molecular biology. Dixie Pelluet Hayes became a full professor only three months before her retirement in 1964, but her late career protests led to a ban on married women faculty members at Dalhousie.[10] Not the legacy that she—or the federation—would have hoped for.

Another CFUW scholarship winner who was financially handicapped by her marriage was botanist Silver Dowding, the 1928 winner of the Travelling Scholarship, who was forced to stay on the margins of her field. She earned a Master of Science degree at the University of Alberta, spent a year at Birkbeck College, London, and completed her PhD in 1931 at the University of Manitoba. She worked briefly as a research assistant at the Dominion Experimental Farm in Edmonton and taught at the University of Alberta without salary because she was married to mathematics professor Ernest Sydney Keeping. She made significant contributions to scholarship as associate editor of the *Canadian Journal of Microbiology* and created a diagnostic service in association with the Alberta provincial laboratory of public health and faculty of medicine. The University of Alberta claims that the lab was the first in the British Commonwealth to collect medically important fungi.[11]

Dorothea Sharp took a long time to gain an academic post. With the help of her 1924 scholarship she earned her doctorate from Oxford's Somerville College in 1928.[12] A year later she expressed regret that there were so few scholarships open to women in Canada and cautioned that one year was not enough time to complete a research project. She added that the amount was insufficient to cover the high fees in the expensive English tutoring system. Aware of such concerns, the committee nonetheless kept the scholarship as a one-year program in the hopes of spreading their limited financial resources among many women. In 1929, they also voted to create a loan program to help candidates fund a second year. In addition, the federation helped Sharp find alternate funding to complete her research. The *Chronicle* later noted that Sharp's thesis, *Franciscan Philosophy at Oxford in the Thirteenth Century* had been published and, in 1949, announced that she was teaching Greek and medieval political ideas at the London School of Economics. During the war, she was principal in the ministry of health in England, responsible for maternity and child welfare. When she was asked about her publications she answered candidly, "During the war years I worked a 7-day week of usually 14 hours a day and since the war every spare moment from work has had to be devoted to house and food hunting."[13]

Alice E. Wilson, who received the 1926 Travelling Scholarship, is not only noteworthy for her contribution to science, but also for her creation of a new CFUW award in 1964. As mentioned in a previous chapter, her experience also pushed the organization to advocate for women in the civil service. As a child, Wilson had enjoyed exploring rock formations on canoe trips with her father and brothers but she followed gender conventions in studying languages and history at Victoria College and expected to have a teaching career. She did not like languages, however, and after an illness, took a job at the University of Toronto Museum.[14] In 1909, she joined the staff of the Geological Survey of Canada in Ottawa as a clerk, cataloguing limestone specimens containing million-year-old fossils. She finished her degree and in 1911 was appointed to a permanent position on the survey's technical staff. By the end of World War I, she was an assistant paleontologist. Excluded from all-male survey parties, she was determined to undertake field research and recruited a recent graduate, Madeline Fritz, to accompany her. Travelling on foot and by canoe, they explored comparable varieties of limestone in the Lake Manitoba and Lake Winnipeg areas. Fritz later had a distinguished career as a paleontologist at the Royal Ontario Museum and the University of Toronto.

Alice E. Wilson,
1926 Travelling Scholarship winner.

Wishing to pursue further research, Wilson asked for educational leave from the Geological Survey, but, despite her supervisor's praise and the fact that she was handling responsibilities well above her job classification, she was repeatedly refused. Even after winning the CFUW Travelling Scholarship in 1926, her employer placed numerous obstacles in her path. But she persevered and, with the intervention of CFUW, was granted leave from her position to study and earn a doctorate in geology and paleontology from the University of Chicago in 1929. Over the course of her career, Wilson wrote more than twenty-five scientific publications, produced geological maps of the St. Lawrence Lowlands between Montréal and Kingston, and named more than sixty new fossil taxa (biological classifications). She also wrote a children's book called *The Earth Beneath Our Feet* to bring geology to a wider readership.

Alice Wilson, who could often be seen exploring the Ottawa area on foot, by bike, and, later, by car, became the first female fellow of the Royal Society of Canada in 1938. She was forced to retire from the Geological Survey in 1948, when she turned sixty-five but continued to work at her office until just months before her death. An inspired teacher, she lectured at Carleton College (Carleton University after 1952), which awarded her an honorary doctorate in 1960. In 1952, the Ottawa Club, of which she was a long-standing member, began awarding an annual scholarship to a Carleton student in her name.[15] She looked upon the CFUW scholarship as a trust

E. Marie Hearne Creech,
1935 Travelling Scholarship winner.

to be returned with interest and bequeathed $1,500 from her modest estate to the federation to create "grants-in-aid" to a maximum of $500 for CFUW members who wished to upgrade their education. Following her death on April 15, 1964, the federation thus created the Alice E. Wilson fellowship. In 2019, this fellowship offered four awards of $5,000 each and an additional two awards of the same value to mark the organization's 100 anniversary.

By 1930, when the *Chronicle* first reported on winners' careers, the obstacles women faced had worsened due to the Depression. While four women among the 1920s winners had already attained professorships and another did so after waiting until 1948, only one among the 1930s recipients found the same success and many of them took teaching jobs at girls' academies. Lillian Hunter undertook research into plant pathology under the University of Toronto's Dr. H. S. Jackson, but it was only when she was granted research leave at Harvard Laboratories through Radcliffe College that she was able to work on her topic of plant rusts other than on evenings and weekends. After earning the CFUW scholarship in 1932, she had to delay taking it up because the University of Toronto's botany department, where she worked as an assistant, refused to give her a year's leave. The records show later that she was teaching at Moulton Ladies College in Toronto, then a girls' academy and now a centre for music.

In 1935, Marie Hearne Creech became the first woman with a completed PhD to receive the Travelling Scholarship. With a 1930 MA from Queen's and a 1933 PhD from McGill, she used her scholarship to study genetics at Strangeways Laboratory in Cambridge, England. While she was there, she married her fellow scientist and collaborator, Hugh J. Creech. As many women were now doing, she refused to choose between her career and her marriage. She was later reported to be researching carcinogenic substances in tissue culture as a research assistant at the Banting Institute in Toronto.[16]

Like Wilson in 1926, the 1937 winner, Gwendolyn Toby, first studied modern languages at the University of Alberta but later branched into biochemistry. Working with Drs. James Collip of insulin fame and David Thompson at McGill, she became a demonstrator and published her work on adrenal insufficiency. As with many women who had been first channelled into the humanities,

Constance MacFarlane,
1933 Travelling Scholarship winner.

her references made a virtue of necessity by speaking of the happy combination "of a fine critical and scientific mind and a broadly human personality."[17] Jobs opened up during the war, and Toby worked with Dr. Collip on sensitive war-related research for the National Research Council (NRC) subcommittee on shock and blood substitutes; their work contributed to the World War II technologies that improved the survival rate of wounded soldiers.[18]

Constance MacFarlane used her 1933 scholarship to study marine algae at the Liverpool Biological Station, University of Liverpool. A Dalhousie graduate from Prince Edward Island, she had also studied at the University of Toronto and, following her scholarship year, she taught at Branksome Hall in Toronto and Mount Allison School for Girls in Sackville, New Brunswick. MacFarlane contributed substantial research and publications to her field and, from 1949 to 1970, she was director of the seaweeds division of the Nova Scotia Research Foundation. She also taught one course at Acadia.[19] Phyllis Brewster, the 1939 winner from Vancouver, had a BSc in pharmacy from the University of Alberta and a MSc from the University of Minnesota. Working in industry, she became the chief chemist of the penicillin pilot plant for Hyland Laboratories until she was forced to take leave because of her husband's transfer to San Francisco.[20]

Mary White, a Queen's University classics scholar, used her 1930 award to study at St Hugh's College, Oxford. She began her career, like many academic women, teaching at girls' schools including Moulton Ladies' College in Toronto. But she persevered, taking advantage of wartime and postwar openings, and was appointed chair of the department of classics at the University of Toronto in 1953.[21] In 1931, Dorothy Blakey of UBC and the University of Toronto used her funding to study Wordsworth and the romantic period of English literature at the University of London and was appointed assistant professor of English at UBC. She published *The Minerva Press, 1790–1820*, a book on the late eighteenth-century and early-nineteenth-century publishing house noted for its sentimental and Gothic fiction, in 1939.

Mary E. White, 1930
Travelling Scholarship winner.

Marion Mitchell Spector, a UBC graduate, was working as a teacher and spending her vacations at the Dominion Archives when she discovered previously untouched records of the Colonial Department in London and used her 1934 scholarship to produce a thesis on the American Revolution. She married Russian historian Ivar Spector from the University of Washington in 1937, and the *Chronicle* reported that she planned to continue her research, and, "we may rest assured that she is not lost to the army of intellectual workers...."[22] By 1940, she was taking an active role in the Seattle American Association of University Women (AAUW) and had her thesis published in the series Columbia Studies in History, Economics and Public Law. During the war, having just published her second book on the American Revolutionary War for which she won an award from the American Historical Association, Spector became a historian at the Seattle army service forces depot.

During the war years, the number of applications increased and the applicants were younger, perhaps reflecting greater opportunities for graduate study. The winners seemed to be predominantly in non-traditional fields and may have been chosen for their potential to contribute to the war effort. The number of BSc degrees earned every year by women in Canada jumped from fifty-one in 1941 to ninety in 1945. Similarly, the percentage of women graduating as physicians jumped from 4.4 per cent to 7.9 per cent.[23] As women often applied for more than one scholarship, a kind of "musical chairs" sometimes ensued. In 1948, for example, the Travelling Scholarship was awarded to Enid G. Goldstine of Winnipeg, who had originally been awarded the Junior Scholarship to study French at the University of Paris, but, when the first and second choices turned down the Travelling Scholarship in favour of the Royal Society fellowship of a higher value, the award went to Goldstine.

The federation funded a number of women in the 1940s who contributed to the war effort. Jeanne Starrett Le Caine, the 1940 winner, studied mathematics and economics at Queen's and Radcliffe before taking a leave of absence from Smith College to work for the Military Research Council in Ottawa. Barbara Underhill from UBC, who had degrees in chemistry and physics from the University of Toronto, studied astrophysics and was appointed to the National Research Council in Montréal. Anne H. Sedgewick, who won the Marty Memorial Scholarship at Queen's University in 1940 and the CFUW Travelling Scholarship in 1941, took time off from her studies to work with the research section of the Commodity Prices Stabilization Corporation, the subsidy-paying agent of the WPTB. There she served as assistant to the economist Irene Spry. Cathleen Synge, who later married Herbert Moravetz, won the Junior Scholarship in 1945 to study mathematical theory at the Massachusetts Institute of Technology. Barbara Mary St. George Craig, a French student from Queen's who had won a scholarship from the French government and studied at Bryn Mawr, worked in the Censorship Department in Ottawa during the war, and then taught at Mount Royal College in Calgary before winning the Travelling Scholarship in 1946–1947.[24]

A few outstanding winners such as 1949 Travelling Scholarship recipient, Carol Evelyn Hopkins, did find university appointments. Hopkins who had won, as an undergraduate, seven scholarships, medals in Latin and Greek, and an arts research resident fellowship became an assistant professor of classics at the University of New Brunswick. But there were many more who made significant contributions to their fields without achieving an academic appointment.

Research positions in government or university labs were a common career path, as was collaboration with their husbands, especially in the sciences. The work of 1940 winner and McGill graduate Christiane Dosne on the physiology of the adrenal cortex with Canadian scientist Hans Selye led to a number of discoveries relating to shock. After moving to Buenos Aires in Argentina, she quickly learned Spanish, studied at the Institute of Physiology, won a Rockefeller research fellowship, and published numerous articles. She married Rodolfo Pasqualini, with whom she collaborated, and had a prolific career with the National Scientific and Technical Research Council of Argentina. It does not appear that she ever held an academic post, although she taught and mentored students. In her autobiography, she stressed that her five children were of equal importance to her research in making hers a long and happy life.[25] There were some winners who took circuitous career routes, delaying their work for the important roles of wife and mother, but it appears that the majority returned to some sort of research or teaching work.[26]

In 1952, the word *scholarship* was changed to *fellowship* to conform with IFUW usage on the understanding that the term denoted advanced research. Fellowship age limits were generally quite liberal. In the 1950s travelling and other "senior" fellowship applicants had to be under thirty-five years of age, while junior fellowship applicants had to be under twenty-five.[27] No doubt the age allowance for the former was in recognition of the interrupted careers that many women experienced.

CFUW created a Professional Fellowship in the 1940s for women who, after working in a particular field, wanted to resume their education and earn a master's degree or equivalent. Many of these were in more traditional fields, such as English major Moira S. Thompson from Fredericton, New Brunswick, who went to the University of Toronto Library School.[28] Tensions occasionally arose within CFUW over which scholarship was more important, with some competition between support for advanced research in the hope of gaining academic appointments versus support for professional training. In 1958, the Scholarship Committee reported a strong preference for the Junior Fellowship over the Professional Fellowship, complaining that "Jr. scholarship applicants with excellent academic standing are continually being turned down," while

Professional Fellowship applicants were "not outstanding and generally gained well-paid positions."[29] The committee did concede that the Professional Fellowship should be retained, but they reserved the right to not award it if no suitable candidate arose.[30] As is reflected in a note in the 1958 minutes, this was "a highly controversial matter with no hope of unanimity."[31]

Beginning in the 1950s and picking up steam by the 1960s, the expansion in women's university attendance was opening up more academic appointments for women. The *Chronicle* reported in 1955 that twelve former scholarship winners were teaching in universities, including Margaret Crichton, who was teaching German at the University of Wisconsin; Enid Goldstine and Margaret Cameron, who were teaching French at the University of Manitoba and the University of Saskatchewan, respectively; Dorothea Sharp, as mentioned earlier, teaching Greek and medieval political ideas at the London School of Economics; Jeanne Le Caine, teaching mathematics at Oklahoma A&M College; Gladys Downes and Barbara Craig teaching French at Victoria College and University of Kansas respectively; Naomi Jackson, teaching fine arts at McMaster University; Doris Saunders and Joyce Hemlow, teaching English at the University of Manitoba and McGill respectively; Dixie Pelluet, teaching biology at Dalhousie; and Mary White, teaching classics at the University of Toronto.[32]

In the 1960s, well-qualified women from the humanities and sciences continued to apply although both applicants and winners were predominantly in the humanities.[33] In 1966, for example, the winners were studying psychology, town planning, English, and history. The family status of winners was changing, too. No longer were women required to be single in order to be admitted to graduate programs, and it was not at all unusual to see married women among the recipients. In 1961, Dr. Camilla Odhnoff, who was married and the mother of three children, won the Vibert Douglas Fellowship, which had been established in 1956 to honour the first Canadian to serve as IFUW president. Still, the event of a woman declining a fellowship when she married was not unheard of, as one 1963 fellowship winner did.[34]

Administered by IFUW and paid for with CFUW funds, the Vibert Douglas Fellowship was awarded to applicants at the PhD level who were studying in a country other than the one in which they were educated or habitually resided. This reflected the wishes of the founders to encourage international experience for women scholars and contribute to worldwide understanding. In 2016, the CFUW/Vibert Douglas Fellowship was awarded to Laura Jan Obermuller from Guyana, who was studying at the University of St. Andrews in the UK, looking into ways that forest preservation could mitigate climate change.

In 1966, CFUW archivist Edna Ash contemplated a centennial publication in honour of these scholarship holders. She sent out a questionnaire to 105 of them, covering the years 1921 to 1963. Although a publication did not materialize, Marion Mann reported on the survey in the 1969 *Chronicle*.[35] The overwhelming majority of these scholarship winners held three degrees each, and half of them had PhDs. Among the seven earliest winners, four had been granted honorary LLDs. They represented nearly every discipline and all Canadian universities established before 1960. Almost all had published works. The most frequently named profession was professor, and the majority of these were working in Canada.

Such numbers reflected a considerable achievement toward one of the major goals of the organization, as well as an improvement over the early years. A booming economy in the postwar years had clearly helped women make inroads into the academic professions, even if many were still at the lower echelons. Among those who were not professors, many worked in teaching, library work, and research. Not one of them held an elective office, however. The *Chronicle* report highlighted pioneers such as Alice Wilson and noted that many, including Doris Saunders and Dr. Marion Mitchell Spector—the latter a second vice president of AAUW, were leaders in the organization.[36] It was also reported that many of the winners were married—half of the Travelling Fellowship recipients, four-fifths of the Junior Fellowship holders, and two-thirds of the Professional Fellowship winners. Of these, half of the winners of the Travelling McWilliams Fellowship, created in 1968 by a merger of the Margaret McWilliams and Travelling Fellowships,[37] had children, while two-thirds of Junior and Professional Fellowship winners did. Marital bliss was no longer impossible for the female professor, if not without its challenges. CFUW proudly reported that regardless of family size, the vast majority of winners had pursued their professional careers largely without interruption.

Like CFUW, IFUW tried to keep track of its winners. In 1956, A. Vibert Douglas, former IFUW president and convenor of the committee set up to award international fellowships, conducted a survey of award winners. Ninety-eight fellowships and twenty-six grants had been given from 1928 to 1956 to applicants from at least twenty-eight nations and proposed by twenty-four national associations. Of these, sixty-two studied in the arts, music, literature, archaeology, and social sciences, and the exact same number, sixty-two, went to scholars in mathematics, physical sciences, and biological and medical sciences. Out of the forty-five questionnaires returned, the organization found that all but one was active in education or research, and thirty-eight listed publications. Many listed their occupation as professor or lecturer.[38]

The CFUW scholarship program expanded in the postwar years, no doubt due to the increasing demand of more and more women attending university. The 1969 Scholarship Committee chair reported that the "war babies" had grown up and were "knocking on every possible door for financial assistance to continue their studies."[39] This made the committee a target for a multitude of inquiries throughout the year, which significantly increased its workload. As the number and value of the scholarships grew—by 1959 there were five fellowships that together were worth $9,000 a year—it was necessary to hire staff to help manage the program and to formalize its management. In 1967 the Charitable Trust was established as a registered Canadian charity to receive donations, manage funds, and issue charitable tax receipts. The Trust also administered the Library Award, which had begun in 1946 as the Reading Stimulation Grant administered by the Library and Creative Arts Committee. The Creative Arts Award began as a small grant in support of young music composers, making it possible for the winner's composition to be performed professionally and a copy of it deposited with Canadian Music Centre in Toronto. Both of these latter awards were moved to the Trust's management.[40]

In a late 1970s internal review of its fellowship program, CFUW noted that at least one provincial human rights commission had rejected the notion that women-only scholarships were discriminatory and the organization asserted that its awards were still relevant. Long overdue increases kept the amounts in line with comparable awards from other agencies such as the Canada Council, the Social Sciences and Humanities Research Council, the Natural Sciences and Engineering Research Council, and the Medical Research Council of Canada—now the Canadian Institutes of Health Research.[41]

The administrative costs of running the program increased as well.[42] For the 1982–1983 year, Margery Trenholme of the Fellowships Committee reported receiving seven hundred inquiries and needing help processing twenty-one French-language applications, as well as experts to assess the four McWilliams Fellowship applications. The committee benefitted enormously from the establishment of a national office in the 1990s, as well as the hiring of Betty Dunlop, whose efficient administration of the program has led to improvements over the years.[43] Recently, most of the work has moved online, substantially reducing the amount of paperwork and staff time. In 2019, CFUW started accepting applications and administering the selection process electronically, which also proved to be more appealing to applicants.

Over the years, new awards have been added, and new names have been given to older awards. The Margaret McWilliams Pre-Doctoral Fellowship is now open to any woman who has a master's or equivalent degree from an accredited university and is well advanced in her doctoral program. The small Alice E. Wilson grants given to women to upgrade their education, originally restricted to club members, had to be opened to all applicants to meet charitable status requirements. The Alumnae Association of the Collège Marguerite Bourgeoys donated $8,000 to the Trust to create the Georgette LeMoyne Fellowship. LeMoyne was one of the first women to receive a university degree in French Canada. In the new millennium, the Massey Award was created by late CFUW member Elizabeth Massey to be presented to a postgraduate student in art, music, or sculpture.[44] In 2005, the Canadian Home Economics Association transferred its two postgraduate awards, the Ruth Binnie Award and the Home Economics Association Award, presented to master's and PhD students in home economics and human ecology, to CFUW. Binnie had been a founding member of the Nova Scotia Home Economics Association. CFUW national office also created the Polytechnique Commemorative Award as a memorial to the victims of the Montréal Massacre of December 6, 1989, with special consideration given to those studying issues relevant to women. In 2015, the Linda Souter Humanities Award was presented to a master's or doctoral student studying in the humanities. CFUW's Aboriginal Women's Award (AWA) was a reiteration of an earlier award honouring Marion Grant and was launched in March 2015, with a transfer from the Wolfville Club to CFUW Charitable Trust.

CFUW has kept its awards relevant to its wider goals. The AWA award, for example, reflects the organization's commitment to service and advocacy, especially to its national initiative on Indigenous Peoples. For Alana Robert, the 2019 recipient who attended Osgoode Hall Law School, the award allows her to continue doing work "focused on combatting gender-based violence and enhancing opportunities for Indigenous peoples. ...the AWA allows me to use my legal education to advance the individual and collective potential of Indigenous women."[45] Her studies in the test case litigation clinic focused on creating new legal precedents that will bring about social change. Co-president of the Osgoode Indigenous Students' Association, Alana Robert participated in the Kawaskimhon National Aboriginal Law Moot and testified before the House of Commons standing committee on the status of women.

Clubs have played an important role in supporting CFUW scholarly awards, not only by contributing to the federation awards through their dues, but also in creating and managing their own scholarships and bursaries. The Ottawa Club launched its first scholarship in 1935,[46] and the Queen's University Alumnae Association in Kingston established the Marty Memorial Scholarship in 1936, named for Dr. Aletta Marty, who earned her MA in 1894 and was Canada's first female school inspector, and her sister, Sophie, who was the head of modern languages at Stratford Collegiate.[47] Over the years, the scholarships have grown and have been primarily awarded to local women in post-secondary institutions or those planning to attend, as most clubs felt that this helped foster "a potential leader."[48] Such local awards complement the federation's postgraduate focus. Like CFUW, some clubs—such as Saskatoon, for example—have also created trust funds to provide for long-term investment that allows them to offer tax receipts for donations, and to keep the financial administration of the award separate from the club's regular activities.[49] A few club awards are administered through the Charitable Trust, including the Margaret Dale Philip Award sponsored by the Kitchener-Waterloo Club. In 1990–1991, the University Women's Club of North York donated money for the Beverley Jackson Fellowship, which is open to women over the age of thirty-five.[50] The Wolfville Club established the Dr. Marion Elder Grant Award in 1992 out of a bequest from Grant's estate, intended for graduate work in Canada or abroad, with preference going to Acadia graduates.[51]

CFUW has been especially sensitive to the needs of mature women returning to school in the postwar era. Locally, these took many forms.[52] The Regina Club established the Harried Housewife Scholarship for at-home mothers wanting to upgrade their education. Although some members objected to the name, it caught on. Many clubs used scholarships to honour prominent women. In 1964, for example, Regina created a scholarship in the name of Helena B. Walker, one of the club's first presidents and the city's first female alderman, who had died that year.[53] The club created another one to commemorate Maureen Rever, a student of Luther College who won Olympic medals in track in 1956 and later earned a PhD and taught biology at the University of Saskatchewan.[54]

A 1991 study conducted by the Weston Club found that clubs of a median size of sixty members had donated an impressive $230,000 in scholarships and bursaries, with the amounts awarded ranging from $25 to $8,000. A typical award was granted to a female high school student with a high average who was headed for fulltime post-secondary study, with a wide variety of priorities such as mature women, the disabled, Indigenous students, women studying engineering, or Canadian studies. Many clubs took into account leadership qualities, community involvement, sportsmanship, and extracurricular activities. A small but growing trend was to support community college and part-time students and a few awards were even given to men. Some clubs had emergency funds for special cases and often worked with a university registrar in these situations. Typically, the selection of candidates was made by the high school staff, who then notified the club and arranged to have a representative at the commencement to present the award. Some of the awards for larger amounts had a selection committee to which the students were required to submit application forms; following this process, the club then invited the students to attend a dinner, club meeting, or commencement.[55]

At the beginning of the 1990s, the federation expressed their hope that, in the future, they could offer more and larger fellowships and they were disappointed when the recession prevented that from happening.[56] Success did come later, however. As part of its 100th anniversary celebrations, the federation set a goal of the raising of an additional $100,000 for the Charitable Trust. By May 2019, the combined total of donations to the Trust and additional local awards was $214,169, making it possible to grant additional awards.[57]

Today, CFUW clubs together with the Charitable Trust award about $1,000,000 annually in fellowships, scholarships, and bursaries, supporting women financially and emotionally while they pursue postgraduate education. Governed as a separate entity from CFUW with its own board of directors, including the sitting CFUW president, there have been only minor changes to the composition, structure, and terms of the directors of the Trust since 1976, when it was allowed to build a reserve fund for future awards and award increases. The Trust is funded through a portion of members' dues, through club and individual donations, and memorial gifts from clubs, as well as fundraising events such as the Charitable Trust Breakfast at the AGM, at which a fellowship winner is invited to speak.[58]

Today, the volume of awards presented and the greatly increased number of winners who have gone on to successful careers makes it difficult to pay the same close attention to each woman as was possible from the 1920s to the 1950s. The world has changed immeasurably since then. While the early pioneers who inspired the formation of the CFUW were a special, rare, and very small minority, that is no longer the case today. Indeed women outnumber men at most campuses, constituting 68 per cent of undergraduates in 2009, with nearly as many in the master's category and only slightly less than 50 per cent of PhD students.[59] While this does represent progress, women are still congregated in certain areas of study and the small minority who become professors remain at the lower levels of the academic pay scale, often in non-tenured or sessional appointments. CFUW's fellowships promote women's equality and improved economic wellbeing. As long as women continue to earn significantly less than men do, they are disproportionately affected by rising educational costs and rising student debt.

CFUW's fellowships go a long way toward ensuring that the Dixie Pelluets and Alice Wilsons of today will be able to achieve the true equality they, and indeed all women, strove for.

Footnotes for this chapter can be found online at:
http://secondstorypress.ca/resources

Chapter 14
THE INTERNATIONAL STAGE

Just after the Canadian Federation of University Women (CFUW) was established in 1919, it joined the International Federation of University Women (IFUW), now Graduate Women International (GWI). IFUW was founded largely through the efforts of British and American academic women such as Caroline Spurgeon from the University of London and Virginia Gildersleeve from Barnard College. In the wake of the devastation of World War I, there was a strong impetus toward promoting "understanding and friendship between the university women of the nations of the world."[1] Founding Canadian federation president and IFUW vice president, Margaret McWilliams, articulated her belief that university education developed an "understanding mind" that made the college-trained woman "conscious of the two sides of every question" and thus able to seek out mutual agreement.[2]

This sketch of CFUW/IFUW history draws primarily upon the same sources used in the rest of this book, as well as two additional sources on IFUW history and one on women at the United Nations. Unfortunately, there are few scholarly or even popular treatments of IFUW but perhaps future historians will tackle the role IFUW played in international feminism and humanitarianism. *Lamp of Friendship*, written by IFUW member Edith C. Batho, speaks to the organization's history during the period from its founding in 1919 to 1968.[3] Christine Von Oertzen's more scholarly treatment, *Science, Gender and Internationalism: Women's Academic Networks*

1917–1955, includes a fascinating account of IFUW efforts to rescue Jewish academic women during the Nazi era. Reflecting both the realities of the time and its author's interests, the book focuses primarily on IFUW's academic leaders such as Carey Thomas, president of Bryn Mawr, Mary Woolley of Mount Holyoke in addition to the above-mentioned Gildersleeve and Spurgeon.[4] Neither study goes very far past the post-World War II period when the organization substantially shifts its focus. This aspect of IFUW/CFUW international work is less well documented, although author Hikka Pietilä's *The Unfinished Story of Women and the United Nations* does provide some context.[5] IFUW contributed to the drafting of the UN conventions to protect women's rights and promoted women's representation in the new international body amid changing political realities such as the Cold War and the expansion of membership to many nations outside of Europe and North America.

Despite its founding rhetoric of peace and internationalism, IFUW found that in the 1920s, discussion of war and ways to promote peace were likely to cause disagreements.[6] Although founded by women from the Allied powers—Britain, the United States, and Canada—the organization quickly reached out to former enemies, convincing Austrian and German women, in 1922 and 1926 respectively, to form national affiliates. Still, the tensions between former enemies remained. The only consensus that the IFUW members could reach in that period was that peace should be taught in schools and universities and that clubhouses and scholarships would facilitate understanding. The organization also addressed less lofty but still contentious issues such as whether German should be recognized as an official language at IFUW meetings, along with English and French.

As discussed in Chapter 3, clubhouses, where women could meet, collaborate, study, and form friendships were an especially significant part of this internationalist vision. Membership in IFUW was a source of pride for CFUW, one that allowed members to obtain letters of introduction to visit a club in any affiliated country.[7] In its early years, the Canadian federation contributed a substantial amount of money—£1,000—to building the British clubhouse, Crosby Hall. Purchased in 1927, the mansion dated to 1466, and was associated with Richard Plantagenet, Duke of Gloucester (later Richard III); Catherine of Aragon; and Sir Thomas More. Clubhouses established in Paris (Reid Hall) and Washington provided "accommodation for about 50 women with reasonably priced meals, library and clubrooms."[8] In 1937, CFUW created a hospitality scholarship to allow women from other IFUW clubs to come to Toronto or Montréal to study, providing them with board and lodging at their clubhouses.[9]

Many academic women wanted to pursue degrees in other countries, in part due to academic limitations at home. The German PhD, for example, was widely respected in the United States.[10] British and American women's colleges were not as well-recognized academically as ones that were part of co-educational systems, such as those in Germany—or for that matter, Canada. For Canadians the appeal of studying abroad related to the lower prestige of the relatively new Canadian universities. CFUW members created their own Travelling Scholarship, and in the 1950s added the Vibert Douglas Fellowship for an international student. In 1923, IFUW had established a million-dollar endowment fund ($14,000,000 in 2019) to support thirty annual fellowships meant to foster cross-cultural friendships and promote women in academic positions.[11] The international federation also investigated international teacher exchanges, although few of these took place in Canada.

While professional advancement, especially in academic posts, was the goal of IFUW and its affiliates, another early concern—and one that engendered heated debate—was that of combining professional work with motherhood. In the mid-1930s, IFUW did a survey on the issue. At the 1926 IFUW meeting, American member Lillian Gilbreth, of *Cheaper by the Dozen* fame, said that although she remained active in her profession, their large household ran efficiently. A psychologist, Gilbreth partnered with her engineer husband on innovative studies on motion and ergonomics. They undoubtedly had "help" and she conceded that it was necessary to have a cooperative husband. At the same meeting, Professor Jessica Blanche Peixotto approached the topic of equal pay for equal work, noting that, "women would always be bad bargainers because they tended, especially in academic work, so to love their work as to disregard its monetary reward. Joy in work is always a bad element in bargaining power."[12] In 1918, Peixotto was the first female full

Some Canadian women attending the 1922 IFUW meeting in Paris. Top row, left to right: Misses A. Macleod, Hunter, Walsh, Rowell, J. MacLeod, and Stock; second row, left to right: Misses Gregg, Anderson, Barnstead, Mrs. Hallam, Misses P. Anderson, Grant, Patterson, and Mason; front row, left to right: Misses Tesky, Moore, Dr. Marty, Margaret McWilliams, and Misses Addison, Bollert, and Hadrill.

professor—in social economics—at the University of California and later became its first department head.[13] In the animated discussion that followed Gilbreth and Peixotto's remarks, Ida Smedley McLean stated, "A nation cannot be made virtuous by an act of Parliament, so women cannot be made satisfactorily to bear children if all interesting occupations are closed to them."[14] Not everyone agreed, although other CFUW members did speak in favour of combining motherhood with careers.

As in Canada, many goals for equality were temporarily put aside by the economic Depression and, especially in Europe, by the coming war. At the 1930 IFUW meeting in Geneva, for example, women discussed the growing restrictions against women in civil service positions. The British Parliament was then debating a proposed reorganization of civil service hiring practices, which favoured men, that led to the establishment of the National Association of Women Civil Servants in 1932.[15] With the 1933 election of the National Socialist (Nazi) government under Adolf Hitler, however, conditions under which women could achieve equality just as quickly deteriorated. In 1936, CFUW President Laura Newman went to the IFUW meeting in Kraków, Poland. When she returned, she reported that the delegates had been surrounded by Nazi propaganda designed to keep women at home, to deprive university women of facilities and jobs, to persecute Jews and other minorities, and to erode intellectual freedom. Many of them came back deeply saddened. Newman fell back on her faith in education, urging CFUW to "play its part in building up a public opinion, which will demand that some other solution than war be found to the problems of the nations of the world."[16]

As ominous threats from Europe increased, CFUW continued to encourage Canadian clubs to study peace and internationalism in conjunction with IFUW initiatives. Although many Canadians—still war-weary from the last global conflict—did not pay attention, by the mid-1930s some clubs were beginning to take heed. Alice Keenleyside of the Vancouver University Women's Club (UWC) was active in the International Women's League for Peace and Freedom, the League of Nations Society, and the Pan-Pacific Women's Association.[17] Several clubs invited speakers to discuss the world situation. The Ottawa Club sponsored Agnes Macphail and Lester B. Pearson, while Regina hosted Laura Jamieson, Mary Dingham, and Winnifred Kydd.[18] Kydd was a McGill alumna who had been named as a Canadian delegate to the 1932–1934 conference for the reduction and limitation of armaments in Geneva. The conference unfortunately represented a failed bid by member states of the League of Nations, including Canada, to prevent the coming war, but to support this effort CFUW signed a petition and passed a resolution calling for disarmament.[19]

In Europe, IFUW was busy dealing with the persecution of professional and academic women, particularly Jewish women, following the 1933 German election. In 1934, IFUW tried to pass the Budapest Resolution that denounced the suppression of minority opinion and discriminatory measures against the citizens of any country. The proposed resolution did not pass, however, due in part to American opposition. That year, CFUW passed a version of the same resolution at home. When the German Federation of Academic Women (Deutscher Akademikerinnenbund, or DAB) pressured IFUW to expel Jewish women from the organization, the conflict led to DAB's departure. The grave state of world affairs did finally push IFUW to pass the Budapest resolution at its 1939 meeting in Stockholm, Sweden,[20] affirming IFUW's purpose in promoting understanding and friendship between the university women of the nations of the world, irrespective of their race, sex, religion, or political opinions.[21] IFUW President Lektor-Dr. Stanislawa Adamowicz returned to Poland just days before German armies marched into her country and she found herself unable to leave. Through much of the war, little was known of her, except that she was alive. She did provide one reply to anxious queries: "Your kind enquiry recently received. Many thanks. Working in the [Hygiene] Institute till now. Irene [daughter] returned Warsaw some days ago. Home destroyed. Health poor."[22] Working in German-occupied Warsaw under Nazi supervision, her situation seemed to symbolize the fate of many European women. From this time forward IFUW *Bulletins* contained "many heart-rending stories of the evacuation of these Polish women and many are still unaccounted for."[23]

Beginning in 1933, the British Federation of University Women (BFUW) and IFUW put considerable resources into helping academic, primarily Jewish, women escape Germany. Many lost their jobs as soon as the Nazi's came to power, while others followed later as the purges intensified. As the German government gained control over other territories, Austrian, Polish, Hungarian, and Czech women joined them in trying to escape. Some who were aging, or had parents or other family members to care for, chose to remain at home; they faced a gloomy future and, sometimes, death. Christine von Oertzen notes that "between 1933 and 1945 the academic networks of the female international community functioned efficiently to assist persecuted members in escaping Nazism."[24] This story of bravery in which IFUW, in particular British and American members, helped women escape persecution and death, is one that has been largely overlooked in science studies and exile studies, especially in contrast to the much better known rescue of male academics and scientists from the Nazi regime.

This rescue work was carried out in a number of ways. In 1933, the BFUW began working with the Academic Assistance Council to help refugee women come to Britain. In 1936, IFUW established an emergency fund to assist in the work, and, after 1938, humanitarian assistance was extended to women graduates from Germany, Austria, and Czechoslovakia who were not professionally active in the university sphere. In the fall of 1939, with the outbreak of the war, the British borders closed, and BFUW concentrated on helping the women who were already in the country. After the United States entered the war in December 1941, American women set up a War Relief Committee and raised substantial funds, some $3,000 of which went to Canada to help with their "war guest" work and $12,000 went to Britain.[25] In 1938, Dr. Erna Hollitscher, a graduate from the University of Vienna who had just escaped herself, was put in charge of an ad hoc refugee committee in Britain to which IFUW referred cases.[26] Hollitscher quickly became the heart and soul of the London-based relief operation.[27] She corresponded with hundreds of women colleagues from across Europe, handling, for example, some 226 requests for help between September 1938 and April 1939. Each case involved bureaucratic formalities and negotiations that she handled with "commitment, reliability, and professionalism."[28] During those months, BFUW arranged for fifty-three academic women and seventeen children to escape Germany, and also helped settle another seventy-five who managed to reach Britain on their own. By April 1939, Hollitscher had found employment for twenty-four women, most often secretarial or domestic work.

Many BFUW clubs also provided help, often by adopting a refugee to offer more personal assistance and mentorship. Together, IFUW/BFUW helped refugees integrate professionally and socially, offering many of them sanctuary at Crosby Hall, "which became the social and cultural hub of IFUW." Until BFUW moved, after 1939, "large receptions, workshops initiated by the guests themselves, and study groups gave Crosby Hall an open, international, intellectual, and sociable ebullience that very soon earned the 'spirit of Crosby Hall' a legendary status not unlike the 'spirit of Geneva.'"[29] A surprising number of the women who had arrived before the war, including those who were given assistance to emmigrate to the United States, actually found teaching or research jobs. To their credit, the organizations tried hard to keep women working in academic roles—between 1933 and 1938, a total of ten university lecturers from Germany received longer-term support through the coveted one-year fellowships awarded by BFUW, IFUW, and the American Association of University Women (AAUW). The stories of these women are a testament to the faith that university women throughout the world had in each other and the contribution they could make, and to their resourcefulness, sacrifice, and perseverance.

Canada took part in this work. As Canadian immigration had all but closed, especially to Jewish immigrants in the 1930s, CFUW could not participate in rescuing women to the same extent as Britain and the United States. It did help bring a Latvian teacher from Austria to Canada and, at the request of the Swedish federation, a Polish judge and her two relatives.[30] Had they been able to do so, CFUW would also have given shelter to the children of BFUW members, but the evacuations were considered to be too dangerous after the sinking of the SS *City of Benares* in the North Atlantic in September 1940.[31]

CFUW members also did what they could to help IFUW recover from the difficult war years. In 1942, CFUW President Dorothy Turville, a professor of romance languages at the University of Western Ontario, arranged for a Christmas message from the women of Canada to the women of France to be broadcast on BBC through the program *France libre*. When she heard that French classic books were being destroyed in Europe, she asked Canadian university women to send theirs to France, Czechoslovakia, and Poland after the war.

Under the leadership of Vibert Douglas's Committee on War Guests, Canadians also helped women stranded in Canada during the war. The Montréal Club hosted Madeleine Francés, a visiting instructor at Wellesley, who could not return to France; she was given an honorarium and room and board at McGill's Royal Victoria College. The club later assisted a Russian doctor studying at the Université de Montréal as well. The Queen's Alumnae Association helped Madame Zbieranska from Poland, whose husband had come to Canada with a Polish delegation. Described as a woman of great culture, she spent a year at Queen's, which the group hoped would allow her to continue her work on French-Canadian literature. Zbieranska later received CFUW financing, supplemented by a grant from the National Committee on Refugees, to study at the McGill University's library school and eventually got a job at the Toronto Public Library. It is not known what became of her husband, or whether she continued her research.

The wife of an English doctor serving with an ambulance corps and her two children were accommodated in Toronto, where she offered to exchange housekeeping for room and board. The Toronto Club also provided guest memberships to eighteen war guests and helped them find employment, buy clothing, and arrange outings for their children.[32] By 1942, the War Guests Committee reported that two of these women held teaching positions without salary in return for room and board, and a law graduate from Dublin was given financial help to take a business course. Others found jobs in war industries and education, or office work. In 1943, one woman was doing scientific laboratory work "of value to the war effort."[33]

The war was almost catastrophic for IFUW. Ten European associations were lost and the fall of France killed plans to reopen Reid Hall in Paris as a centre for refugee work in Europe. In 1940, things looked so bad that American Virginia Gildersleeve, immediate past president of IFUW, requested that women be prepared to serve on an emergency committee should one be needed to carry on the organization's work in North America if the situation further deteriorated in Europe. Canada attended a regional meeting held in Havana, Cuba in 1941 after the IFUW triennial planned for 1942

IFUW members meet at Crosby Hall for the first time following the war, London, 1946. In the centre (front) is Lektor-Dr. S. Adamowicz from Poland, Past IFUW President.

was cancelled. Still, IFUW continued to award scholarships and maintained a skeleton headquarters in London under the guidance of treasurer Marguerite Bowie-Menzier.

Finally, in 1945, the war was over and France, Belgium, and Italy re-joined IFUW. Poignant stories emerged of how members had managed to stay in contact and carry on some of their activities. Edith Batho writes in *A Lamp of Friendship* that the Polish members who stayed at home conducted underground schools for children during the occupation of their country.[34] Some ninety exiled Polish women formed the Polish Federation Abroad in Teheran, and Dutch women created a similar organization in the West Indies.[35] Many more organizations re-emerged and Adamowicz, who survived the war, resumed her interrupted presidency. The British Refugee Office in London, still run by Hollitscher, continued to provide refugee and emergency assistance for distressed university women in the liberated regions, to which CFUW donated clothing, food, money, and books that flowed steadily once shipping restrictions were lifted. Canadians also helped fund sanatorium treatment in the Swiss Alps for university women suffering from tuberculosis and for the care of displaced persons or concentration camp survivors.

In recognition of Canadian efforts to help liberate Europe, Canadian astronomer Dr. A. Vibert Douglas, was elected the first Canadian president of IFUW in 1947, although Douglas thought the honour should go to her British colleague, Marguerite Bowie-Menzier, who had managed much of the work in Britain. A fuller biography of Vibert Douglas and description of the 1947 IFUW meeting in Toronto may be found in Chapter 5.

Canadian members were enthusiastic supporters of refugees and displaced persons during World War II, politically as well as financially. The 1960 CFUW delegation to the prime minister's office requested that the federal government continue to admit refugees, including those who were handicapped.[36] The IFUW Relief Fund that was created to help women escape from Nazi Germany was renamed in honour of Dr. Blanche Hegg-Hoffet in 1968, and CFUW members continued to support it long after the war. By 1961, the *Chronicle* reported that CFUW had donated a total of $4,771.04 to the IFUW fund, an amount that is approximately $40,000 dollars in 2019 currency.[37] Indeed, much of the money raised for this fund

IFUW Board of Officers 1947–1950 at the Ninth IFUW Conference
held in Toronto, Canada in 1947. From left to right: Jeanne Chaton
(France), Second Vice President; Lektor-Dr. Stanisława Adamowicz
(Poland), Past President; Dr. A. Vibert Douglas (Canada), President;
Marguerite Bowie-Menzier (Great Britain), First Vice President; Dr.
Jeanne Eder (Switzerland), Treasurer.

was said to come from Canadian sources. By 1980, the Hegg-Hoffet International Relief Fund was helping eleven aged and infirm women as well as two young refugee protégées in England and France respectively who were expecting to complete their doctorates soon. In 1998, members were saddened to hear that the last recipient, Mrs. Fekete of Germany, had died. In 2004, CFUW members were again raising money for the Hegg-Hoffet fund, this time earmarked for victims of the earthquake and tsunami in the Indian Ocean. As BFUW had done, some clubs "adopted" one or more refugees, providing gifts of food, clothing, and books and with an exchange of personal letters.

In the postwar period, priorities shifted away from Europe, and Canadians supported Third-World women through the Counterpart Aid Programme, later renamed Partners in Development, to help associations in the developing world to pay their IFUW dues. They also supported the Virginia Gildersleeve International Fund for University Women, founded in 1969, to support worldwide projects in women's education, leadership training, and community development. In 1963–1964, members donated more than $3,000 to a fund for sending teachers to emerging countries to work and live with locals. They reported back to the supporting clubs, speaking at their meetings about their experiences upon their return.[38] All of these efforts were directed toward academic women, an otherwise neglected group in society.

After World War II, IFUW expanded geographically from its predominantly European base. At the 1947 meeting, President Adamowicz had welcomed thirty-two nations, including the Austrian, Czech, and Greek federations that were readmitted after the war. From 1945 to 1968, the number of national affiliates rose to more than fifty and many of the new members were from Asia and the Middle East, including Japan, Hong Kong, Turkey, and Iran, as well as from African nations. Under Vibert Douglas' guidance, IFUW shifted its political focus as well. It was announced at the Toronto meeting that IFUW had been given permission to send an accredited observer to all the constituent bodies of the newly established United Nations. It would have consultative status with the Economic and Social Council of the United Nations and the United Nations Educational, Scientific and Cultural Organization

(UNESCO). Vibert Douglas organized the 1950 IFUW meeting in Zurich on the theme of human rights and applied to UNESCO for funds for travel expenses and the publication of reports. Dr. Jaime Torres Bodet, director-general of UNESCO, was one of the distinguished speakers at that gathering.[39]

After her presidency ended, Vibert Douglas continued her international work. She was named Canada's representative to the 1954 UNESCO conference in Montevideo, Uruguay, and later described, with a Eurocentric viewpoint typical of the era, the cultural tensions between the Anglo-Saxon nations and the representatives from other parts of the world. There were also new political realities to be cognizant of—the Cold War was casting suspicion on internationalism at home and political posturing and bloc voting at international meetings. Conflicts between have and have-not nations also emerged as Third World countries—many of them just emerging from colonialism—demanded to be heard.[40]

Although IFUW history following World War II is not well documented, it appears that the organization focused its energies on bringing women's issues to the international stage and ensuring that they were represented on international bodies. As Edith Batho sums up in *A Lamp of Friendship*, by 1968, the IFUW had contributed fellowships, an international glossary of academic terms, and twenty years of "co-operating with international organizations in collecting and distributing information on relevant matters and urging action on behalf of women and against various kinds of discrimination that hamper them."[41] Not long after the United Nations was formed in 1945, women pushed for conventions that recognized women's rights internationally and could be used to pressure governments domestically.

The UN Commission on the Status of Women, established in 1947, was originally a subcommittee of the Commission on Human Rights, but women's groups successfully pressured for status as a full commission. One of its earliest successes was the gender neutral and relatively woman-friendly wording in the 1948 Universal Declaration of Human Rights, guided by the indomitable wife of the American president, Eleanor Roosevelt, who chaired the drafting commission.[42] While the declaration established a human rights framework, women found that it did not always ensure their rights. In 1958, when the Canadian government finally ratified the UN Convention on the Political Rights of Women, Canada was able to gain a seat on the then eighteen-member UN Commission on the Status of Women when it met in Geneva. As noted earlier, CFUW had asked the government to do so in 1953, but it delayed until 1957, when it had improved its records on women's rights by lifting the ban on the employment of married women in the federal civil service in 1953, passing equal pay legislation, and then setting up the new Women's Bureau in the Department of Labour.[43] Mrs. Harry Quart of Québec City was appointed Canada's representative and Marion Royce, director of the Women's Bureau, attended as advisor to the Canadian delegation. The UN Commission on the Status of Women also worked to ratify the 1958 Convention on the Nationality of Married Women, a measure that IFUW had proposed to allow married women to retain their citizenship of birth as early as 1930.[44]

In the mid-1950s, France's Jeanne Chaton, IFUW president from 1956 to 1959, worked with UNCSW to draft the Convention on the Elimination of all forms of Discrimination against Women (CEDAW). The details were hashed out in the 1960s, it was adopted by the UN General Assembly on December 18, 1979, and signed by Canada on July 17, 1980, at the Second World Conference on Women in Copenhagen. A mechanism later negotiated to handle complaints—the Optional Protocol to the CEDAW Convention— gave the Committee on the Elimination of Discrimination against Women the authority to receive and consider complaints from individuals or groups within its jurisdiction.[45] The Ontario Council lobbied its MPs and MPPs to encourage Ontario, and then Canada, to sign on and was pleased when Jean Augustine, secretary of state for multiculturalism and the status of women, announced at the Ontario Council's AGM on Persons Day in 2002 that Canada had accepted the Optional Protocol.[46]

By the 1990s, IFUW had consultative status with ECOSOC, UNESCO, the United Nations Children's Fund (UNICEF), and the International Labour Organization (ILO), providing its national affiliates with access to these bodies. Priorities were changing. Jeanne Chaton, for example, who had represented IFUW at UNESCO for many years after the war, worked on women's issues and the eradication of illiteracy.[47] IFUW was very active in illiteracy projects—which may not have resonated as well with Canadian women as with other member nations, given the high level of education in relatively wealthy North America. After attending a 1970s Canadian-hosted international seminar on eliminating discrimination against women, Ruth Bell, CFUW president at the time remarked there were some insurmountable differences between wealthy nations and countries in which 80 per cent of women were illiterate and survival took precedence over human rights.[48]

Just as CFUW promoted the appointment of women to various boards and commissions at home, IFUW had advocated for women's appointments to the League of Nations by creating the Joint Standing Committee of Women's International Organizations for Securing Appointment of Women to Expert and International Committees. IFUW renewed this effort in 1954–1955 by asking national associations to encourage qualified women to put names forward for public appointments to United Nations committees and delegations, and to bring these applicants to the notice of their governments.

By the 1980s and 1990s, the international women's movement was pressing ahead on numerous issues including poverty and violence against women. On October 31, 2000, they convinced the United Nations Security Council to unanimously adopt Security Council resolution 1325 (SCR1325) on women, peace, and security. This represented the first time that the council had addressed the disproportionate—and unique—impact of armed conflict on women and the need for their participation in peacekeeping.[49] In the 2000s, CFUW urged the Canadian government to honour it and used it to bolster their efforts to have women participate in the peace process at home, such as the 2015–2016 meeting with officials on Afghanistan and Syria.[50] In her address to UNCSW in 2001, Canadian Louise Fréchette, the first deputy secretary-general of the United Nations, emphasized the importance of resolution 1325.[51]

UN resolution 1820, which calls for the elimination of rape and sexual violence as a weapon of war, also represents international recognition of the violence women suffer in military conflicts. Similarly, CFUW called for endorsement of the Convention on Cluster Munitions, explosives that scatter sub-munitions, smaller explosives or other weaponized material, over a geographic area. Like landmines, on which CFUW had lobbied successfully, they do a great deal of harm to civilians, often long after they have been planted. While Canada signed the convention in 2008, it was not ratified until 2015.

As part of the international body, CFUW was also asked to help assess the Canadian government's own record on international issues. Toward that end, CFUW worked with the National Council of Women on a joint submission on Canada's Second Universal Periodic Review at the United Nations. CFUW recommendations to the Canadian government all reflect issues on which CFUW had advocated at home, including reducing inequality for disadvantaged groups; poverty and homelessness; violence against women; and racism and discrimination.[52] In 2017, CFUW made a submission to the Third Universal Periodic Review and gave its input into Canada's eighth and ninth periodic reports on CEDAW. In 2005, CFUW asked the Canadian government to meet its UN Millennium Development Goals—an increase of its Official Development Assistance to at least 0.7 per cent of Canada's gross national product and other measures.[53] In 2016, CFUW asked the government to ensure that these goals were accelerated and achieved before 2030.[54]

Work with IFUW and the UN opened the way for CFUW involvement with other international women's organizations and in the 1990s, the organization began to join some of its public rallies. Consolidating the movement's focus on poverty and violence against women was the World March of Women that got its start with the Fédération des femmes du Québec (FFQ)'s successful 1995 Bread and Roses March Against Poverty, and was followed by the 1996 cross-Canada Women's March Against Poverty—For Bread and Roses, For Jobs and Justice.[55] In 2000, the World March of Women Against Poverty and Violence covered two hundred kilometres in Canada, beginning on International Women's Day, March 8, and ending on the International Day for the Eradication of Poverty on October 17. Millions of people all over the world took part in these marches and CFUW members were among the Canadians, most of them women, who joined the rally in Montréal on October 14, 2000, and the 35,000 who marched in the Ottawa March to the Hill. Many other cities participated as well.[56] Times had certainly changed since Laura Sabia expressed doubts that she could get two, let alone two million women to march in demand of a royal commission!

For some women in Third World countries, the march was their first major feminist demonstration and it helped bring about some initial reforms. In Canada, however, budget-conscious governments pointed to existing programs and offered little new support. In 2005, the World March of Women drafted a Women's Global Charter for Humanity and some CFUW clubs requested copies of the document to study. The charter encompassed seventeen demands based on five values: equality, freedom, solidarity, justice, and peace.[57] The women who drafted it sought to create a world in which exploitation, oppression, and intolerance were abolished and integrity, diversity, and the rights and freedoms of all women and men were respected.[58] In September-October of 2010, the Fredericton Club participated in the fourth World March of Women by drafting a list of demands, making speeches on the grounds of the New Brunswick legislature, and holding teach-in sessions.[59] A 2018 CFUW advocacy survey found that among the sixty-eight CFUW clubs that responded, more that 70 per cent had participated in International Women's Days events, and 40 per cent had participated in the 16 Days of Activism Against Gender-Based Violence that was first organized in 1991 by the Centre for Women's Global Leadership and others. It was held from November 25, the International Day for the Elimination of Violence against Women, to December 10, Human Rights Day.[60]

CFUW continued to work in coalitions internationally as well as domestically. In the 2000s CFUW worked with international NGOs such as the Canadian Network Against Nuclear Weapons and CARE Canada, the latter on issues of gender and peace-building in Nepal and earthquake relief in Haiti. Chitra Copra, vice president Québec, represented CFUW at the large international Refugee Women Fleeing Gender-Based Persecution Conference in Montréal in 2001.[61]

• • • • • • • • •

Since its founding in 1919, IFUW encountered tensions with its national affiliates over payment of fees or dues and the related issue of voting rights.[62] Perhaps this is a given in international organizations.

Nonetheless, IFUW dues come from member organizations, who in turn levy them from their own members. In a per capita fee system, the wealthiest nations who have the most highly educated populations—and thus a larger membership—pay much more than smaller nations. Particularly by the post-World War II era, the United States and Canada felt that they were paying more than their share. Their geographic distance from other affiliates, which in the early years were European, created some feelings of alienation, and this was compounded by the Cold War, when McCarthyism was casting suspicion on internationalism. CFUW members continued to support IFUW relief efforts, especially as directed toward post-World War II refugees and displaced persons, but interest in international issues lagged. In 1969, CFUW president, Margaret Orange, proposed that the IFUW executive attend a CFUW meeting in Edmonton and suggested that more Canadians be elected to the international body.[63] The IFUW president did attend the meeting, where she reminded Canadians of the stellar contributions of Margaret MacLellan on the IFUW Status of Women Committee and Vibert Douglas as president and encouraged Canadians to put forward candidates for election. In the mid-1970s, Ruth Bell continued this conversation in an exchange of letters with her friend Bina Roy, IFUW president. In their discussion of the animosity between their respective organizations, Bell wrote to Roy that Canadian members feel:

> ...very much put-upon. We gave a substantial amount to IFUW, not only in actual fees but in a fellowship, and I understand the Canadian Federation gives more to international relief than any other federation regardless of size. We do not have the benefit that the American federation has of reduced fees for a large number of members; nor do we have any representation on IFUW committees...[64]

Bell also made a reference to the dim view that Europeans took of what she called the "housewife syndrome" in North America. The perception was that the European national affiliates had more professional women active in their organizations, as women were apparently better at maintaining their professional standing after marriage. In the Canadian organization, executive positions were increasingly held by women who did not work outside the home except as volunteers. As early as 1926, there were hints of a minor cultural clash. Mrs. W. T. Hallam, for example, expressed outrage at one European conference delegate she described as coarse and who contributed to what she called "sex antagonism." She also complained that the women at these meetings smoked, which offended her view that the educated woman must be ladylike. Canadians also complained that, unlike Europe, Canada was too big for everyone across the country to know one another, and, unlike the United States, its revenues were too small to hire a large staff. All of these factors led some Canadians to feel at a disadvantage.

International participation was certainly time- and resource-consuming. When Ruth Bell was nominated to the IFUW Standards Committee, Bina Roy told her that she would have to attend annual meetings over the three-year period, and that IFUW covered only 40 per cent of travel expenses and nothing for accommodation or meals. In this case, personal communication was certainly helpful in breaking down barriers and the exchange of letters led to an invitation for Canada to host the IFUW meeting that took place in Vancouver in 1980.[65]

By the end of the 1970s, a period that saw rampant inflation, IFUW and CFUW were both experiencing escalating costs. IFUW increased its fees at the same time that it moved its headquarters from England to Geneva, Switzerland, which required payment in Swiss francs (CHF). The modern installment of this story begins in Stirling, Scotland in 1977, when the international organization voted on a per capita fee increase from 3.50 CHF to 5.00 CHF. Although it carried, both CFUW and AAUW opposed it, and Britain abstained. Not long after, the CHF deteriorated rapidly against the American and Canadian dollar, and CFUW was granted an alleviation of fees, allowable, under IFUW Bylaw 32.4, when a substantial change in exchange rates occurred. Still unhappy, CFUW wrote to IFUW to notify them that the increase was aggravating their existing financial problems and if the situation was not addressed, they would reassess their membership in IFUW.[66]

Of course, anger toward IFUW was not unanimous among members. In an article in the Winter 1980 *Journal*, which had replaced the *Chronicle*, L. Gladys Harvey of the Ottawa Club observed:

When we cry poverty, other nations despise us. ...I'm a Canadian. I was embarrassed and humiliated to learn that we have been guilty of sharp practices in using 1977 exchange rates to pay our fees for the last two years.[67]

In 1978, CFUW and AAUW met in Toronto to develop a united stance. AAUW objected to a per capita fee because it meant that it had to pay 67 per cent of IFUW's budget, and argued that no one affiliate should have to pay more than 25 per cent. CFUW, which had the second largest membership, adopted a similar position and recommended that IFUW reduce its costs; relocate their head office; concentrate on more "action-oriented" programs; and support more regional conferences, increased visibility, and more effective communications. The joint meeting produced four recommendations to revise IFUW bylaws to reduce their expenses and change the dues structure. CFUW President Eileen Clark negotiated a settlement of this dispute at the Vancouver meeting that allowed CFUW to pay nine CHF per person for the first six thousand members and 3.6 CHF per person for the rest. Other measures included cutting costs and restructuring the international body, although the head office would remain in Switzerland.[68]

These measures alleviated CFUW's financial problems and opened the way for greater Canadian participation in IFUW. In 1985, CFUW President Margaret Strongitharm co-chaired a successful Asia-Canada Women in Management Conference held in Victoria and the International Women's Peace Conference in Halifax. IFUW was still having difficulty achieving consensus on peace proposals. So, when a resolution to state "our common horror of nuclear war and our world-wide will for peace" was defeated, CFUW answered the call and established its own Committee on Peace and Security. The committee's goals were to promote awareness and study of and action on the issues of war and peace, and to urge Canada to continue its role as an international mediator and peacekeeper.[69]

The Asia-Canada Conference in Victoria, funded through the Canadian International Development Agency and IFUW, was attended by women from Burma, Nepal, China, Pakistan, India, Bangladesh, Indonesia, Sri Lanka, Thailand, Malaysia, Singapore, Fiji, Philippines, and Canada. When the topic of entrepreneurship

The IFUW Board, 1986–89. Front row, left to right: Ritva Luisa Karvetti (President), Helen Dunsmore, (Past President), and Mary Purcell (First VP); back row, left to right: Eileen Clark (Third VP), Chitra Ghosh (Second VP), and Margaret Calvert, (former Treasurer).

came up, one Canadian woman raised the issue of banks in Canada that refused to lend money to women without their husbands' signatures. Isabel Kelly, British Columbia's deputy labour minister for women's programs argued that governments missed the boat by not sending women on trade missions. The conference led to a number of research projects, including the creation of a *Small Business Management Handbook* produced by CFUW, funding for a hotel in Malaysia, the development of a University of New Brunswick marketing program directed toward Pakistan, India, and Bangladesh and initiatives to launch a Women's World Bank.[70]

The 1990s saw an end to the Cold War, dramatically culminating in the fall of the Berlin Wall in 1989 and the collapse of the USSR. These events brought a renewed optimism for peace, and IFUW welcomed an influx of new affiliates from Eastern Europe. Regional groups also came together during this period with the formation of the new Federation of University Women of Africa and the University Women of Europe. Although CFUW did have sporadic meetings with AAUW over the years, there was no organized movement to form an Americas chapter that could have included Central and South American affiliates. In August 1988, AAUW and CFUW held their first national-level joint conference in Ottawa on the theme of Environment and Sustainable Development, and AAUW President Sarah Harder came to the meeting along with 170 women from the two countries. There were also some smaller meetings between the two organizations. In October 1992, for example, a joint meeting in Ogdensburg, New York explored the two health-care systems, and in 1990, the Brockville Club sponsored a CFUW-AAUW environmental conference, For Land's Sake II, that explored the question of acid rain.

Hopes for global peace were unfortunately short-lived, and CFUW President Peggy Matheson noted the irony that the end of the Cold War should so be so closely followed by the beginning of the Gulf War. In 1990–1991, the Peace Committee (renamed the Global Peace and Security Sub-Committee on Legislation) voiced its opposition to the war in the Persian Gulf.[71]

Nonetheless, domestic and international feminism made substantial gains in the 1990s. During these years, Canada sent larger delegations to IFUW meetings, organized workshops, passed

CFUW delegates attending the United Nations Commission on the Status of Women in New York, March 2019. President Grace Hollett is seated third from right.

resolutions, and served on the executive. In 1989, former CFUW President Linda Souter helped organize a fifteen-day conference on Women in Management, Marketing and Development held in Accra, Ghana. CFUW received substantial funding and support to work with several African women's associations from numerous organizations.[72] The work primarily involved transferring such beneficial skills as proposal writing, project development, doing feasibility studies, marketing, and budgeting, and Dr. Comfort Nwabara from Nigeria described the experience as immensely enriching.[73] With more support from the Canadian International Development Agency, three African women were also able to attend IFUW's 1990 Helsinki conference. In 1993, Linda Souter and Enid Hinchley organized a joint CFUW-IFUW workshop in Harare, Zimbabwe on Organizing Change: Leadership and Organizational Management & Programme Development Training for Women as Decision Makers. Attended by thirty-three IFUW participants from eleven African nations, the workshop was designed to meet the needs of African affiliates for training, managing effective organizations, and developing sustainable projects at local, regional, and national levels.[74]

Seventy-three CFUW members attended the Helsinki meeting, while an even larger number of Canadians came to the 1992 meeting in Palo Alto, California where CFUW sponsored seven workshops and five resolutions dealing with household hazardous waste, literacy, protection of endangered ecosystems, the UN Convention on the Rights of the Child, and violence against women.

Susan Russell, CFUW's executive director from 1999 to 2010, observed that CFUW was well regarded for formulating resolutions, particularly on peace issues.[75] Another of their resolutions that brought Canada to the international stage was their 1986 resolution on child pornography that passed unanimously at the IFUW meeting in New Zealand. As early as the 1970s, an anti-pollution resolution that originated in Edmonton was passed at the 1970 triennial in Toronto and then became IFUW policy at the 1971 conference in Philadelphia.[76] IFUW and CFUW resolutions on the environment always insisted that women be part of solutions. CFUW's 1991 resolution on resource management, for example, called for "national and local energy strategies in collaboration with the women consumers," particularly for policies to develop alternative, affordable energy sources for household use; management programs for fuel wood and other energy resources with women as major participants; and training programs for women in modern forms of resource management. And in 1998, IFUW passed numerous Canadian-based resolutions on sustainable forestry, the right to education, violence against women, human cloning, the trafficking of women and children, and the abuse of women's rights in Afghanistan.

With several high-profile international projects to her credit, it is not surprising that Linda Souter became second vice president of IFUW, and was then elected president in 1999 at the meeting in Graz, Austria. Plans for the 2001 IFUW meeting in Ottawa began soon afterward. Wanting to ensure that they were including Third World affiliates, CFUW secured $100,000 in funding from CIDA to allow women from developing countries to attend the Ottawa meeting. When it turned out that they only needed $80,000, CFUW astonished the government by returning the unused portion! The details of the Ottawa meeting are discussed in Chapter 11.

Through IFUW, CFUW participated in a series of UN world conferences on women, the first of which was held in Mexico City in 1975, International Women's Year. By the time the fourth meeting opened, the 1995 World Conference on Women in Beijing, international delegates had produced the Beijing Declaration and Platform for Action for Equality, Development and Peace, or simply Platform for Action. This declaration consolidated all the recommendations of the previous meetings and provided a comprehensive and demanding program to guide future reforms, fulfilling on the international level the role that the Royal Commission on the Status of Women had played in Canada.[77] The international initiatives reflected in this document—and the degree of progress on them—included using the term "gender" instead of "women" and recognizing violence against women and the feminization of poverty as issues of global concern.

Once issue that found its way into the PFA was the girl-child initiative. While the UN had adopted the Convention on the Rights of the Child in 1989, women's organizations were only too aware that girl children around the world are often not treated as well as boy children.[78] To highlight these distinctions, the initiative addresses such issues as discrimination against girls in the areas of labour, education, health and security, and the prevention of violence and/or sexual exploitation. CFUW executive director Susan Russell, on behalf of IFUW, brought the initiative to the floor of the World Conference, Education for All, in Thailand in 1990, the first in a series that also included the 1995 Beijing meeting.[79] Russell recalled that,

> The World Bank had done a study and they brought it to the floor at the request of IFUW. However, as we prepared for the World Conference on Women we began to push harder and harder to make sure it was part of the agenda. I seem to remember that the African women really took it on.[80]

In 2012, the International Day of the Girl Child was launched by the UN, an initiative meant to promote girls' empowerment by highlighting the challenges that they face throughout the world.

Both CFUW and IFUW also participated in the GEAR (Gender Equality Architecture Reform) Campaign, a global initiative to create a stronger UN entity to advance gender equality.[81] This resulted in the creation, in 2010, of UN Women, the United Nations Entity for Gender Equality and the Empowerment of Women. Amalgamating a number of other UN bodies, UN Women had a broad mandate to address equality issues. Former president of Chile, Michelle Bachelet, was its first executive director. Later, CFUW's International Relations Committee worked with UN Women to lobby for women's appointments to the all-male UN Advisory Board on Climate Change and for gender equality in all UN appointments.[82]

The successes of the 1990s, symbolized by the Beijing meeting and its Platform for Action, were difficult to sustain in 2000s and 2010s when the combined forces of economic recession and the rise in fundamentalism and isolationism saw women struggling to maintain previous gains. As well, the focus of international feminism and humanitarianism shifted to southern or Third World countries, leaving less incentive for women in northern developed nations to participate.[83]

Showing increasing confidence and independence in international affairs, CFUW applied for its own membership on the Economic and Social Council of the United Nations. The organization received the designation in 1998 and CFUW's Committee on International Relations began participating in the work of UNCSW and attending their annual two-week meetings at UN headquarters in New York.[84]

CFUW continues to support women internationally. In 2005, when CFUW gave a tuition grant to a Ukrainian refugee in Israel who was studying nursing, the IFUW Relief Fund convenor noted that "most of our grants are small (between about $500 and $1,200) but that amount of money goes a long way in some countries, and the moral support we provide, letting refugees know that other women care about their plight, is very important."[85] CFUW is also making more and more charitable efforts independent of IFUW. Perth CFUW raised funds to buy solar lamps for women and girls in Ethiopia through the International Organization of Migration.[86] In 2010, Dr. Sima Simar, an Afghani physician, human rights advocate, former cabinet minister in the Afghan interim government, and chair of the Afghanistan Independent Human Rights Commission, gave an inspiring speech at the CFUW AGM held in conjunction with the Ottawa Club's 100th anniversary while she was on a fundraising tour for a girls' school in Kabul.[87] As a result, the Ottawa Club formed an interest group called Women Helping Afghan Women to raise funds for Afghan girls' schools. Other clubs have contributed to similar projects.

• • • • • • • • •

Two major events occurred in the period between 2005 and 2015 that led CFUW to again assess its relationship with IFUW. The first was AAUW's 2005 decision to withhold its dues, which left Canada as IFUW's largest member and reduced the latter's operating revenues by approximately 40 per cent. The second event was IFUW's 2015 decision to transform itself into Graduate Women International (GWI), an idea first discussed at the 2013 IFUW meeting in Istanbul. IFUW proposed spending its reserve funds to revive the organization by addressing visibility, activities, and fundraising. Rebranding, a name change, and a new website addressed the issue of visibility, but critics argued that there would be few other positive results. Then, in 2015, Germany and the Netherlands withdrew from the organization, leaving Canada to provide GWI with approximately 50 per cent of its income.

The question of whether to go or to stay sparked a heated debate within CFUW, an analysis of GWI's finances and programs, allegations, emotional pleas, support groups, and information sessions.[88] The first vote on the issue was held at the 2016 AGM when the St. Thomas Club proposed a resolution calling for deleting Article 4—Membership in Graduate Women International (GWI)—from the constitution. AGM votes on constitutional change or financial motions require a 66 per cent, or two-thirds, vote to pass. The 2016 AGM vote to remove the constitutional requirement that CFUW be a member of GWI was 55 per cent in favour. In 2017, a second AGM vote to remove the constitutional requirement regarding CFUW membership in GWI was 57 per cent in favour. In 2018, the AGM voted 61 per cent in favour of a motion that would have given members the option of paying dues either to both GWI and CFUW, or only to CFUW. A similar proposal in 2019 was also defeated.

During these troubled years, Karen Dunnett, elected president in 2016, decided to resign in December of that year, along with Brenda Robertson, who was VP Advocacy. The two women felt that this was the best course to help the organization heal from the divisive dispute. Dunnett was a New Brunswick teacher, former business owner, and previous president of Save the Children Canada. Like most CFUW presidents, she had extensive experience within the organization, having previously served as regional director for New Brunswick and V P Atlantic, on various national committees, including the Ad Hoc Committee on Governance, Advocacy, Finance, and Risk Management, and had chaired the Human Relations Committee. Well-known and respected throughout the C F U W community as a consensus builder, "who many hoped could fix the divide," Dunnett remains disappointed that she was unable to do so.[89]

In the meantime, G W I passed a dues increase at their 2016 Triennium that led to a great deal of opposition from its national federation affiliates (N F A), many of whom did not pay the increase while others left G W I. As President Grace Hollett acknowledged, board members became frustrated with a perceived inability on the part of G W I to supply answers to their questions "relating to finances in the previous Triennium, the spending of G W I resources without being able to turn the organization around" or conducting an evaluation "at some point before the funds were exhausted."[90] Ongoing negotiations between C F U W and G W I concluded with a Memorandum of Understanding in July 2019. While the constitutional relationship between the two organizations remains unchanged, a new payment schedule with reduced per capita dues for C F U W and repayment of outstanding dues was agreed on.[91] President Hollett also announced the launch of a new chartered club, C F U W CANADA G W I.[92]

The relationship between I F U W/G W I and C F U W has long been a troubled one, as international relationships often are. It has been episodic, with active periods interspersed with two major disputes— perhaps more accurately called one ongoing dispute—regarding finances. Despite this, the relationship has been productive. In the post-World War I period, the two organizations joined in a spirit of internationalism, combining clubhouse construction and scholarship foundation to facilitate exchanges and to help women gain academic appointments. During World War II, C F U W assisted I F U W in its efforts to rescue female scholars persecuted by the Nazis and, later on, displaced persons. C F U W consistently contributed to relief funds to support the education and wellbeing of women and girls worldwide. There was a lull in the 1960s and 1970s, when the Cold War and a fee dispute dampened enthusiasm. But after the resolution of the dispute in 1980, CFUW members renewed their interest in international feminism and humanitarian activism, and were active as IFUW executives and volunteers. Linda Souter's election in 1999 as the second Canadian IFUW president and the IFUW meeting in Ottawa in 2001 were highlights. This period, which coincided with the 1990s' spirit of optimism and gains by women, saw CFUW and IFUW participate in a number of important women's meetings, help launch the Girl-Child initiative, and promote the formation of UN Women. CFUW members may be proud of the role they played in promoting education and equality for women and girls worldwide.

Footnotes for this chapter can be found online at:
http://secondstorypress.ca/resources

WHAT IS CFUW'S FUTURE?

Alice Evelyn Wilson
(1881–1964)

Alice Wilson helped pave the way for women in scientific fields and within the federal civil service. This persevering scientist, teacher, and popularizer made significant contributions to paleontology and geology, undertaking extensive studies of the Ottawa–St. Lawrence Lowlands. With support from the Canadian Federation of University Women, she earned a doctorate in 1929 and was the first woman employed as a geologist at the Geological Survey of Canada, formerly located here. In recognition of her achievements, she was made a Member of the Order of the British Empire and was the first female Fellow of the Royal Society of Canada.[1]

—Historic Sites and Monuments
Board of Canada plaque

The above text is inscribed on a bronze plaque commemorating Alice Evelyn Wilson that was unveiled on Persons Day, October 18, 2018, at the Canadian Museum of Nature in Ottawa.[2] Wilson is one of the many women who exemplify what CFUW's scholarship programs have achieved over the last one hundred years.

CFUW's past strengths and forward-looking vision offer hope for its future. The work of the original twelve clubs, along with the scholarships and bursaries at the local club and federation levels, financed the education of promising women and gave them confidence and a sense of community—gave them the knowledge that other women believed in them. CFUW support inspired women to achievements in teaching and research that led to professional, community, and even political success. More than just a financial contribution, the organization made efforts to place its scholarship winners in academic and other jobs.

There were so many other ways in which the federation and its clubs helped to inspire women. Before the introduction of guidance counselling in high schools, when young women were routinely steered into traditional jobs and discouraged from following their true passions, CFUW members went into classrooms to present them with better educational and career possibilities and even published vocational leaflets to help students and teachers to make informed choices. No one else was doing this. Later, CFUW established mentorship programs to bring out the best in young women, even enlisting Roberta Bondar, Canada's first female astronaut and an honorary CFUW member, to inspire young girls to study science and math. CFUW was among the earliest of the first-wave feminist groups to argue for changes that would allow women to combine motherhood with work outside the home while arguing that the voluntary roles many women play in their communities remain worthy of greater respect. Further, the valuable experience and expertise women acquire in those occupations train them for roles on boards and commissions, and in politics, business, and the professions.

Many CFUW programs anticipated the needs of educated women and were thus taken over by much larger players. CFUW's early efforts to further the advancement of professional women, especially academic women, teachers, librarians, social workers, and civil servants, also laid the foundation for work that was assumed by the Canadian Association of University Teachers, by teachers' unions and federations, by the Canadian Library Association, and by the Professional Institute of the Public Service. CFUW's commitment to research has also produced significant results. Some of the more notable studies include the 1967 Continuing Education Study, and the 1992 Women in Universities study with its follow-up report twenty-five years later. In accordance with CFUW's longstanding concern with post-secondary education for women, they helped women find a more hospitable place within university settings both as teachers and as students.

Throughout its history, CFUW has effectively advocated for senior appointments for women in the academy, in government, and in business; for social welfare measures that recognize women's contributions in the family; for ways to address poverty and violence against women, and so much more. Local clubs have partnered with other organizations in their communities in rallies and fundraisers, in support of women's shelters, and they have joined marches for domestic and international initiatives. In a 2019 survey, club executive members stressed how rewarding it was to work with like-minded women on projects that encourage social change.[3] Cultivating women's political involvement has factored, sometimes ambivalently, in CFUW advocacy. In 2015, CFUW President, Doris Mae Oulton, asserted that politics was an effective way to ensure equality for women. Speaking of Justin Trudeau's gender-balanced Cabinet, she said,

> Women, when they see they have the potential for significant input, will be encouraged to run. The electorate will see that women are regarded as serious contributors—and they will elect more women. Change happens in many forms and through many influences—this is an historic change for the role of women in Canada. It certainly spoke to long time concerns by CFUW on getting women appointed to senior positions.[4]

The founding president, Margaret McWilliams, made a similar plea and backed it up with several terms on Winnipeg city council. The 2019 survey also found that most respondents gave an emphatic yes to the question of whether CFUW members should run for political office, although they have continued to insist that CFUW itself remain non-partisan. Political leadership within the organization was found to be beneficial at both the club and national levels. CFUW coalitions led to such notable successes as the 1954 creation of the Women's Bureau in the Department of Labour, with CFUW member Marion Royce its first director. And connections with influential and sympathetic members could often make a difference—Judy LaMarsh, a Liberal cabinet member, lobbied within government for the Royal Commission on the Status of Women and Flora MacDonald, Progressive Conservative cabinet member, worked for pay equity and constitutional protections for women.

For a century, CFUW has attracted, fostered, and trained community leaders in politics—not just in the feminist movement, but, in many other fields. Helen Gregory MacGill and Evlyn Farris led a campaign for legal reforms in family law in British Columbia that provided a model for other provinces to follow. MacGill, Laura Jamieson, Thérèse Casgrain, and others contributed to the suffrage campaign.[5] Margaret McLellan made the leap to thinking of women's status within the new human rights framework that developed through international bodies after World War II. June Menzies made a contribution to family law reform through tax measures such as pension splitting. Ruth Bell helped foster the placement of women in prominent positions, including the boardrooms of corporate Canada.

Countless less famous but equally effective CFUW pioneers who served as school board trustees, scientists, prison wardens, environmental activists, and members of government bodies have also led through example. And on the collective rather than individual level, coalition building has contributed to CFUW efforts in successful advocacy with regard to gun control and the ban on the use of landmines. With a relatively small membership, CFUW cannot take sole credit for many of its lobbying efforts, but when the federation has joined voices with similar organizations and contributed excellent research and networking, good things have happened.

CFUW has achieved an enviable longevity. The glue that keeps the organization together is built on the friendships forged by working on common causes and enjoying the benefits of chosen interest groups. A group of friends might want to play bridge, do walks, learn tap dancing, investment, or gourmet cooking, take home repair classes, or entertain in the elegant Ralph Conner House in Winnipeg or Hycroft in Vancouver. Over the years, the membership question has haunted CFUW and many have wondered why, among the pool of millions of women that qualify, only a small percentage join. Perhaps that is because the organization reflects a cultural homogeneity that is both its downfall and its strength. Members share a desire to keep up to date on current events, to retain a generalist's knowledge of what is happening in the world, and a desire to pursue excellence.

Historically, CFUW members have come from an educated, middle-class milieu, and many have pursued a liberal arts education rather than a scientific or technical one. Not surprisingly, considering its early roots in the social gospel, a disproportionate number of its leaders have been involved in humanitarian work, often influenced by Christian, usually Protestant, churches. Despite efforts to be more inclusive—Québec has four English clubs and two French clubs, with AFDU Montérégie of Saint-Lambert being the most recently formed club in CFUW and some women of colour have become members—CFUW is aware that its membership needs to expand from its primarily middle-class, white, anglophone, and heterosexual composition within a mainstream, moderate feminism.

Clubs are the first point of entry for new members. A flexible, decentralized structure and a broad mandate have allowed the organization to respond to members' needs. As such, clubs jealously guard their autonomy. Financial independence has been another source of CFUW's strength, although that is not without its pitfalls. Fundraising brings women together as clubs balance moneymaking ventures with programs that enrich their members' lives. Independence has protected CFUW from the fate of women's groups funded by the state. While Doris Anderson and Laura Sabia both contended that governments got their money's worth from the women's organizations they funded because they received much good advice, they were also the first to be cut when times were bad. Conversely, fundraising does assume that women have the time and interest to hold book sales and house tours. For some women, these events are uncomfortably close to the traditional volunteer role they want to escape. The annual dues also require a certain level of affluence among members.

Balancing fun and friendship with advocacy and more serious goals has sometimes produced tensions, and the level of advocacy within CFUW has waxed and waned with world events and economic conditions. Federation executives have occasionally made disparaging remarks about non-activist members, trying to fire them up for the battle against injustice. But some women do not want to change the world—like former president Margaret Orange, they feel that the feminist battle has largely been won, or they feel that they are privileged just to have an education and to be able to serve their families and communities. Still, all members who pay their annual dues are financing a paid staff member at national office to carry out duties associated with CFUW's advocacy and to support scholarships for women.

The 2019 questionnaire also revealed that many members are worried about the organization's future because of its declining membership, financial difficulties, and conflicts with Graduate Women International. But history does teach us that CFUW is no stranger to challenging times. The organization certainly did some soul-searching in the 1970s when the noisy new women's liberation groups made—for them—embarrassing and militant demands that were much at odds with CFUW's own philosophy and modus operandi. But the federation regrouped, found its niche, and enjoyed a resurgence in the 1980s and 1990s by gaining the ear of government. When other women's organizations were severely hurt by government program cuts in the late twentieth century, CFUW had a reserve of financial self-sufficiency to fall back on. Later, when the government of the day refused to meet with the federation delegates, they cultivated opposition leaders, presented their well-researched resolutions, and found coalitions to work with to further their agenda.

No one can predict what changes the next one hundred years will bring. New developments continue to bring new challenges and new opportunities—the #MeToo Movement and women's determination to achieve equality in all areas of life countered by the backlash against women's equality; the full acceptance of different family arrangements and gender identities; Indigenous issues highlighted by the Truth and Reconciliation Commission of Canada and the National Inquiry into Missing and Murdered Indigenous Women and Girls; and continuing efforts to eliminate violence against women and cyber-bullying. Still, one thing is certain. As long as CFUW continues to offer opportunities for lifelong learning; for identifying and meeting community needs; and for socializing with other women who have the same interests, CFUW will continue to foster excellence and leadership and train women for roles in education, science and engineering, politics, international aid, and social reform.

CFUW has had a strong, proud, and productive one hundred years. As long as the core remains strong—learning, friendship, advocacy, and the will to empower women and strive for equality and excellence—CFUW will continue to be relevant. The Canadian Federation of University Women may not appeal to all women, but it fills a need among a committed group of women who want to make the world a better place, just as their founders had envisioned they would.

Footnotes for this chapter can be found online at:
http://secondstorypress.ca/resources

ACKNOWLEDGEMENTS

There are so many people to thank at the end of a long, laborious task such as this one and I will try not to forget anyone. In contemplating taking on this project I received support and encouragement from many important colleagues and friends, including Deborah Gorham, Constance Backhouse, Donna Neff, Beth Atcheson, and Tina Bates. My Ottawa feminist history reading group, a larger manifestation of that support network, also listened patiently when I detailed some particular roadblock on the journey. I also want to thank my colleagues at Parks Canada who taught me how to be a public historian, to write for a general audience, and who provided me with a wealth of experience in documenting Canadian women's history. Thanks also for sharing such a collegial and rewarding work environment for over twenty years.

Many thanks to the women who make up the Canadian Federation of University Women, who shared the lessons of their past, consciously or otherwise. I enjoyed the inestimable benefit of their foresight in preserving and organizing their archival records in a way that made them easy to access. To Robin Jackson, Betty Dunlop, and the rest of the staff at CFUW offices—where I often camped out to use their smaller archives and their photocopier, I am grateful. Thank you to Jasmin Strautins for facilitating the questionnaire that helped with the final section of the book. And, finally, thanks to the CFUW History Committee—Gail Crawford, Grace Hollett, Eleanor Palmer, and Doris Mae Oulton—who oversaw the production of the book, gave sage advice, timely edits, quick answers to sometimes stupid questions, and directed me to the right person to talk to. Sometimes they even wrote little bits of the book. Interviews with Susan Russell and Teri Shaw provided me with insights into the modern period when historical sources were scarce. Many clubs also responded to questions, requests for photographs, bits of information, and questionnaires. Volunteers Gail Crawford, Dorothy Phillips, and Susan Russell helped collect photographs used in the book and the staff at the Library and Archives Canada were always helpful in facilitating access to CFUW's records. Thanks also to the editorial and production staff of Second Story Press— Margie, Melissa, Natasha, and Kathryn—and to the Feminist History Society, for believing in the value of this ambitious history of a women's organization that bridged early and later feminism in Canada. But especially I want to thank Beth Atcheson and Andrea Knight for their edits—both of them, in very different ways, made this a much better read than it otherwise would have been.

And last but not least, I want to thank my good friend, Rhona Goodspeed, for her courage and inspiration, never wavering in her enthusiasm for "The Book" even through chemo and other indignities. It saddens me that she didn't get to read it. Special thanks also go to my family—Michael, Liz, Brian, Kathleen, Mel, and especially Evan and Hayden—for putting up with a too-often distracted wife, mother, and grandmother. You all kept me sane and grounded during a hectic several years, and for that I am truly grateful. This book's for you.

INDEX

Note: Page numbers in italics indicate a photograph.

191; as moderate feminists, 191, 224, 239, 321; relative wealth of, 55, 74, 144–45, 218, 320–21; volunteers, 75, 132, 145, 154, 160–61, 184, 192, 199, 218, 235, 306, 318

Canadian Federation of University Women (CFUW), political activities: and Canadian constitution, 191, 194–97, 209, 219; coalitions with women's groups, 172–73, 176, 224, 246, 253, 254–55, 259, 304, 319; contacts in government, 208–11, 226, 230, 240, 246–47, 258; national initiatives, 165–66, 183–86, 249, 253, 257–58, 259–61, 263; as non-partisan, 93, 246, 319; protests, 88–92, 157–58, 223, 226, 246, 249, 252, 253–54, 303–4; working with opposition parties, 246–47, 249, 254, 322. *See also specific issues.*

Canadian Federation of University Women (CFUW), social initiatives: the arts, 57–58, 115, 123–24, 131–32, 135, 140, 145, 151, 181; bilingualism, 145–46, 147, 149, 159, 161, 188, 240, 256; community service, 53, 62–64, 96, 160, 167, 177, 179, 188, 200, 214; environmentalism, 169, 180, 204, 205, 214, 217, 219, 226, 232, 237, 240, 243, 255, 259, 263, 309, 311; events, 55, 56–59, 81, 97–98, 130–31, 144–46, 145–46; friendships among women, 48, 53, 55, 177, 200, 218, 248, 321, 322; fundraising, 57, 62, 71, 76, 99, 131, 147, 179, 297, 299; mentorship, 201–3, 217, 257–58, 318; public lectures, 57, *58*, 71, 81, 96, 131; social aims, 49, 51–52, 54–55, 56–57, 82, 160, 167; study groups, 56, 57–58, 81–82, 97, 108, 131–32, 144, 188, 201; war efforts, 42–43, *43*, 95–97, 98–102, 104–5, 110–11, 294–95, 315

Canadian Federation of University Women (CFUW), structure: annual general meetings (AGM), 192, 208, 213–14, 216, 224, 227, 235, 245, 248, 250–51, 257, 262; autonomy of clubs, 49, 54, 97, 131–32, 146, 192, 321; biennial meetings, 213–14, 215;

clubhouses, 59–62, *63*, 77–78, *79*, 98, 99, 147, 201; constitution, 49, 51–52, 115, 121, 143–44, 177, 216–17, 250, 314; executive, 54, 75, 121, 123, 145, 166, 192, 200, 210, 215–16, 235; finances, 60–62, 75, 85–87, 99, 166–67, 188–90; financial troubles, 212–13, 215–16, 222, 232, 245, 250, 306–7, 322; funding, 167, 173, 189, 212–13, 215–16, 217, 227, 232; meetings, 53–54, 55, 57, 60–61, 75, 81, 112, 115, 199; membership fees, 49, 60, 62, 71, 74–75, 77, 147, 190, 191, 193, 219, 252; modernization of, 249, 256, 256–57; permanent offices, 123, 132, 143–44, 189, 192, 207–8, 213, 217, 235, 245, 281; policies, 54–55, 59, 63, 64, 75, 93, 115, 173, 235, 238, 240, 250; procedures, 97, 99, 115, 121, 123, 172–73, 176, 200, 224, 226; provincial councils, 143–44, 203–4, 218, 226–27; regional conferences, 97, 98–99, 115, 121, 125, 135, 138, 145–46, *146*, 179; resolutions, 49, 53–54, 75, 97, 123, 234–35, 250–51; triennial conferences (1920s), 51, 55, 60, *61*; triennial conferences (1940s), 97, 105, 108, 110; triennial conferences (1950s), 120, 132, 135, 138; triennial conferences (1960s), 143, 147, 152, 153, 160; triennial conferences (1970s), 161, 167, 178, 180, 188, 190; triennial conferences (1980s), 196, 198, 199, 201, 205, 207

Canadian legislation: Bill of Rights (1960), 152, 194; Charter of Rights and Freedoms, 194–97, 207, 211, 219, 243, 252, 260; and constitution reforms, 190, 191, 193–97, 209, 219; *Criminal Code*, 164, 171, 206, 241, 255; and equal pay, 133–34, 163, 183, 212, 231, 247, 301; and family law, 108, 139–40, 151, 153, 155–56, 185–86, 244, 320; and gun control, 228, 229, 231, 232, 234, 240, 242, 254, 320; and human rights, 175, 193–94, 241, 255, 300–301; and immigration, 104–5, 175, 241; and landmines, 228, 230, 320; and penal reform, 126–27, 242–43; and technology,

207, 221–22; and women's careers, 37, 59, 82, 93, 108, 133–34, 163–64; and women's education, 21, 23, 38, 39–40, 64; and women's rights, 45–47, 59, 63–64, 108, 134, 193–97, 233, 300–301
Canadian Library Association, 65
Canadian Mental Health Association, 217
Canadian Panel on Violence Against Women, 229
Canadian Pension Plan (CPP), 204, 230, 231
Canadian Radio-Television and Telecommunications Commission (CRTC), 205, 250
Canadian Red Cross Society, 76
Canadian Research Institute for the Advancement of Women (CRIAW), 175, 246
Canadian Women's Army Corps (CWAC), 100–101
Canadian Women's Auxiliary Air Force, 100, 192
Canadian Women's Press Club, 26
Cardin, Lucien, 157
careers for women: business, 55, 66, 73, 75, 128–29, 156, 163; civil service, 27, 75, 85, 111, 112, 128, 158; domestic service, 36, 80, 88, 106, 108; during WWII, 95–96, 99–102, 106–9; government, federal, 93, 129–30, 162, 204, 208–9, 257, 319; government, municipal, 115–16, 152; government, senate, 128–30, 151, 156, 170, 183, 197; industry, 36, 82, 88, 101–2; law, 66, 86–87, 93–94, 129, 134, 186, 187, 197, 211, 282; medicine, 187, 218, 230, 276; micro-technology, 198, 240, 248; military, 99–101, 112, 152, 192; nursing, 39, 66, 69, 75, 88, 100, 101, 112, 199; teaching, schools, 19, 56, 64, 67–68, 74, 133–34, 151; teaching, Universities, 37, 88–89, 104, 187, 220; wartime industries, 101–2, 110. See also women's rights; workplace inequality.
Carey Brewster, Harlan, 46
Carleton University, 198
Carman, Bliss, 71

Carnegie, Andrew, 65
Cartwright, Mabel, 29
Casgrain, Thérèse: and suffrage, 101, 320; and women's rights in Québec, 109, 110, 121, 157, 159, 189
Casselman, Cora, 115–16
Catholicism, 149, 151
Catholic Women's League, 156
Cazelais, P., 126
CFUW–FCDFU *Journal*, 195, 203, 223, 224, 306–7. *See also Chronicle* (CFUW publication).
Charitable Trust, 189, 280, 282, 283, 284
Charlottetown: women's club of, 120
Charlottetown Accord (1992), 219
Charter of Rights and Freedoms, 194–97, 207, 211, 219, 243, 252, 260
Chatelaine (magazine), 141, 194, 201
Chaton, Jeanne, *298*, 301–2
Chilacombe, Eleanor, *209*
child care: and CFUW, 80–81, 131, 155, 163, 203, 241, 246–47, 260; daycare, 36, 95, 108, 162, 170–71, 203, 210, 213; expense of, 163, 170, 201, 224, 241, 263; funding for mothers, 94, 106–7; legislation, 46, 102, 133, 163, 170, 245; and women's equality, 245, 246–47. *See also* women's rights.
children: CFUW studies of, 81, 110; child abuse, 190, 205, 224, 260; education of, 64, 123, 125–26, 137, 149, 180, 201, 217; effects on mother's careers, 87, 95, 144, 163, 203, 218, 279–80; International Year of the Child (1979), 187, 189, 201; and pornography, 205, 206, 311; rights of, 152, 235, 241, 254, 260, 311, 312, 316
Children's Aid Society, 260
Chisolm, Shirley, 248
Chrétien, Jean, 194, 237
Chrichton, Margaret, 278
Chronicle (CFUW publication): on CFUW activities, 143, 167, 297; during WWII, 95, 98, 101, 107; on education, 125, 146, 149; evolution of, 144, 166–67, 188, 192; inception

and aims of, 51, 54, 75–76; and
RCSW, 170, 174, 176; on scholarship
winners, 94, 266, 270, 273, 275, 278,
279; on women's careers, 85, 87, 91,
112, 115, 129; on women's rights, 114,
160, 185. *See also* CFUW–FCDFU
Journal.
Civil Employment Reinstatement
Act (1942), 107–8
civil service: discrimination against
women, 64, 67, 83, 87, 91–93, 111,
128, 163, 291, 301; reforms to, 91–92,
134, 163, 301; women working in,
27, 75, 87, 111, 112, 128, 158
Clancy, Mary, 227
Clarke, Edwin, 203
Clark, Eileen: as CFUW president,
190, 192–93, *193*, 196, 199; and
IFUW, 307, *308*
Clark, Joe, 195, 210, 219
Clark, Susan, 206
*The Clear Spirit: Twenty Canadian
Women and their Times* (CFUW
publication), 159
Coallier, Suzanne, 143, *209*
Cockburn, Pat, 154
Cody, H.J., 54
Cold War, 118, 288, 300, 305, 309, 315
Collins, Mary, 224, *225*
Collip, James, 273–74
Committee for the Equality of
Women in Canada (CEWC), 156–57
Connor, Ralph, 78, 99, 320
Conservative Party of Canada:
Harper administration, 232, 241,
242, 244, 247, 257; and non-profit
advocacy, 241–42, 244, 252; and
women's rights, 45, 46, 130, 247, 257.
See also Progressive Conservative
party.
Convention on the Elimination of
All Discrimination Against Women
(CEDAW), 194, 207, 301
Cook, Deborah, 241
Cooke, Katie, 174–75
Co-operative Commonwealth
Federation (CCF), 82, 94
Cooper, Mrs. John, 49
Cooper, Pat, 198
Copra, Chitra, 304

Cornwall: women's club of, 120
Couglin, Daniel, 127
Council of Jewish Women, 156, 157
Crabb, Sharon, 264
Craig, Barbara, 278
Crawford, Mary, 26, 44
Creech, Marie Hearne, *272*, 273
Creighton, Edith, 96
Criminal Code, 164, 171, 206, 241,
255
Crosbie, John, 207
Crosby Hall (BFUW clubhouse),
59, 99, 288, 294, *296*
Crummy, Ruth Harrap, 109–10
Cugnet, Margaret, 215
Cullis, Winnifred, 48–49
Cummings, Alice, 42
Cureton, Elizabeth, 207, *212*, 217, *225*
Curie, Marie, 57, *58*

Dalhousie University, 40, 114, 269,
274, 278
Dartmouth: women's club of, 96
Davidson, Agnes, 201
Davidson, Jean Gertrude (True):
and CFUW membership, 74, 77, 86;
and Vocations Bureau, *84*, 85–87
Dawson, John William, 19, 21
Deneault, Rachel, 250
Denne, Lexa, *50*
Department of Labour, Women's
Bureau of, 112, 132–33, 154, 166, 301,
319
the Depression: impact on society,
73, 74, 78; impact on women's
groups, 62, 72, 76–78, 82, 85–87, 114;
and lack of government aid, 73, 82;
and unemployment, 73–74, 77, 80,
82, 86–89, 93; and women's careers,
67, 72, 80, 82, 85, 87–89, 95, 268,
273, 291
Derrick, Carrie, 36, 57
Desmond, Viola, 137
Dewey, John, 125
Dickie, Donalda, 83, *83*, 85, 125
Diefenbaker, John, 130, 139, 194
Dingham, Mary, 291
Divorce Act (1968), 164
Dosne, Christiane, 277
Dowding, Silver, 269

feminism: and CFUW, 34, 54, 114, 172, 176–77, 187; divisions within, 224, 239; first-wave, 177, 318; generational gap, 172–73, 176; opposition to, 158, 207, 214; in Québec, 196, 214; second-wave, 141, 153, 176–77; and women's rights, 31, 167, 206, 221, 231, 304
Ferguson, Margaret, 127
Fergusson, Muriel McQueen, 129, 156, 157, 159, 165, 183
Firearms Act (1995), 229
Fischer, Tara, 252
Fisk, Pat, 241
Flaherty, Dorothy, *122*
Fontaine, Tina, 261
Forsythe, Heather, 246
Foster, Stuart, 104
Foster, Theodora Carroll, 205, *209*, 213
France, and IFUW, 294–95, 297, 299
Francés, Madeleine, 295
Fraser, Paul D.K., 205
French, Mabel, 37
Fritz, Madeline, 159, 271
Frost, Leslie, 140, 155
Fullerton, Margaret, 138

Gardiner, Ella, 17, 21
Geological Survey of Canada, 67
Germany, and IFUW, 288–89, 292–94, 314
Ghosh, Chitra, *308*
Gibson, Mrs. G. Ross, *119*
Gilbreth, Lillian, 289, 291
Gildersleeve, Virginia, 48–49, 287, 288, 295, 299
Gilleland, Margaret, *122*
Gill, Phyllis Marjorie, 77
Gilman, Charlotte Perkins, 31
Glassford, Sarah, 100
Goldstine, Enid G., 276, 278
Gold, Sylvia, 212
Gould, Karina, 257
Graduate Women International (GWI) *see* International Federation of University Women (IFUW)
Grant, George, 19
Grant, Marion: awards of, 159, 282, 283; as CFUW president, *113*, 114,

118–20, *119*, 178, 199, *290*
Greenhill, Margaret, 138
Green Party of Canada, 243, 257
Gregg, Milton F., 134, *290*
Gregory, Phyllis *see* Turner, Phyllis (née Gregory)
Griffin, Mrs. W.H., 46
Griffiths, Naomi, 198
Guthrie, Nora, 91–92, 112, 128

Haige, Kenneth, 86
Halifax, women's club of, 96, 126, 263
Hallam, Mrs. W.T., 306
Hamilton, women's club of, 75, 81, 125, 179, 200
Harder, Sarah, 309
Hardman, Lyn, 203
Harper, Stephen, 232, 241, 242, 244, 249
Harvey, L. Gladys, 165, 306–7
Hayward, Constance, 105, 128
Hegg-Hoffet, Blanche, 297, 299
Hemlow, Joyce, 278
Hemmeon, Ellen, 267–68
Henripin, Jacques, 159
Himmel, Barbara, *236*
Hinchley, Enid, 310
Hind, Cora, 73
History and Heroines (CFUW publication), 199, 248
Hitler, Adolf, 291
Hitschmanova, Lotta, 104
Hobbs, Margaret, 89
Hogg, Helen, 159
Holland, Dorothy, 235
Hollett, Grace, 257, *258*, 261–63, 315
Hollitscher, Ernam, 293–94, 297
Hooper, Thomas, *147*
Hopkins, Carol Evelyn, 276
Houston, William, 21
human rights: in Canada, 175, 193–94, 241, 255; and CFUW, 131, 137, 151–52, 156, 167, 170, 173–74, 263; gender identity, 241, 322; healthcare, 217, 237, 253–54, 258; homelessness, 255, 260, 302; landmines, 217, 228–29, 231, 234, 303, 320; LGBTQ rights, 206, 223, 241, 263; poverty, 255, 263, 302; race, 33–34, 137,

Ross, George, 21
Ross, Phyllis see Turner, Phyllis Ross (née Gregory)
Rowles, Winnifred, 112
Royal Commission on Bilingualism and Biculturalism (1963–1969), 149
Royal Commission on Education, 123
Royal Commission on Education and Youth (Warren commission), 149
Royal Commission on Education in the Province of Québec (Parent commission), 144, 149
Royal Commission on National Development in the Arts, Letters and Sciences (Massey commission) (1951), 118, 123–24, 131
Royal Commission on New Reproductive Technologies, 221
Royal Commission on Taxation (Carter Commission), 152, 163
Royal Commission on the Status of Women (RCSW): and CFUW, 154, 158, 167, 231, 242; hearings of, 161–62, 175; implementation of, 172–74, 176, 212; inception of, 152, 320; legacy of, 175, 312; recommendations of, 108, 166, 170, 178, 181; release of, 158, 164, 178
Royal Victoria College (McGill), 21, 69
Roy, Bina, 305, 306
Royce, Jean, 133
Royce, Marion, 133, 138, 154, 166, 301, 319
Ruffo, Andrée, 206
Russell, Ruth, 101, 102
Russell, Susan (née Mohamdee): advocacy of, *212*, *225*, 227, 228–29, 230; role in CFUW, 235, 246, 249, 312
Rutherford, Ernest, 102

Sabia, Laura: career of, 172, 174–75, 185; as CFUW president, *142*, 144, 146, *146*, 153–59, 176; politics of, 176, 178, 185, 188, 304, 321, 323; and RCSW, 141, 162, 164, 166
Sackville, women's club of, 96, 169

St. Catharines University Women's Club, 76, 98, 153
Sainte-Anne-de-Bellevue, women's club of, 143
St. George Craig, Barbara Mary, 276
St. Hilda's College (UofT women's residence), 21, 25, 29, 41, 68, 69
St. John's, women's club of, 75, 96, 104, 145, 149, 189, 201, 262
Saint John, women's club of, 23, 48, 81, 153, 181
St. Laurent, Louis, 128, 129
St. Thomas, women's club of, 127, 132
Salter, Mary, 102
Salvation Army, 62, 78
Sangster, Joan, 32
Sarnia, women's club of, 75
Sarson, Jeanne, 255
Saskatchewan: provincial council of, 192, 218; women's clubs in, 126, 149. *See also* University of Saskatchewan; University Women's Club of Saskatoon.
Saskatoon see University Women's Club of Saskatoon
Saunders, Doris: career of, 69–70, 99, 199, 278, 279; as CFUW president, 121, 123, 128, 134–35, *135*, *136*, 268
Saunders, Mary, 221
Savage, Mrs. J.L., 111
Sawyer, Artemus Wyman, 18
scholarships: Rhodes Scholarship, 28, 51, 265; Travelling Scholarship, 51, 54, 71–72, 94, 266–77, 289; of university women's clubs, 28, 31, 70–71, 76, 80, 99, 179, *238*, 263, 282–84, 318; winners of CFUW, 266, 267, 268, 270, 274–75, 276, 278–79, 280, 281–84; women excluded from, 28–29, 51, 186, 265. *See also* Canadian Federation of University Women (CFUW), awards; *specific university women's clubs.*
Schreiner, Olive, 31
Schreyer, Edward, 201
Science, Gender and Internationalism: Women's Academic Networks (Von Oertzen), 287–88

Turner, Phyllis Ross (née Gregory), 97, 101, 149, 268
Turville, Dorothy (Ada), 96, 108, 294–95

Underhill, Barbara, 276
The Unfinished Story of Women and the United Nations (Pietilä), 288
United Nations: Commission on the Status of Women (UNCSW), 137, 153, 300–301, 313; Convention on the Political Rights of Women (1953), 137, 301; Economic and Social Council (ECOSOC), 301, 313; Educational, Scientific and Cultural Organization (UNESCO), 299–300, 301; International Children's Emergency Fund (UNICEF), 179, 301; International Women's Year (1975), 165–66, 176, 185, 187, 312; and women's groups, 116, 156, 287, 288, 311–13
United States: women's education in, 17–18, 25, 41, 55, 64, 266, 289; women's groups in, 25, 48–49, 59; and women's rights, 91, 205, 239
Universal Declaration of Human Rights (1948), 137, 151, 157, 159, 193–94, 300. *See also* human rights.
Université de Montréal, 135, 143, 193
University of Alberta, 26, 64, 114, 133, 181, 187, 267
University of British Columbia (UBC): and campus sexual assault, 263; female faculty at, 36, 68, 80, 149, 221, 268, 275; founding of, 26, 38, 94, 132; and women's education, 39, 46, 71, 135, 174, 199
University of Manitoba, 30, 39, 69, 90, 104, 128, 135
University of New Brunswick (UNB): Alumnae Association, 26, 39–40, 56; and women's education, 21, 23, 29, 152–53, 276
University of Ottawa, 23, 27, 250
University of Regina, 27, 94
University of Saskatchewan: and CFUW, 123, 135; female faculty at, 124, 230, 267, 268, 278, 283
University of Toronto (UofT): and

CFUW, 30, 57; female alumni of, 35, 67, 83, 118, 151, 160, 267, 274–75, 276; female faculty at, 48, 89–90, 270–71, 278; opposition to women's education, 17–19, 40–42, 57; St. Hilda's College, 21, 25, 29, 41, 68, 69; Trinity College, 18, 21, 29, 41, 68–69, 111, 114; United Alumnae Association, 25, 40
University of Western Ontario, 66, 96
University Women's Club of Edmonton: education initiatives of, 28, 65, 82, 114, 125, 187, 189; events of, 57, 97, 131, 145, 185, 259; membership of, 26, 28, 51, 120; recommendations to RCSW, 162, 181; scholarships of, 28, 71; social initiatives of, 125, 126, 145, 180, 181, 187, 189; and women's careers, 114, 133, 214
University Women's Club of Montréal: clubhouse of, 60, 61, 77, 98–99, 147; demographics of, 56, 99, 109; during WWII, 98–99, 109, 295; regional conferences held by, 98–99, 115; social initiatives of, 63–64, 126, 184, 258. *See also* Québec.
University Women's Club of Ottawa (UWCO): and CFUW offices, 208, 235; demographics of, 27–28, 56, 75, 96, 129–31; during WWII, 96, 98–99, 105, 291–92; establishment of clubhouse, 61; events of, 30–31, 55, 57, 81, 259; and formation of CFUW, 48; membership of, 28, 120–21, 166; regional conferences held by, 98–99, 138; scholarships of, 80, 271, 282; social initiatives of, 82, 93, 111, 115, 121, 126, 134, 154, 183, 313
University Women's Club of Québec, 126, 179, 181, 189. *See also* Québec.
University Women's Club of Regina: advocacy of, 90, 126, 186; during WWII, 291–92; and education, 125–26, 149, 252; events of, 31, 58, 80, 81, 180; membership of, 27, 94; recommendations to RCSW, 161; scholarships of, 76, 131, 283

PHOTO CREDITS

Page 20: Victoria University Archives (Toronto), 1991.161/738

Page 22: Victoria University Archives (Toronto), 1991.161/409

Page 25: University Women's Club of Toronto

Page 39: University of British Columbia Archives, Frank Nowell photo (UBC 1.1/1643)

Page 43: University Women's Club of Toronto

Page 45: City of Vancouver Archives, R. H. Marlow photograph P114.05 Ref Code AM54.S4.

Page 50: British and Colonial Press/ Library and Archives Canada/ PA-186441

Page 58: University Women's Club of Toronto

Page 61: Library and Archives Canada / PA-212228

Page 63: Photo courtesy of Gerry Crawford

Page 79: University Women's Club of Winnipeg

Page 83: City of Edmonton Archives EA-10-100

Page 84: Toronto Star – Frank Lennon / Contributor

Page 103: R2770 Vol. 151, CFUW Library and Archives Canada

Page 113: CFUW Archives

Page 119: Library and Archives Canada

Page 122: Dorothy and Frank Flaherty 1986–014, Library and Archives Canada

Page 124: University of Saskatchewan, University Archives and Special Collections, Photography Collection A 3321

Page 135: CFUW Archives

DIANNE DODD, who holds a PhD in history, was first introduced to women's equity and justice issues as a young adult in 1975, when the United Nations declared International Women's Year. She later studied history at Carleton University and the Ontario Institute for Studies in Education, specializing in women's history, and has published on the history of birth control, domestic technology, nursing, and healthcare. After a post-doctoral fellowship at the University of Ottawa (Hannah Institute on the History of Medicine), she worked at the National Archives (now Library and Archives Canada) and later moved to Parks Canada, where she researched and wrote reports for the Historic Sites and Monuments Board of Canada. The latter led to the designation of persons, places, and events of national historic significance, including the founding of the Canadian Federation of University Women.

THE FEMINIST HISTORY SOCIETY SERIES

The Feminist History Society is committed to creating a lasting record of the women's movement in Canada and Québec for the fifty years between 1960 and the year of the Society's founding, 2010. Feminism has a history that predates the 1960s and continues long after 2010.

The energy that women brought to their quest for equality in these decades is beyond dispute, and it is that energy that we capture in this series. Our movement is not over and new campaigns are upon us. But the FHS series presents an opportunity to take stock of the wide-ranging campaigns for equality that occurred in Canada between 1960 and 2010. There was much transformative social, economic, civil, political, and cultural change.

We maintain an open call for submissions (https://secondstorypress.ca/submissions/) across a full range of approaches to the period, including autobiographies, biographies, edited collections, pictorial histories, plays and novels. There will be many different authors as all individuals and organizations that were participants in the movement are encouraged to contribute. We make every effort to be inclusive of gender, race, class, geography, culture, dis/ability, language, sexual identity, and age.

Beth Atcheson, Constance Backhouse, Lorraine Greaves, Diana Majury, and Beth Symes form the working collective of the Feminist History Society. Margie Wolfe, Publisher, Second Story Feminist Press Inc. and her talented team of women, are presenting the Series.

The Abortion Caravan: When Women Shut Down Government in the Battle for the Right to Choose Karin Wells
ISBN 978-177260-125-1

Inside Broadside:
A Decade of Feminist Journalism
Philinda Masters and the Broadside Collective
ISBN 978-177260-112-1

Two Firsts: Bertha Wilson and Claire L'Heureux-Dubé at the Supreme Court of Canada Constance Backhouse
ISBN 978-1-77260-093-3

Personal and Political: Stories from the Women's Health Movement 1960–2010 Lorraine Greaves
ISBN 978-1-772600-79-7

White Gloves Off: The Work of the Ontario Committee on the Status of Women
Edited by Beth Atcheson and
Lorna Marsden
ISBN 978-1-77260-049-0

Fairly Equal:
Lawyering the Feminist Revolution
Linda Silver Dranoff
ISBN 978-1-77260-022-3

Resilience and Triumph:
Immigrant Women Tell Their Stories
Book Project Collective
ISBN 978-1-927583-85-2

Marion Dewar: A Life of Action
Deborah Gorham
ISBN 978-1-77260-009-4

Queen of the Hurricanes:
The Fearless Elsie MacGill Crystal Sissons
ISBN 978-1-927583-53-1

Writing the Revolution Michele Landsberg
ISBN 978-1-897187-99-9

Playing It Forward:
50 Years of Women and Sport in Canada
Guylaine Demers, Lorraine Greaves,
Sandra Kirby and Marion Lay, Editors
ISBN 978-1-927583-51-7

Feminist Journeys/Voies féministes
Marguerite Andersen, Editor
Forthcoming as an ebook

Feminism à la Québécoise
Micheline Dumont, Trans. Nicole Kennedy
Forthcoming as an ebook

https://secondstorypress.ca/feminist-history-society-series/